REGIMENTAL HISTORY OF THE 45th RATTRAY'S SIKHS 1914-1921.

REGIMENTAL HISTORY
OF THE
45TH RATTRAY'S SIKHS
DURING THE GREAT WAR AND AFTER. 1914—1921.

COMPILED BY
LIEUT-COLONEL R. H. ANDERSON.

The Naval & Military Press Ltd

Published by
The Naval & Military Press Ltd
5 Riverside, Brambleside, Bellbrook
Industrial Estate, Uckfield, East Sussex,
TN22 1QQ England
Tel: +44 (0) 1825 749494
Fax: +44 (0) 1825 765701

www.naval-military-press.com
www.military-genealogy.com

In reprinting in facsimile from the original, any imperfections are inevitably reproduced and the quality may fall short of modern type and cartographic standards.

CONTENTS.

CHAPTER		PAGE
	A Short Epitome of the previous History of the 45th Rattray's Sikhs : 1856—1914	8
I.	August 4th, 1914, to February 29th, 1916. The N.W. Frontier, Provision of Drafts, Etc.	23
II.	Mesopotamia—March 1st to December 12th, 1916. The Summer of 1916	30
III.	Mesopotamia—December 13th, 1916 to February 19th, 1917. The Crossing of the R. Hai. The Operations in the Hai Salient, and the Attack of February 1st, 1917	47
IV.	February 20th, 1917, to September 30th, 1918. On Lines of Communication at Amara, and Bgailah. The 17th Division, on the Euphrates and up the Tigris to Samarra and Tekrit	82
V.	October 1st to December 31st, 1918, including the Operations in front of Fat-Hah, the Pursuit and the Battle of Shergat	110
VI.	January 1st to October 31st, 1919. Baghdad and Hillah	140
VII.	November 1st to End of 1919, including the Operations in Kurdistan	154
VIII.	January 1st to June 30th, 1920, in the Kirkuk Area	164

CONTENTS

CHAPTER	PAGE
IX.— July 1st to September 30th, 1920. The First Phase of the Arab Rebellion, including the two Battles of Rumaithah, the Retreat from Diwaniyah, the Fighting round Hillah, and the Operations round Shahroban	173
X.—October 1st, 1920, to March 3rd, 1921. The Final Stages of the Arab Rebellion, until the return of the Regiment to India	218
XI.—The Experiences of certain of our Prisoners-of-War, who escaped from the Turks	236

APPENDICES.

APPENDIX	PAGE
I.—British Officers who Served with the Regiment 1914–21	245
II.—Indian Officers who Served with the Regiment, 1914–21	250
III.—Yearly Casualty Return	252
IV.—Reinforcements, Indian Ranks	254
V.—Honours and Awards	256
VI.—Actions for which Awards were Given	257

LIST OF PLANS AND MAPS.

Fig.		Page
1.—The Pentagon		38
2.—Aqra Panorama		159
3.—Diwaniyah		186

1.—Shaikh-Saad and Kut-el-Amara		32
2.—Falahiyah–Shumran–Zenabrijah		40
3.—Hai Bridge-Head Defences		52
4.—Shatt-el-Hai		62
5.—Do. (further north)		64
6.—Jift Post		112
7.—Fat-Hah Position		118
8.—Qalat-ash-Shargat and Fat-Hah		122
9.—Shargat		130
10.—Country round Aqra		156
11.—Country North of Baghdad		173
12.—River Euphrates—Hillah to Rumaithah		178
13.—Baqubah to Shahraban		206
14.—Hillah to Feluja		226
15.—River Hai–Kut-el-Amara to Karachi		232
16.—Mesopotamia—Key-map		*At end*

A SHORT EPITOME OF THE PREVIOUS HISTORY

OF THE

45TH RATTRAY'S SIKHS

1856—1914.

THE Regiment was raised at Lahore in January, 1856, by Captain Thomas Rattray (afterwards Colonel Rattray, C.B., C.S.I., Commandant 42nd Regiment Native Infantry), as the Bengal Military Police Battalion and has always been known as "Rattray's Sikhs." **1856.**

The original strength of the Battalion was :—

    500 Cavalry
    1,000 Infantry composed of 500 Sikhs,
                           300 Punjabi Mahomedans,
                           200 Dogras.

During the Mutiny of 1857-58 four mountain guns were captured from the mutineers by the Regiment and afterwards until the end of the mutiny became a recognized unit of the Regiment and manned by Sikhs.

Many of the Sikhs enlisted had seen service under Ranjeet Singh.

The Regiment was raised under the orders of the Government of Bengal for services in the Santal Pergumahs and in September, 1856, marched down country, arriving in Bengal in February, 1857.

When the Indian Mutiny broke out the only troops between Calcutta and Benares were the 10th Foot (a very weak battalion) and Rattray's Sikhs. **1857.**

For fourteen months the Regiment was continually engaged in active operations against the mutineers, and during 1857-58-59 shared in upwards of thirty engagements with the enemy, besides many minor affairs under the civil officers of the district.

In a despatch from the Government of India—thanking Colonel Rattray and his Sikhs—it was stated "that it was to the loyalty and bravery of the Regiment that the Government owed the power of protecting the provinces, on which depended the integrity of the finances of Bengal, and without the Regiment it would not have been possible to have preserved the hold on Behar." The most famous action of the Regiment during the mutiny was the defence of Arrah from July 29th to August 2nd, 1857, when eleven British civilians and fifty of Rattray's Sikhs, under the command of Jemadar Hookam Singh, successfully defended themselves in the Billiard Room House, near the Judge's Bungalow at Arrah, against some three thousand mutineers from native infantry battalions at Dinapore under the leadership of Keor Singh, until relieved by a force under Major Vincent Eyre.

The Billiard Room House was of two storeys; the Europeans held the upper and the Sikhs the lower storey. Among the mutineers were some Sikhs, who tried in vain by promises and threats to induce the men of Rattray's Sikhs to desert the Europeans and join them. They nobly spurned all inducements to secure their own safety by abandoning the Europeans and held out, in spite of great hardships, till relieved.

For its services during the Mutiny, Government granted the Regiment the honour to bear the words "Defence of Arrah" and "Behar" on the regimental colour. Captain Daunt and Lieut. Baker received V.C.'s and the Regiment the Indian Mutiny medal and a grant of sixteen months Batta to all ranks, besides monetary rewards for the capture of certain rebel chiefs; the garrison of Arrah received extra Batta in addition.

1860. In 1860 the Regiment marched from Arrah to Calcutta and from there a detachment proceeded to Chittagong for active service against the Kookies, whilst the Headquarters and remainder of the Regiment proceeded to Darjeeling and joined the Sikkim Force for service against the Bhootias in 1861.

In 1862 the Cavalry were detached from the Battalion under the orders of the Bengal Government. 1862.

In 1862-63 the Regiment was on service in the Khassia Hills and took part in three important engagements.

In May, 1864, the Regiment was transferred to the Regular Army as the 45th (Rattray's Sikh) Regiment Bengal Native Infantry and marched from Sylhet, Assam to Jullundur. 1864.

The uniform was red; facings—light buff; blue loongies; buff leather belts and muskets (Victoria pattern).

The Sikh Quoit was introduced and worn on the pugri six years later.

In 1866 the Regiment marched to Peshawar and two years later to Multan, and thence, via Delhi, to Moradabad in 1872, where the Enfield rifle was issued in place of the musket and the white uniform dress introduced for summer wear instead of khaki. The Snider rifle replaced the Enfield in 1875. Shortly after its receipt the Regiment marched to Delhi for the camp of exercise and afterwards proceeded to Alipore. It was here in 1877 that the first colours were presented to the Regiment. These colours are now in the Officers' mess. The Band was sanctioned the same year. 1866. 1872. 1875. 1877.

In October, 1878, the Regiment left Alipore for active service in Afghanistan, arriving at Peshawar on November 19th and joined the 4th Brigade Khyber Field Force under Lieut.-General Sir Sam Browne. A detachment of the Regiment took part in the attack on Ali Musjid Fort, but the main body remained at Jamrud till March, 1879. 1878.

In 1879 a detachment under Lieut. H. N. McRae took part in the First Bazaar Valley Expedition and the Regiment served in the Second Expedition. Afterwards the Regiment was stationed at Landi Kotal till the end of the first campaign, September, 1879, when the Regiment joined the Kabul Field Force and advanced on Jellalabad and after several engagements proceeded to Kabul with Sir Frederick Roberts' Force and was present at the battle of Charasiah on May 25th, 1880. On the evacuation of Kabul the Regiment formed part of the rear guard, under Lord Gough, from Kabul to Peshawar, which place was reached in September, 1880. 1879. 1880.

12 HISTORY OF THE 45TH RATTRAY'S SIKHS

For its services in the Afghan War the Regiment was permitted to inscribe on its colours "Ali Musjid" and "Afghanistan, 1878-80."

1882. The Regiment moved to Jhelum in January, 1882, and to Quetta in May, 1884, whence it proceeded on the Zhob Valley Expedition in September of that year and left Sibi by troop train for Agra in December.

In February, 1885, a draft of volunteers left the Regiment to join the 15th Sikhs in the Sudan and were present at the action of McNeil's Zariba and other actions. Subadar Gurditt Singh, I.O.M., was presented with a sword of honour by Lord Wolseley for gallantry at Tofrek.

Up to July, 1885, there had been a Mahomedan company in the Regiment; it was now allowed to die out and the company of Dogras was discontinued a few months later.

1886. The Regiment under the command of Colonel Waterfield left Agra for Delhi in January, 1886, for the camp of exercise at Delhi and afterwards proceeded to Rawalpindi. In October the Regiment joined the 2nd Column of the Hazara Field Force against the Akazais and Khan Khel and destroyed many villages. Subadar Major Tara Singh and Subadar Lehna Singh received the 1st and 2nd Class India Orders of Merit, respectively, for this campaign. The latter's decoration was presented on a ceremonial parade by H.R.H. Prince Albert Victor. Both these Indian Officers had taken part in the Mutiny and Subadar Lehna Singh had been present at the relief of Arrah.

1890. In December, 1890, the Regiment proceeded to Jhansi.

1894. In 1894-95 a detachment of the Regiment under Lieuts. F. T. Stewart and G. de H. Smith, attached to the King's African Rifles in British Central Africa, distinguished itself in several actions for which four Indian Orders of Merit were granted.

1895. In October, 1895, the Regiment left Jhansi for Mian Mir, where it was stationed until April, 1896, when it left for Nowshera *en route* for Malakand, furnishing a detachment of two companies, under Lieut. H. B. Rattray (son of Colonel Rattray, who raised the Regiment) and 2nd/Lieut. L. L. Wheatley at Chakdara.

On July 26th, 1897, the Fort of Chakdara was suddenly attacked by a large force of tribesmen, Swatis and Utman Khels, estimated at 10,000. The garrison, consisting of the two companies of the Regiment and forty sabres of the 11th Bengal Lancers, was closely besieged for seven days, during which time the enemy made repeated vigorous attacks on the walls of the Fort, even using ladders to scale the walls, but were always defeated with great slaughter. When the relieving troops from Malakand approached, the garrison, led by Lieuts. Rattray and Wheatley, made a most gallant sortie with the bayonet and did great execution, Lieut. Rattray being severely wounded in the neck.

One of the many brave actions of the siege was that of Sepoy Signaller Prem Singh, who was afterwards promoted to Jemadar for his gallantry. Telegraph communication with Malakand had been cut on the first night of the siege and the only means of signalling to that place was from a spur on the hill near the signal tower outside the fort. Repeatedly during the first three days of the siege the signallers with great gallantry had run out, regardless of the murderous fire, and had endeavoured to send a message for help. Each time they had been forced back with casualties. At last, on the third day, Prem Singh ran out alone, set up his helio and signalled the words "Help us" before his helio was smashed by a bullet, and he succeeded in returning to the tower unhurt. Meanwhile the same night at 10.30 p.m., the Fort at Malakand was also suddenly attacked by several thousand tribesmen; the fighting continued with the greatest ferocity till 2 a.m., when the enemy was repulsed with great loss.

The British Officers were still in the mess, when news was received by the Political Agent that the enemy was already near the top of the Pass. Lieut.-Colonel Sawyer, the Commandant of the Regiment, was on leave. Lieut.-Colonel H. N. McRae, the Second in Command, and Major W. W. Taylor rapidly collecting some twenty men, ran down to a cutting on the Bhuddist Road and for twenty minutes held "the neck of the bottle" against overwhelming odds (it was estimated that the enemy were over one thousand strong), thus enabling the rest of the Regiment to get under arms and eventually saving the whole of the Kotal Camp. When morning broke the Regiment was holding a line of piquets across the Pass, which kept the enemy at bay, but it was not till August 2nd, after incessant fighting that the Malakand Column, having been reinforced, was able to advance, fighting its way, and relieved the sorely pressed garrison of Chakdara.

Our casualties were Major Taylor and four Sepoys killed and twenty-eight other ranks wounded. A memorial stone has been erected in the cutting on the Bhuddist Road, where Major Taylor fell, and the regimental crest, together with the crests of the other regiments who took part in the defence of the Crater Camp, have been emblazoned on the rocks of the hill called " Gibraltar " in memory of the gallant defence.

After the relief of Chakdara the Regiment formed part of the 1st Brigade of the Malakand Field Force, under General Sir Bindon Blood, and took part in the expedition to Upper Swat and afterwards to the Mahmund country.

1898. In September the Regiment joined the Tirah Field Force at Peshawar and proceeded up the Bara Valley and afterwards to the Khyber Pass, returning to Jamrud in April, 1898, *en route* to Multan.

For its services in the operations of 1897 the Regiment was granted the honour to bear on its colours the words " Punjab Frontier " and " Malakand." Lieut. McRae was awarded the C.B., Lieuts. Rattray and Wheatley the D.S.O., and fourteen Indian Orders of Merit were presented to Indian Officers and Other Ranks.

1902. The Regiment proceeded to Dera Ismail Khan in July, 1900, and took part in the Mahsud-Waziri Blockade of 1900-02, and was present in many actions and suffered many casualties. For these operations the Regiment received the Indian General Service medal, 1895, with clasp " Waziristan." Captain McVean was awarded the D.S.O., and three Indian Orders of Merit were presented to Indian Officers and men.

The Regiment was re-armed with the Lee-Enfield rifle in February, 1902.

In November, 1902, Jemadar Ishar Singh and a detachment of the Regiment proceeded to Somaliland on active service with the mounted infantry.

1904. In October, 1904, the Regiment marched to Nowshera.

HISTORY OF THE 45TH RATTRAY'S SIKHS 15

The following year the Regiment was re-armed with the short magazine Lee-Enfield rifle.

In April, 1905, and again in 1906 the Regiment marched as far as Chakdara with the moveable column for the Chitral Reliefs. In January, 1905, and again in November the Regiment marched to Rawalpindi and took part in the Reviews for the Amir of Afghanistan and H.R.H. the Prince of Wales (H.M. King George V) respectively.

1905.

The average height of the trained soldier in the Regiment in January, 1906, was five feet nine inches, and the chest measurement—thirty-five inches.

1906.

On February 12th, 1908, the Regiment joined the 2nd Brigade, Bazaar Valley Field Force, at Peshawar and three days later led the advance into the Bazaar Valley and took part in the actions from Walai and Chora Camps against the Zakha Khels, returning to Nowshera on March 3rd.

1908.

On May 1st, a detachment of 500 rifles from the Regiment joined the Mohmand Field Force and was employed in protecting rail head of the Loi Shilman Railway, whence it returned to Nowshera in June.

For this campaign the Regiment received the Indian General Service Medal, 1908, with the clasp "N.W.F. India, 1908."

On December 19th the Regiment entrained for Nasirabad. Whilst at this station on February 15th, 1911, new colours were presented to the Regiment by General Sir Edmond Barrow, G.C.B., Commanding the Southern Army, the old colours being transferred to the Officers' mess.

1911.

On November 21st, the Regiment proceeded by rail to Delhi to attend the Coronation Durbar of H.M. King George V, held on December 12th, and on December 14th furnished with the Seaforth Highlanders the King Emperor's Camp Guard and, Guard of Honour. Colonel H. C. Bernard being in command of the Guard and Escorts for that day. 116 Coronation medals were presented to Officers and Indian Other Ranks of the Regiment.

A representative detachment of the Regiment, under Major H. B. Rattray, D.S.O., was present at Arrah on December 17th, during the visit of H.I.M. the King Emperor.

On December 22nd the Regiment entrained for Darya Khan and marched into Dera Ismail Khan on the 24th.

16 HISTORY OF THE 45TH RATTRAY'S SIKHS

1912.   In May, 1912, the Regiment proceeded to Tank and furnished garrisons for seven frontier posts ; it was relieved in September when it marched back to Dera Ismail Khan.

1913.
1914.   The Regiment returned to Tank and the outposts in September, 1913, and on relief in January, 1914, returned to Dera Ismail Khan.

HISTORY OF THE 45TH RATTRAY'S SIKHS

LIST OF COMMANDANTS.

45TH RATTRAY'S SIKHS.

Rank	Name	From	To	Remarks
Capt.	Rattray, T.	1.56	58	Afterwards Colonel, C.B., C.S.I.
Lieut.	Baker, V.C. ..	58	61	
Lt.-Col.	Thompson, R. L.	1.5.62	1. 5.72	
Col.	Basden, C.B.,		2.11.78	Hon. Major-Gen., Colonel of the Regt., 17.10.13.
Col.	Armstrong, F. M.	11.11.78	22.6.85	
Col.	Waterfield, H. G.	8.7.85	5.4.92	Major-Gen., C.B., Command P.F.F.
Col.	Sawyer, H. A.	6.4.92	18.4.99	
Col.	McRae, H.N., C.B., A.D.C.	19.4.99	27.1.03	Colonel on Staff Assam Bde.
Lt.-Col.	Fryer, L. C. ..	18.3.03	24.4.09	
Col.	Bernard, H. C.	25.4.09	25.4.14	Killed in action, France, 1916.
Lt.-Col.	Stewart, F. T.	26.4.14	28.7.16	
Lt.-Col.	Rattray, H.B., D.S.O.	29.7.16	1.2.17	Killed in action, 1.2.17, Mesopotamia.
Col.	McVean, D. A. D., C.S.I., D.S.O.	2.2.17	29.7.21	
Lt.-Col.	Keen, F. S., D.S.O.	31.7.21	8.5.22	Colonel, General Staff.
Lt.-Col.	McRae, H. St. G. M. McRae, D.S.O., O.B.E.	11.5.22		

LIST OF SUBADAR MAJORS.

45TH RATTRAY'S SIKHS.

Rank on Retirement	Name	From	To	Remarks
Sub.-Maj.	Attar Singh	1864	5.2.77	Deceased
Sub.-Maj.	Tara Singh, Sardar Bahadur, A.D.C. to Viceroy.	9.3.77	30.6.93	Deceased
Sub.-Maj.	Lehna Singh, Sardar Bahadur	1.6.91	1.7.93	
Sub.Maj.	Mangal Singh, I.O.M.	1.7.93	1.11.00	Deceased
Sub.-Maj.	Ishar Singh	1.11.00	15.3.01	
Capt.	Jiwand Singh, M.V.O., Sardar Bahadur, I.O.M.	15.3.01	1.8.04	A.D.C. to H.M. King Edward VII.
Capt.	Jawala Singh, Sardar Bahadur	1.8.04	1.2.05	Deceased
Sub.-Maj.	Budh Singh	1.2.05	10.4.09	Deceased
Capt.	Bhagat Singh, Sardar Bahadur	11.4.09	30.6.15	
Capt.	Sundar Singh, Sardar Bahadur I.O.M.	1.7.15	6.1.21	
Lieut.	Narain Singh, Bahadur, I.O.M.	6.1.21	1.2.22	
Sub.-Maj.	Labh Singh, M.C.	1.2.22	10.12.22	
Sub.-Maj.	Wattan Singh	11.12.22		

STATEMENT OF HONOURS AND REWARDS GAINED BY THE 45TH RATTRAY'S SIKHS FOR OPERATIONS FROM 1856 TO 1908.

Campaign	V.C.	C.B.	D.S.O.	Bt. Lt.-Col.	Bt. Major	Order B.I. (1)	Order B.I. (2)	I.O.M. 1st	I.O.M. 2nd	I.O.M. 3rd	B.O.'s	I.O.'s	I.O.R.	Other Promotion
Indian Mutiny, 1857	2				1	2	1	3	1	20				
2nd Afghan War, 1878		1		1						4	3			
Sudan (Tofrek), 1885										1				Attached 15th Sikhs
Hazara Field Force, 1888											1			
Peshawar Valley F.F.											1			
B.C. Africa, 1894					1					4	2		2	
Shaudur Pass, 1896											1			
Defence of Malakand, Defence and Relief of Chakdara and Operation, 1897		1	2							13	5	2		
With Malakand F.F., N.-W. Frontier, 1897, 1898			1		1						4	1		
Mahsud Waziri Blockade, 1901							1			3				
Tibet Mission, 1904														1
Bazaar Valley F.F., 1908				1							7	3	2	1
Total	2	2	3	1	3	2	2	3	1	45				

20 HISTORY OF THE 45TH RATTRAY'S SIKHS

HONOURS AND DISTINCTIONS OTHER THAN FOR OPERATIONS GAINED BY THE 45TH RATTRAY'S SIKHS UP TO 1915

A.D.C.—Lieut.-Colonel H. N. McRae, C.B.

Order British India, 1st Class.
Subadar Major Tara Singh.
Subadar Lehna Singh.
Subadar Jawala Singh.
First Class Senior Hospital Assistant Mahbub Khan Khan Bahadur.
Subadar Major Jawand Singh.
Subadar Major Bhagat Singh.

Order British India, 2nd Class.
Subadar Hukam Singh, I.O.M.
Subadar Amir Singh.
Subadar Lehna Singh.
Subadar Major Tara Singh.
Subadar Major Jawand Singh.
Subadar Bhagat Singh.
Subadar Teja Singh, I.O.M.

Honorary Captains.
Subadar Major Jawand Singh, Sardar Bahadur.
Subadar Major Jawala Singh, Sardar Bahadur.
Subadar Major Lehna Singh, Sardar Bahadur.

Royal Humane Society Stanhope Gold Medal.
Captain H. N. McRae.

Royal Humane Society's Silver Medal.
Captain H. N. McRae.

Royal Humane Society's Bronze Medal.
Sepoy Jiwan Singh.
Havildar Naranjan Singh.

HISTORY OF THE 45TH RATTRAY'S SIKHS 21

MacGregor Memorial Medal.
Major H. A. Sawyer.
Havildar Gurdit Singh.
Captain F. C. Waterfield.

BRITISH AND INDIAN OFFICERS WHO GAINED HONOURS AND REWARDS FOR OPERATIONS FROM 1856 TO 1908

V.C.—Captain Daunt ; Lieut. Baker.
C.B.—Lieut.-Col. F. M. Armstrong ; Lieut.-Col. H. N. McRae.
D.S.O.—Lieut. H. B. Rattray ; Lieut. L. L. Wheatley ; Capt. D. A. D. McVean.
Bt. Lieut.-Col.—Major C. L. Woodruffe.
Bt. Major.—Captain Miles ; Captain G. de H. Smith ; Captain H. B. Rattray, D.S.O.

Order of British India, 1st Class.
Subadar Major Sheikh Hadayat Ali Khan Bahadur.
Risaldar Wazir Ali Khan.

Order of British India, 2nd Class.
Risaldar Wazir Ali Khan.
Subadar Sangat Singh.

I.O.M., 1st Class.
Subadar Major Sheikh Hadayat Ali Khan Bahadur.
Jemadar Hukam Singh.
Subadar Nihal Singh.

I.O.M., 2nd Class.
Jemadar Seodyal Singh.

I.O.M., 3rd Class.
Subadar Attar Singh.
Jemadar Seodyal Singh.
Subadar Gurditt Singh.
Subadar Major Mangal Singh.
Jemadar Uttam Singh.
Subadar Ala Singh.

Mentioned in Despatches.

Lieut.-Col. F. M. Armstrong.
Lieut.-Col. C. D. Woodruffe.
Lieut. H. N McRae.
Colonel H. G. Waterfield.
Major H. N. McRae.
Lieut. F. T. Stewart.
Lieut. G. de H. Smith.
Surgeon Captain H. B. Luard.
Colonel H. A. Sawyer.
Lieut. R. M. Barff.
Lieut. H. B. Rattray.
Lieut. L. L. Wheatley.
Subadar Jawala Singh.
Jemadar Ala Singh.
Captain D. A. D. McVean.
Captain F. T. Stewart.
Lieut. L. L. Wheatley, D.S.O.
Colonel H. N. McRae, C.B., A.D.C.
Subadar Sangat Singh.

MARCHES

The Regiment has always been famous for its marching powers—amongst the most famous marches are :—

1. May, 1857.—218 miles in twelve days to quell an insurrection at Patna.
2. 1903.—Pezu to Dera Ismail Khan. Thirty-six miles in six and a half hours. Team race twelve men in marching order—open to the Brigade and race won by this Regiment on time, but lost on the shooting competition at the end of the test.
3. December, 1912.—Dera Ismail Khan to Murtaza—sixty miles in forty-two hours proceeding on Field Service.

CHAPTER I

August 4th, 1914, to February 29th, 1916

The outbreak of the Great War found the Regiment in the 1914. Derajat Brigade, split up into the following detachments :—

Tank .. .. .. Headquarters and	121	Rifles
Jandola	130	,,
Jatta	32	,,
Garhi Manjhi	40	,,
Spinkai Kach	40	,,
Nili Kach	80	,,
Khajuri Kach	150	,,
Drazinda	36	,,
Zam	95	,,
Mullazai	30	,,

to which posts they had marched on May 10th, 1914. The 27th Punjabis relieved them on September 13th, and the Regiment marched into Dera Ismail Khan. The greatest hope was entertained by all ranks of proceeding overseas, but the Regiment saw many Regiments come and go before their turn came.

Captains F. C. Waterfield and B. W. Shuttleworth were at home on leave on the outbreak of War, and were kept at home to assist in the training of the New Armies.

On August 28th, Captain R. H. Anderson proceeded to take over the appointment of Inspecting Officer, Punjab I.S. Infantry.

Calls for drafts for the link Battalions overseas came quickly and frequently, and were a great strain.

The first draft of 75 I.O. Ranks left on October 21st, for the 15th Sikhs in France. Captain W. W. Van Someren, D.S.O., left on October 23rd for the 15th Sikhs, but was on arrival posted to the 47th Sikhs instead. On October 30th, a draft of 30 I.O. Ranks left to join the 14th Sikhs overseas. On November 28th, a third draft consisting of Lieut. K. G. Hyde Cates, Subadar Balwant Singh, and 99 I.O. Ranks left to join the 15th Sikhs in France, and large recruiting parties went out to make good the deficiencies thus caused.

On December 21st, Captain W. W. Van Someren, D.S.O., was severely wounded with the 47th Sikhs in France. He never became·fit for Service again, and after the war retired from the Service.

In accordance with orders received from the Derajat Brigade, the Regiment proceeded to reinforce Tank on December 1st, in connection with disturbances on the Frontier, and returned to Dera Ismail Khan on December 24th.

Captain G. A. Phillips, I.A.R.O., joined the Regiment for instruction on September 29th, and the following Officers also joined:—

>Lieut. J. W. Guise, October 15th.
>2/Lieut. G. H. St. P. Bunbury, December 18th.
>2/Lieut. B. W. Key, December 18th.

Lieut. C. A. M. Tennant left the Regiment on appointment to the Supply and Transport Corps on October 14th.

On January 1st, 1915, the average service of the Regiment was as follows:—

>Indian Officers .. .. .. 23–24 years
>N.C. Officers 15–16
>Sepoys and Drummers .. 5–6

The average height and chest measurement on the same date was 5 ft. 8 ins. and $33\frac{1}{2}$ ins.—$35\frac{1}{2}$ ins. respectively.

On January 28th the following detachments left Dera Ismail Khan for:—

(1) Khirgi Post.—1 Indian Officer and 60 I.O. Ranks.
(2) Girni Post.—1 Indian Officer and 50 I.O. Ranks.

followed on January 30th by the Regiment for Tank. Strength: 6 British Officers, 8 Indian Officers, and 400 I.O. Ranks. A depot was left in Dera Ismail Khan to train recruits.

The Regiment at this time was very hard-pushed for men. In order to keep 550 rifles always ready, leave and furlough at reduced rates was open all the year round. They had also had to furnish 3 drafts overseas and had to maintain large recruiting parties to fill up.

During February, 61 reservists from the 14th and 15th Sikhs joined the Regiment for duty. These were mostly unsatisfactory on account of old age and it was no loss when they gradually drifted off.

On February 25th Captain H. C. Strong, a very fine officer who was seconded for service with the Burma Military Police, was drowned at sea between Calcutta and Rangoon to the great regret of all ranks.

The Headquarters of the Regiment moved out to Zam on March 6th, returning to Tank on March 25th. The detachments at Khirgi and Girni were relieved by the 87th Punjabis and returned to Tank on April 1st when the Regiment was together again.

On April 3rd the Regiment provided a fourth draft for the 15th Sikhs in France. Strength: Jemadar Karm Singh, and 49 Indian Other Ranks, and on May 13th, yet another under Jemadar Lal Singh of 52 Indian Other Ranks. This was the last draft we provided for other units. The Regiment had since November, 1914, provided drafts of 2 British Officers, 3 Indian Officers, and 304 Other Ranks to the 14th and 15th Sikhs, and this was a very severe strain on any Regiment serving in the Derajat.

Captain F. C. Waterfield was dangerously wounded on May 12th, whilst serving with the 15th Sikhs, and he died of his wounds on May 21st.

He was the son of an old Commanding Officer of the 45th, and was a very fine officer. His loss was very keenly felt in the 15th Sikhs, as well as in his own Regiment.

On May 31st, the Regiment furnished detachments for the following posts :—

	British Officers	Indian Officers	I.O. Ranks
Jandola	1	2	130
Girni	Nil	1	50
Khirgi	,,	1	61

These detachments were relieved by the 97th Infantry on September 15th, and the following posts were taken over in their place from the 87th Punjabis on the dates given below :—

Khajuri Kach	150 Rifles.	September	19th.
Nili Kach	80 ,,	,,	19th.
Drazinda	35 ,,	,,	19th.
Zam	50 ,,	,,	15th.
Jatta	35 ,,	,,	19th.

On the morning of the 18th November the Khajuri Kach detachment, when on its way to picquet for the Up Militia Convoy to Tanai was attacked by 100 Mahsuds lying in ambush about two miles from the post.

The enemy was driven off after a stiff fight lasting 20 minutes, and Captain J. G. Wilson, commanding at Khajuri Kach passed the convoy through safely. No rifles or ammunition were lost, and all killed and wounded were brought back safely to Khajuri Kach.

Our casualties were :—

Killed in Action.—5 Indian Other Ranks.

Wounded.—2/Lieut. S. F. Criper, I.A.R.O., and nine I.O. Ranks. Jemadar Mehar Singh and 1121 Sepoy Puran Singh were awarded the I.D.S.M. for gallantry in action on this occasion.

(Extract *Gazette* of India, No. 815 of 1915.)

The following is a copy of the G.O.C. Derajat Brigade report to Army Headquarters dated December 4th, 1915.

"I have the honour to forward the report regarding the attack by Mahsuds on the picquets of the 45th Rattray's Sikhs on November 18th last, a rough sketch is forwarded explaining it. [Not forthcoming.]

The convoy left Khajuri Kach a day later than usual, and the day it should have left Captain J. G. Wilson commanding at Khajuri Kach was informed by the Political Munshi, that 80 Mahsuds had intended to attack the convoy, but not meeting it had gone off into the Hills, north of the Gomal River. Similar reports are constantly received at the posts.

He, however, sent out stronger picquets than usual under 2/Lieut. S. F. Criper, I.A.R.O., who had been out with him several times, and whom he considered capable of command.

"The men behaved very well indeed under very trying circumstances, being fired into from three sides at once, as is

HISTORY OF THE 45TH RATTRAY'S SIKHS 27

proved by their losing no rifles or ammunition, and beating off the attack, and I think that they did all that could be expected of them, and maintained the high reputation the Regiment has always had.

The formation in which the picquets advanced does not appear to have been good, and the flanking party on the right flank should have been out further beyond the nullah, also a flanking party out on the left, but it is difficult to criticize these points without an intimate knowledge of the ground. The Officer commanding 45th Rattray's Sikhs has already given orders on these points.

It is impossible with the comparatively small numbers at the various posts, to do more than picquet the important points or to send flanking parties all over the ground which should be searched, otherwise the convoys would not get through before dark.

Now the posts have been strengthened, orders have been issued for strong supports to be sent with the picquets, and for all the bad ground near the line of advance to be searched as far as possible.

Captain J. G. Wilson did not go out himself that day, as he was preparing a sketch and report on the available camping ground near the Post which I had asked for, and which he had to despatch next day by the down convoy, otherwise he would have been out himself, as he always goes out with the picquets."

The following despatch from His Excellency, General Sir Beauchamp Duff, G.C.B., G.C.S.I., K.C.V.O., C.I.E., A.D.C., Commander-in-Chief in India, on minor operations on the N.W. Frontier of India, dated 9th March, 1916, contained the following allusion to the above fight of the Regiment :—

"THE TOCHI VALLEY AND DERAJAT."

"A Militia picquet was attacked on November 12th, 1915, and on the 18th, a detachment of the 45th Rattray's Sikhs on picqueting duty near Khajuri Kach in the Gomal was attacked by some 80—100 raiders. The enemy was driven off and fled, and the convoy proceeded to its destination in safety. Brigadier-General F. J. Fowler, C.B., D.S.O., Commanding the Derajat Brigade, states that the detachment behaved

28 HISTORY OF THE 45TH RATTRAY'S SIKHS

very well indeed, and maintained the high reputation of the Regiment.

The successful operations mentioned above, combined with pressure brought to bear on the Mahsuds by the Civil Authorities, has prevented any tribal outbreaks on a considerable scale, but raiding has been constant, which necessitated constant vigilance, and action on the part of the troops.

"In conclusion, I attach a list of officers and men, whose names I desire to bring to notice for gallantry, or good service, in connection with the operations dealt with above.

* * * * *

Jemadar Mehar Singh.
Sepoy Puran Singh, 1121."

Captain W. D. Keyworth, I.M.S., joined the Regiment for duty on March 4th, 1915.

In November the following officers joined the Regiment for duty :—

2/Lieut. R. H. L. Minchin.
2/Lieut. A. C. Curtis, M.C.
2/Lieut. W. A. Christie.
2/Lieut. G. Mitchell.

During the year the following officers of the I.A.R.O. joined the Regiment for Training.

Name	Joined the Regt. for duty	Proceeded on F.S. overseas or to other destination
Capt. G. A. Phillips.	Sept. 29th, 1914.	Jan. 27th, 1915.
2/Lieut. N. E. Kirby.	Jan. 31st, 1915.	May 13th, 1915.
,, D. Craik.	Feb. 4th, 1915.	March 6th, 1915.
,, C. W. A. Dunning	Feb. 21st, 1915.	July 1st, 1915.
,, N. C. Wimbush.	Feb. 21st, 1915.	April 22nd, 1915.
,, K. de B. Smart.	April 25th, 1915.	Oct. 26th, 1916.
,, S. F. Criper.	July 28th, 1915.	—
,, A. H. Worster.	July 28th, 1915.	—
,, A. C. Stone.	Aug. 19th, 1915.	—
,, B. W. Murdoch.	Sept. 10th, 1915.	—
,, H. E. Crocker.	Sept. 18th, 1915.	To R.A.F.

HISTORY OF THE 45TH RATTRAY'S SIKHS 29

1916.

The Regiment received the welcome and long-awaited orders to mobilize for Indian Expeditionary Force "D" (Mesopotamia) on January 22nd, and, being relieved on the Derajat outposts by the 121st Pioneers, marched into Dera Ismail Khan for the last time on January 31st.

The month of February was spent in preparation. On the 20th, a draft of 40 I.O. Ranks arrived from the 15th Sikhs Depot to complete the Regiment to War Establishment.

Before proceeding to the story of the Regiment on active service, a word about our drafts who proceeded to the 14th and 15th Sikhs will not be out of place.

Nearly all who proceeded to the 14th were killed or wounded and only five rejoined the Regiment in the field in February, 1917, viz.—Subadar Kehar Singh, No 4538 Havildar Bhag Singh (who afterwards died of pneumonia), No. 665 Lance Naick Gagar Singh, No. 727 Lance Naick Gajjan Singh (afterwards transferred to the 151st Infantry, and demobilized) and No. 4993 Sepoy Santa Singh.

Of the drafts sent to the 15th, Captain K. G. Hyde-Cates held the "Glory Hole" at Festubert very gallantly on May 17th–18th, 1915, until Lieut. Smyth's party reached him with bombs. With Lieut. Smyth, who was awarded the Victoria Cross on this occasion, amongst others were two of our men, No. 1001 Sepoy Ujagar Singh, and No. 1036 Sepoy Fateh Singh, who were both awarded the I.D.S.M., and promoted to Lance Naick for their gallantry.

Our men also took part in three actions fought by the 15th Sikhs, in the Senussi Campaign of 1915–16. No. 4038 Jemadar Mala Singh, who had been promoted for good service in the field in France, unfortunately died of wounds received in the last of these three actions.

Sixty other ranks of the drafts we sent to the 15th, rejoined the Regiment in the field on January 26th, 1917, under Jemadar Lal Singh.

CHAPTER II

MARCH 1ST—DECEMBER 12TH, 1916

1916.
March.

On March 1st, 1916, the 45th Sikhs, strength, British Officers, 13, Indian Officers, 18, I.O.R., 796

British Officers.	Indian Officers.
Lieut.-Colonel F. T. Stewart, Commanding.	Subadar Major Sundar Singh.
Major H. B. Rattray, D.S.O., "D" Company.	Subadar Ishar Singh.
Captain R. Rainsford Hannay, "B". Company.	Subadar Nidhan Singh.
Captain J. E. Waller, "A" Company.	Subadar Wariam Singh.
Lieut. R. A. Macausland, "C" Company.	Subadar Natha Singh, I.O.M.
Lieut. G. H. Atkinson, Adjutant.	Subadar Narain Singh.
2/Lieut. A. C. Curtis, M.C., Qr.-Mr.	Subadar Lehna Singh.
2/Lieut. R. H. L. Minchin.	Subadar Bhag Singh.
2/Lieut. B. W. Key, Machine Gun Officer.	Jemadar Thaman Singh.
2/Lieut. G. Mitchell.	Jemadar Ram Singh.
2/Lieut. A. H. Worster, I.A.R.O.	Jemadar Karam Singh.
2/Lieut. S. F. Criper, I.A.R.O.	Jemadar Lehna Singh.
Captain W. D. Keyworth, I.M.S.	Jemadar Kehar Singh.
	Jemadar Labh Singh.
	Jemadar Buta Singh.
	Jemadar Sundar Singh.
	Jemadar Rur Singh.
	Jemadar Lal Singh.

marched out of Dera Ismail Khan where they had spent four-and-a-half very strenuous years for Darya Khan, en route for active service in Mesopotamia. The Regiment entrained and left for Karachi the same day, arriving at Kiamari Docks on March 3rd. After the usual medical inspection, they at once embarked on the troopship *Ekma* (B.I.S.N. Co.), and were all aboard by 7.45 p.m. Three-hundred of the 2/5th Gurkha Rifles and the 16th Mule Corps were also on board, and the men were very crowded. The O.C. Troops was Lieut.-Col. F. G. Lucas, D.S.O., 2/5th Gurkha Rifles.

The ship sailed at 9.15 p.m., and the voyage to Basra proceeded uneventfully except for a few cases of measles amongst our men. The drums played " Retreat " on the

HISTORY OF THE 45TH RATTRAY'S SIKHS

main deck every evening. The H.M.T. *Ekma* arrived at Basra on March 8th. There was a great deal of shipping in the stream and much congestion, so the Regiment remained anchored in the stream until March 13th, when the *Ekma* went alongside at Magil. The Regiment disembarked at 2 p.m., and went into camp at Magil.

The disembarkation occupied five hours, but there was only one gangway available for men and baggage. Lieut.-Col. F. T. Stewart in Regimental orders congratulated all ranks " on the smart and silent manner in which the disembarkation was carried out."

The camp at Magil was knee deep in mud owing to recent rain, and the arrangements for water were indifferent. Camp was changed to Makina on March 16th, and the Regiment joined the 42nd Infantry Brigade—1/4th Dorsets, 2/4th Gurkha Rifles, 2/5th Gurkha Rifles—at that time without a Commander. Next to us in camp were the 21st Mountain Battery, old friends of the Regiment in the Derajat.

From March 17th to 27th, the Regiment was employed in " bund " building round Magil and Makina, and a detachment of 200 rifles under Captain R. Rainsford Hannay proceeded to Shaiba for guards and escort duties, but rejoined on the 27th. During these ten days all young soldiers under eight months' service, turned out twice daily for training under the Adjutant.

On March 27th, the Regiment was transferred to the 41st Infantry Brigade, commanded by Brig.-General A. Cadell. (The other regiments were the 2/4th and 1/8th Gurkha Rifles.)

On March 28th a draft of Burma Military Police, who had been attached to the 15th Sikhs in France and Egypt, joined us. Strength: three I.O.'s and 131 I.O.R.'s. They were a very fine body of men. On the 29th, a regrettable incident took place in this draft, for a sepoy shot a comrade dead, wounded another and then shot himself. The real motive for the crime was not discovered.

When the Regiment joined the 41st Infantry Brigade, it was announced that the Brigade would move up to the front in the near future, so Brigade tactical exercises were held daily, and all surplus baggage and kits were stored in the Indian Combined Depot at Basra.

April.

Many orders and counter orders to proceed up river were received, and at last on April 4th, the Regiment (less the machine gun section and Officers' chargers, which were left behind to come up later under 2/Lieut. B. W. Key) and a field ambulance boarded a river steamer and two barges, one of which had no awning at all. They sailed at dawn on April 5th and passing Qurnah, the legendary Garden of Eden, reached Amarah after sunset on the 7th, Shaikh Saad early on the 11th, only halting there about twenty minutes, and Wadi at 10 a.m. the same day. There they at once disembarked and pitched camp on the left bank.

During the voyage up the River Tigris, the steamer tied up every night to let the men cook ; the voyage was characterized by very windy and stormy weather, and the steamer broke from her moorings alongside the bank on two or three occasions. On the night of the 9/10th April the steamer was flooded out by torrential rain, as the awnings were not rainproof, and all ranks got very wet indeed. The ship's officers, however, came to the rescue, and some officers had to appear at breakfast next morning in seagoing blue and gold uniform.

Map No. 1.

The Regiment camped on a very dirty site at Wadi, left bank. The Brigade Staff and the other two battalions of the Brigade had already arrived there. There was much aerial activity, as our main aerodrome was situated at Wadi, and gun fire could be continually heard some ten miles west in the Sannaiyat direction.

The Regiment was at last up in the fighting area.

On the 13th, the Regiment moved over to the right bank at dawn, crossing by a new bridge of boats that had just been completed. The camp was pitched near the aerodrome, and our duty was to protect it with a line of picquets.

The 1st Double Company—Captain J. E. Waller—proceeded to Orah on the 15th to occupy a detached post there, and on this date 2/Lieut. B. W. Key arrived with the machine gun section and Officers' chargers, having left Basra on April 7th.

Our life at Wadi consisted for the most part of fatigues, guards and escort duties. The weather was beginning to warm up, and there were many dust storms, which caused much damage to our aeroplanes.

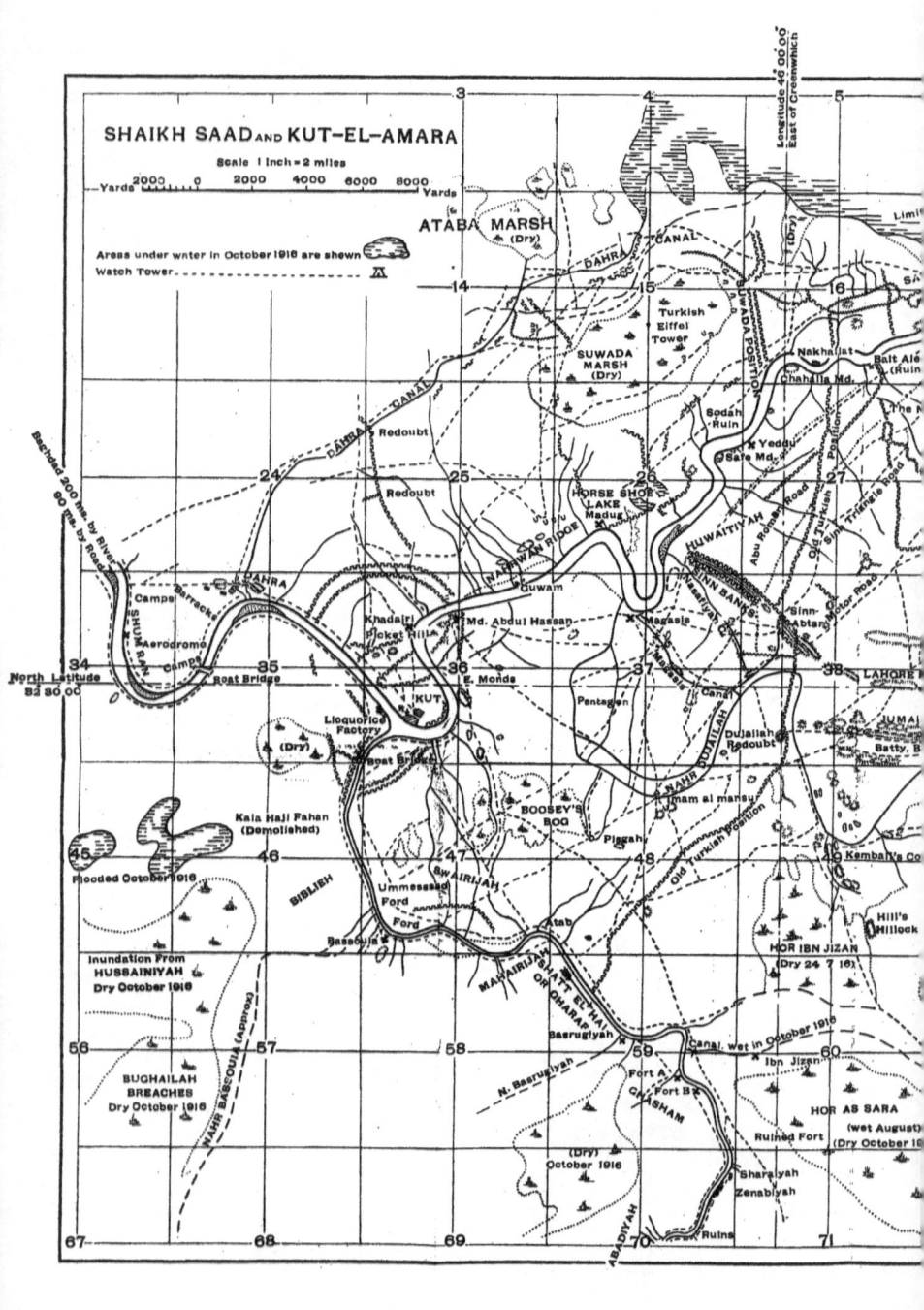

MAP I.

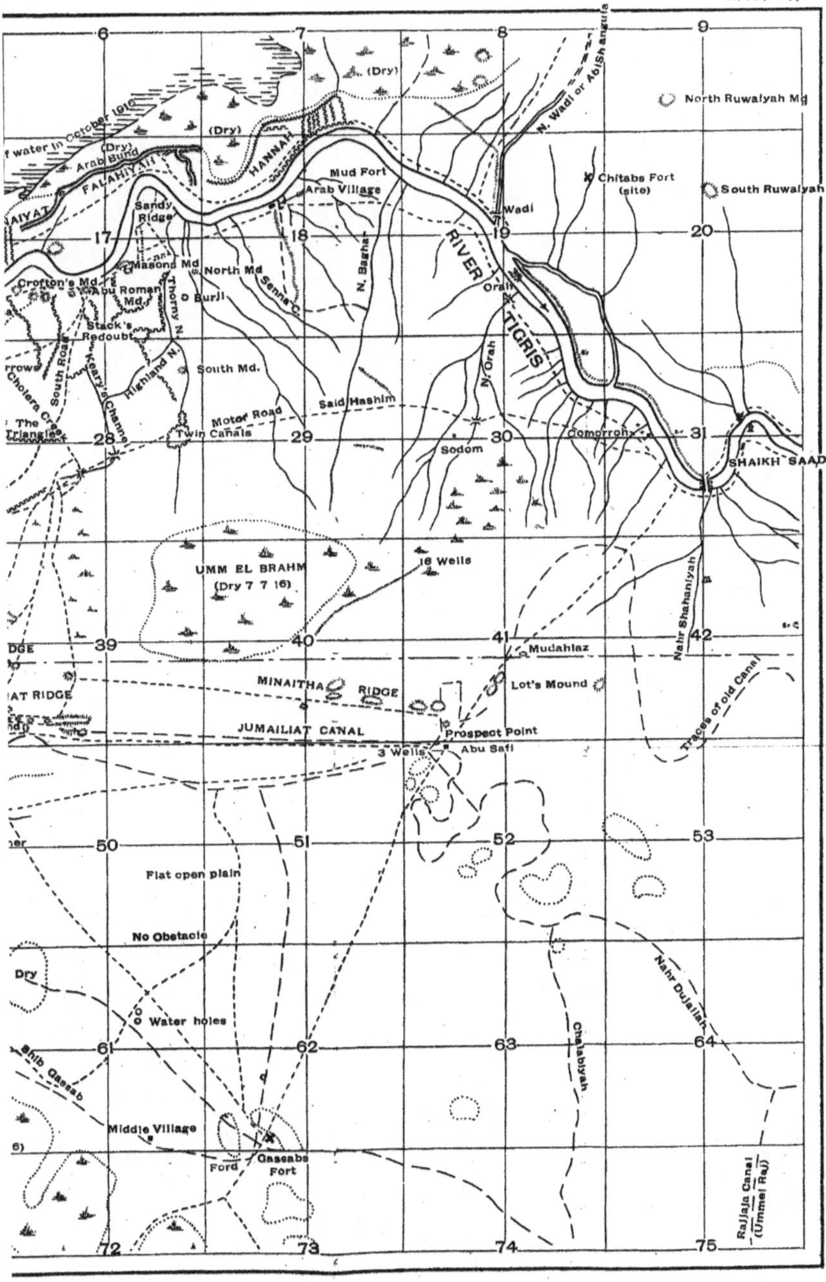

(Dry)
North Ruwaiyah Md
N. Wadi or Abi Shanguia
(Dry)
Arab Bund
HANNAH
FALAHIYAH
Mud Fort
Arab Village
Chitabs Fort (site)
South Ruwaiyah Md
Sandy Ridge
Wadi
RIVER
TIGRIS
Masons Md
North Md
Crofton's Md
Abu Roman Md.
Thorny N.
O Burji
Senna C.
N. Bagha
Orah
Stack's Redoubt
South Road
Keary's Channel
Highland N.
South Md.
N. Orah
Cholera Cr.
The Triangles
Motor Road
Twin Canals
Said Hashim
Sodom
Comorroh
SHAIKH SAAD
UMM EL BRAHM
(Dry 7 7 16)
16 Wells
Nahr Shahaniyah
Mudahlaz
MINAITHA RIDGE
Lot's Mound
Traces of old Canal
JUMAILIAT CANAL
Prospect Point
3 Wells
Abu Safi
Flat open plain
No Obstacle
Dry
Water holes
Nahr Dujailah
Chalabiyah
Shib Qassab
Middle Village
Ford
Qassabs Fort
Rajjaja Canal (Ummel Raj)
6
7
8
9
17
18
19
20
28
29
30
31
39
40
41
42
50
51
52
53
61
62
63
64
72
73
74
75

HISTORY OF THE 45TH RATTRAY'S SIKHS 33

The ill-fated ship *Jalna* passed on the 23rd minus a mast. She was heavily laden with rations for the Kut garrison, and was to run the gauntlet into Kut under cover of darknesss. Unfortunately she ran into a wire hawser stretched across the river near Magasis and was captured by the Turks with all her stores on the night of the 25th, all her crew being killed or captured.

On the nights of the 27th and 28th our picquets fired on parties of marauding Arabs without result, and on the latter date news was received that Major H. B. Rattray, D.S.O., had been promoted to the rank of Lieut.-Colonel.

On the 29th we received the news of the surrender of Kut through a Flying Corps officer.

On the 30th No. 1423 Sepoy Kirpal Singh was tried by a S.G.C.M. for murder. The evacuation of Wadi Post began this day, and Hospitals, Ordnance and S. and T. Dumps, etc., began leaving for Shaikh Saad.

On May 1st a cavalry brigade passed through Wadi on its way to Shaikh Saad, and Major C. H. Watson, I.M.S., our Medical Officer, who was serving in it, came and saw the Regiment. News was received that the Regiment was to be posted to the 37th Infantry Brigade, 14th Division, at an early date, and this was confirmed on May 2nd. The move was to take place when the evacuation of Wadi Post was completed.

May.

On May 5th, Brig.-General A. Cadell and Staff of the defunct 41st Infantry Brigade set sail for Basra, after handing over their documents to the Regiment, on the breaking up of the Brigade. As a Brigade they had not been fortunate enough to see any active operations.

Arabs were very active about this time in the direction of Sodom ; the Cavalry Brigade dealt with them, and they were never formidable.

On the 7th one of our aeroplanes was brought down by an enemy plane close to our camp. There were thirty hits on it, including one in the petrol tank, but the pilot landed her safely.

A case of cholera occurred in the Regiment this day ; all water was boiled and no more cases occurred.

On the 9th the 4th Double Company, Major H. B. Rattray,

C

D.S.O., moved over to the left bank to assist the 12th Pioneers in making a new post on the Wadi.

On the 10th the 3rd Double Company, Captain R. A. Macausland, relieved the 1st Double Company at Orah Post. A Turkish plane came over and was fired at by us, and was believed to have been hit.

The Regiment, less the 4th Double Company, moved over to the new post on the left bank at Wadi on the 13th, the 4th Double Company remained on the right bank.

On May 14th under orders of the Corps, Chittab's Fort was destroyed by the Regiment, aided by an explosive party of the 12th Pioneers, without meeting any opposition; only a few Arab horsemen were seen in the distance.

Captain J. G. Wilson rejoined the Regiment, having escaped from the draft of another regiment by stealth. He had been left at the Depot when the Regiment left India on field service, and had been relieved by Captain K. G. Hyde Cates, after he had been released from duty with the 15th Sikhs.

On May 15th, the 4th Double Company, Major H. B. Rattray, D.S.O., marched to Shaikh Saad, and on the same day the Regiment was visited by Major-General R. G. Egerton, G.O.C., 14th Indian Division, whose division the Regiment was shortly to enter.

On the 20th a party of Arab horsemen moved from a village three miles north of Chittab's Fort towards the Hannah position to loot. The 1st Double Company at once moved out and caused them to disperse by long-range fire. After dark they returned and began digging up the old Wadi camp, making a terrific noise, and they were dispersed by the Sussex Battery T.F. in the post.

On the 21st a reconnaissance was ordered by the Corps towards the Hannah position, in conjunction with one from the 7th Division at Sannaiyat. The 2nd Double Company went out, and, finding nothing, returned by noon.

In the evening the Arabs repeated their performance of the 20th, and were again dispersed by gunfire. After dark they returned to the old camp at Wadi, but were hurriedly dispersed by a machine gun ambush, which we had laid for them.

About this period our picquets frequently fired at night on

HISTORY OF THE 45TH RATTRAY'S SIKHS 35

small parties of marauding Arabs, but never succeeded in killing any.

Orders had been received that the Regiment (less 3rd Double Company at Orah Post and 4th Double Company at Shaikh Saad) would march to join the 37th Infantry Brigade at Shaikh Saad in two marches on the 30th, and on the 29th the 8th Cheshire Regiment (13th Division) arrived, and took over all of our guards and picquets.

On the 30th the Regiment (less 3rd and 4th Double Companies) marched at 4 a.m., via the Hannah position and the bridge of boats at Falahiyah, and camped at Arab Village at 9.15 a.m. The march was cool for the time of year.

The march was continued on the 31st at 3.45 a.m., Shaikh Saad being reached three hours later. Here they pitched camp on a site already marked out by the 3rd Double Company, who had marched in from Orah on the 30th, and the 4th Double Company, who had arrived from Wadi on May 20th.

The camp was pitched on long dry grass, and grass fires were both frequent and dangerous. The Regiment had to turn out and extinguish one near camp within three hours of arrival.

The Regiment now joined the 37th Infantry Brigade, the other three battalions of which were the 1/4th Devon Regiment T.F., the 1/2nd Gurkha Rifles and the 36th Sikhs. Lieut.-Colonel F. T. Stewart was appointed to the temporary command of the Brigade on our arrival, and Lieut.-Colonel H. B. Rattray, D.S.O., assumed temporary command of the Regiment.

The strength of the Regiment according to the A.G. at the June. Base about this time was B.O.'s, 13; I.O.'s, 19; I.O.R.'s, 914, but this number included sick in the country and drafts not yet joined.

During the night of June 1st, Lieut.-Colonel F. T. Stewart's tent was broken into by Arabs. His 80 lb. tent, belt, field glasses and many other articles were carried off, and he woke up to find about eight Arabs in his tent. Colonel Stewart was commanding the Brigade, and had a guard of another battalion in the vicinity.

On June 2nd, Major-General R. G. Egerton, commanding

the 14th Indian Division, inspected the Regiment on parade at 5.30 a.m. The men turned out exceedingly well, and on the 3rd a permanent guard of not less than 40 rifles was ordered as a guard to the Divisional Commander.

The Regiment remained at Shaikh Saad from June 3rd to 13th doing large numbers of fatigues on loading and unloading ships.

Orders were issued for Double Company, Battalion and Brigade Training to commence, and programmes had to be submitted. On the 8th all ranks learnt of Lord Kitchener's death with deep regret. On June 11th the Regiment had a very heavy day escorting an ammunition column to Arab Village and back. The day was a scorching hot one.

On the 13th the Acting Adjutant-General in India visited the Regiment, and at 3 p.m. on the same day the 37th Infantry Brigade was ordered to march to Twin Canals that night on operation scale of kits and tentage. All our surplus kits had to be dumped at Shaikh Saad and small guards left under Brigade arrangements.

We were ordered to pass the starting point at 10 p.m. The Regiment was there to the minute, but had to wait there two hours, as none of the other regiments put in an appearance till much later.

The march was an easy one of ten miles, and the night was cool. The Regiment led the column, and the advanced guard reached Twin Canals at 6.15 a.m. on June 14th, when camp was pitched. Water was four miles away at Falahiyah, and the pakhals arranged for by the Staff did not turn up, so the Brigade got practically no water all this hot day.

The Brigade was at Twin Canals for the purpose of "harvesting" twice a day. Sickles were provided, and the crops dumped in the 39th Brigade area. This "harvesting" went on till June 19th, when the 37th Infantry Brigade marched at 6 p.m. from Twin Canals for Sinn Abtar. The Regiment did rear guard this night, and had to leave the 2nd Double Company—Captain J. G. Wilson—at Twin Canals as guard over the crops.

The Brigade reached Sinn Abtar at 12.10 a.m., on the 20th. The Regiment shared a camp with the 36th Sikhs, and provided a "Sniping Picquet" of 1 I.O., 36 rifles, and one

HISTORY OF THE 45TH RATTRAY'S SIKHS 37

machine gun at the northern end of the Sinn banks. Water in this camp also was both far away and scarce.

On June 21st the 2nd Double Company—Captain J. G. Wilson—rejoined the Regiment. Lieut.-Colonel F. T. Stewart took about 100 rifles to reconnoitre the ground on which a new series of redoubts were to be constructed by the Regiment about one mile westwards of the then established firing line. (See Map 1, 37C.)

Orders were received to send out parties to dig wells on the 22nd, but these were cancelled and the two double companies were ordered to move out permanently. Accordingly, on June 22nd, at 4 a.m., the left wing under Lieut.-Colonel H. B. Rattray, D.S.O., marched to the site of the new work and bivouacked there. They dug two wells that day, and found water at 13 feet. The sides of the wells, however, required to be shored up by experts, and the water turned out was unsuitable for drinking purposes. The canal bank was also put into a state of defence as a temporary measure.

On June 23rd, Headquarters and the right wing marched to the Dujailah Canal, and the whole Regiment took up a frontage of 700 yards on it. The position was divided up into two sectors, each held by a double company with two double companies in support. The days were very hot, and the watering arrangements were at first very sketchy.

On June 24th, the C.R.E. came out and settled the trace of various redoubts, and a R.E. officer came out to live with the Regiment. Water was very scarce, the men felt the heat very much owing to lack of water, hard digging and the effects of the sun. Lieut. and Adjutant G. H. Atkinson, who had been sick for some days, had to go to hospital.

Hand grenades had been issued to the Regiment for the first time a few days previously, and on June 25th the first and last fatal bomb accident took place. The armourer, No. 719 Naick Mohammad Bakhsh, was trying to extract a piece of detonator from a bomb in a dugout, when the bomb exploded, killing him instantaneously, at the same time wounding No. 4755 Sepoy Kala Singh severely, and No. 1012 Sepoy Teja Singh slightly, whilst two other men escaped untouched.

Work on the defences was carried out twice daily till the

end of the month. The Regiment was assisted by working parties from the 1/2nd Gurkhas and 34th Pioneers. A motor lorry commenced to bring in pakhals of water every evening and the water question improved somewhat.

On June 28th, Major-General R. G. Egerton, G.O.C., 14th Division, came out to inspect the Pentagon, which was the

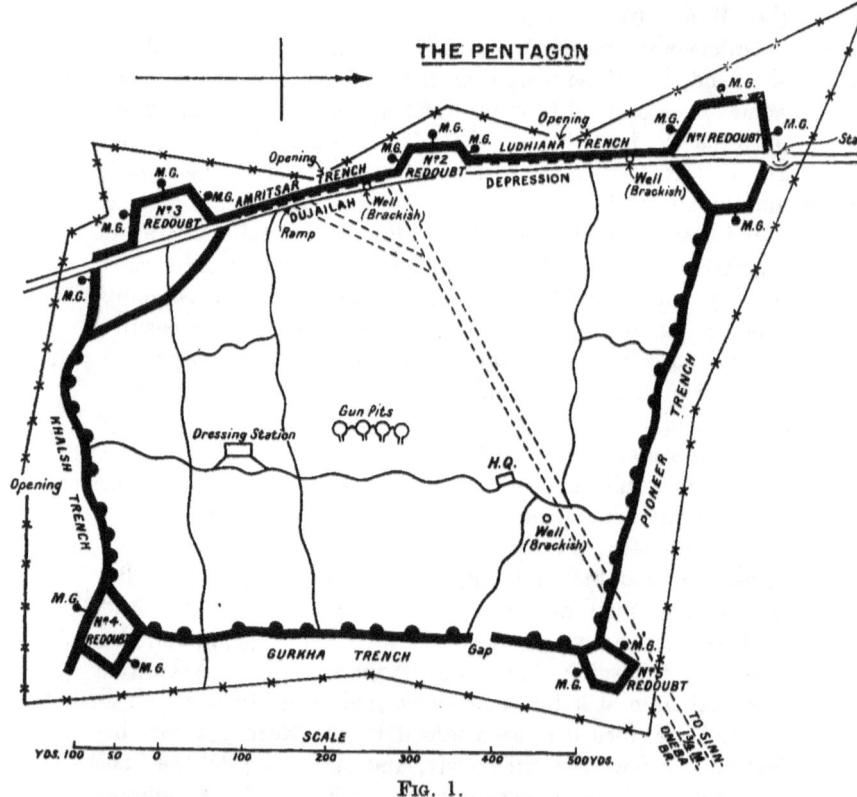

Fig. 1.

new name for the post. (See sketch and its position on Map No. 1.) He also ordered a new covered road to be made along the Dujailah Canal to Imam-Ali-Mansur.

Our patrols were in constant touch with the enemy picquet line to the west.

A lot of sickness occurred during June, three officers, *i.e.*, Captain W. D. Keyworth, I.M.S., 2/Lieut. A. H. Worster,

HISTORY OF THE 45TH RATTRAY'S SIKHS

I.A.R.O., and 2/Lieut. B. W. Key were invalided sick to India. The prevailing ailments were fever, jaundice and dysentery, and there was a lack of fresh meat and green vegetables in the men's rations.

July was remarkable only for the great heat and dust. *July.* The Shamal or N.W. wind had commenced, which raised clouds of dust, though it tempered the heat a little. The work on the Pentagon went on incessantly, twice a day. Numerous communication trenches, dugouts, gun and machine gun emplacements, wire entanglements, etc., were constructed, and the covered road to Imam-Ali-Mansur was completed by July 10th. Escorts to convoys to and from S.P.4 were also frequent.

There was a good deal of aerial activity on the part of the Turk, who had at this time aerial ascendency. Our machine guns frequently fired at his planes, but never had any luck. On July 11th a plane came over and kept dropping coloured lights. The result was that the 36th Sikhs' outpost line near Magasis was shelled, with some casualties. It was felt that the Pentagon would receive attention in the near future, and all working parties were told off to cover.

The Pentagon was visited on July 15th by Lieut.-General Sir F. S. Maude, who was at this time commanding the 3rd I.A. Corps.

About the middle of the month, a medical inspection for scurvy was held, as it was beginning to get prevalent in the Regiment, with the following result : Bad cases, 5 ; slight, 6 ; suspected, 27.

One month's leave to India was sanctioned to 15% of men who had been out of India for one year and over. This in our case only affected some of the B.M.P. men attached, and 34 of them proceeded on leave.

Parades were started twice a week on the last day of the month. No parades other than guards had been held since we took over the Pentagon. The Regiment, however, remained well turned out and as good at drill as ever.

The Regiment was much reduced by sickness during the month, and its strength fell to five British Officers and, roughly, 500 Indian Ranks. The following British Officers were invalided sick to India :—

Captain J. E. Waller, Lieut. G. H. Atkinson and 2/Lieut. S. F. Criper, I.A.R.O.

August. The Regiment remained in the Pentagon for the whole month of August. Parades and musketry were carried out in the morning on most days, and work on the defences in the afternoons.

Morning and evening patrols were sent out in the direction of Kut daily, and were often fired on.

Lieut. J. W. Guise joined the Regiment in the field on August 3rd.

The Turks, during the month, were active in digging and wiring positions in the Mohomed Abdul Hassan bend, and on the Hai Bridge defences, left bank.

There was a good deal of aerial activity in which our planes were generally driven off, but on August 12th and 13th Fokkers were driven off by our planes.

On August 13th one of our planes appeared over the Pentagon in the early morning, and a Fokker at once came out and attacked him.

Our plane took him on single-handed for 15 minutes, when two more of our planes came up. The Fokker then took on all three, and they circled round firing at each other for 30 minutes. To the joy of all ranks the Fokker was hit, and was forced to land on the left bank of the River Tigris, north of Magasis, when our heavy guns quickly wrecked it. We heard that a new airman from the French front was piloting our first machine that went up.

On August 14th in the morning the enemy planes dropped fifty bombs on the 14th Divisional Area, paying particular attention to the 4th Devons, artillery lines and 36th Infantry Brigade Camp, inflicting casualties of two killed and six wounded.

About the middle of the month the Turks commenced and finished a tall white obelisk north of Kut on the Kut Peninsula, which puzzled our force for some time. This eventually turned out to be the Turkish memorial in honour of the capture of Kut in April, 1916.

One Lewis gun was issued to the Regiment for instructional purposes, and was at that time a new and little-known weapon. By the end of the month all British Officers had fired a great deal with it.

MAP 2.

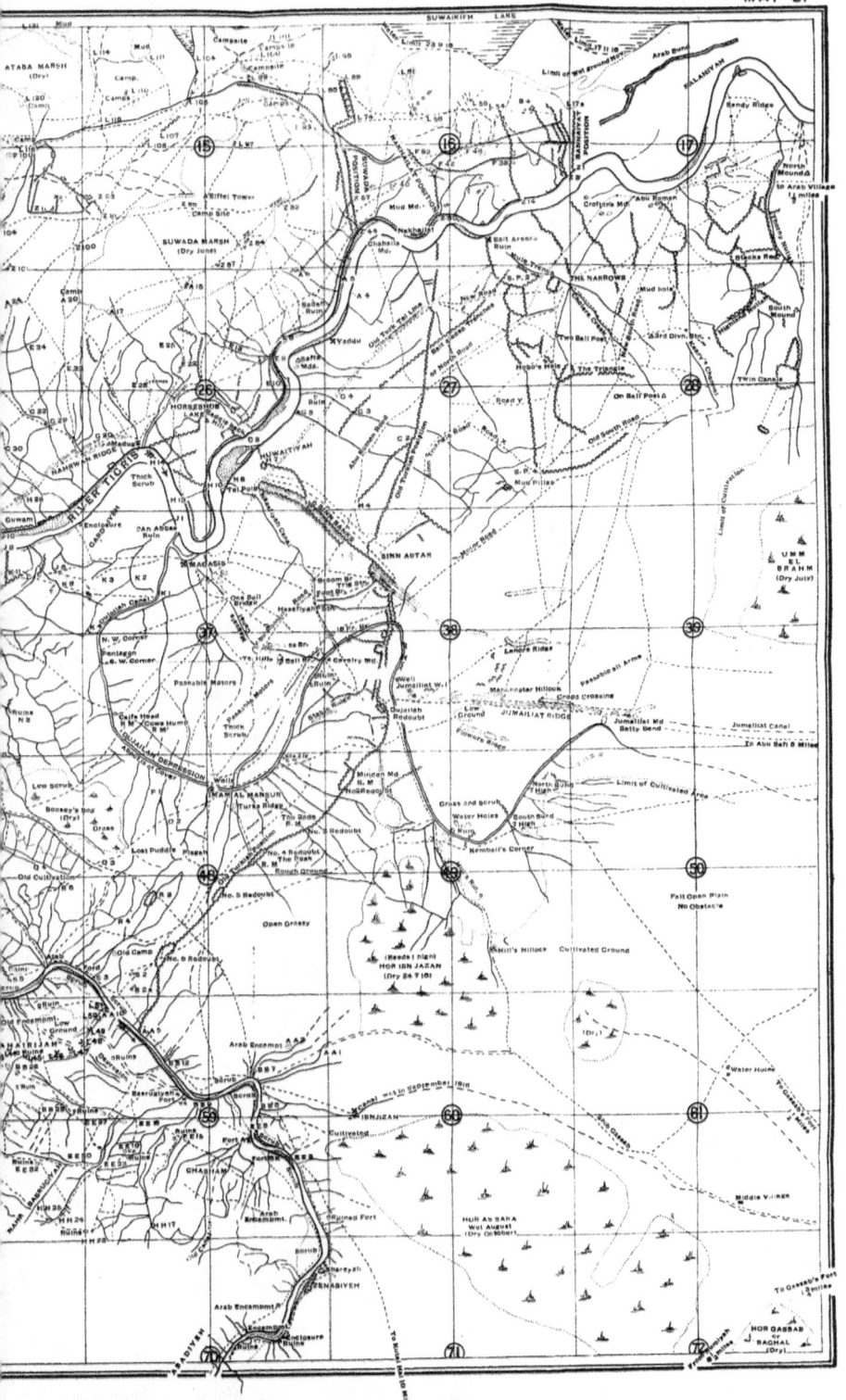

HISTORY OF THE 45TH RATTRAY'S SIKHS 41

The weather was very hot and trying all the month, and sickness and scurvy was on the increase. The men stuck to it very well, and only gave in when they were very bad.

On August 28th the command of the Mesopotamian Expeditionary Force was taken over by Lieut.-General Sir F. S. Maude, K.C.B., and the Force came under the control of the War Office, and from now onwards the fortunes of the Force gradually turned.

The entire month of September was spent by the Regiment *September.* in the Pentagon with the usual parades, patrols and work. Double companies were also able to carry out night firing with the aid of Very lights on three occasions. The heat was lessening, but there was a great amount of sickness, and our strength fell to about 300 Indian Ranks. Early in the month, in consequence of our lower numbers and sickness, parades and work, also the garrisons of redoubts, had to be reduced.

Lieut.-Colonel F. T. Stewart commanded the 37th Infantry Brigade as a temporary measure from September 3rd to 22nd, but on the 23rd instant Colonel O. W. Carey, 27th Punjabis, was appointed to the command of the Brigade vice Brigadier-General F. J. Fowler, C.B., D.S.O., invalided.

On the 6th many of our sick of the captured Kut garrison arrived at Kut in steamers for exchange with Turkish sick, under arrangements made by the army commanders of both sides. They were trans-shipped to our hospital ships near Magasis, and flags of truce were flown for the day at Imam-Ali-Mansur, Magasis, the Pentagon and certain other points.

Captain R. A. Macausland was attached to the 36th Sikhs for temporary duty on September 12th, and on the 13th, 2/Lieut. K. H. Preston, I.A.R.O., 15th Sikhs, joined the Regiment with a very welcome draft of 81 men.

There was some aerial activity during the month, our planes bombed Kut, Shumran and the Hai bridge defences on four occasions during the month. The Turkish planes dropped bombs on the Sinn area with no damage, and on the 25th, at 5 a.m., they dropped twenty-five bombs on the Pentagon, from which the Regiment had three men slightly wounded.

The Turkish artillery was also active. On September 12th,

their heavy and light guns bombarded the Sinn area for one-and-a-half hours. Several shells dropped into the camp of the 1/4th Devons, causing some casualties.

On the 17th and 18th they shelled the 36th Sikhs camp, causing them to move camp on the latter day.

On the 27th they shelled the Pentagon about 4 p.m., for two hours with five-nines, and at the same time shelled Imam-Ali-Mansur and Magasis, firing 480 rounds altogether. They put twenty-five shells into the Pentagon, most of them dropping near No. 5 Redoubt. No. 4114 Havildar Harnam Singh was our only casualty, wounded in the neck.

Our own artillery were not so active, but on the 21st they carried out a bombardment of the Turkish gun positions behind the Nurwan Ridge. On this day, 2/Lieuts. A. C. Stone and B. W. Murdoch, I.A.R.O., joined the Regiment with a draft.

From the 26th to the end of the month the Turks started sniping into the Pentagon from long range at night from the west and south-west. They never caused any casualties, and probably did it with a view to keeping us awake. Their flashes were never observed.

On September 29th the A.G.'s estimate of our strength was 851 Indian Ranks, but barely 500 were present with the Regiment owing to sickness.

October. Work still continued, for certain new strong posts on the line Imam-Ali-Mansur—Pentagon—Magasis were ordered to be constructed.

The Regiment's strength had fallen so low through sickness that the 1/2nd Gurkha Rifles sent out a double company on October 3rd, and took over the reserve.

The Battalion scouts of the 1/4th Devons and 1/2nd Gurkha Rifles also came out to live and train with us.

The Turks carried out their usual night harassing tactics of firing into the Pentagon from the west for the first seven nights. Officers' patrols were out every night, and sometimes all night, and never saw much. They were sometimes fired at whilst retiring.

Orders were received, and carried out in two days, for all tents to be dug down.

The new four company organization came into force in the

HISTORY OF THE 45TH RATTRAY'S SIKHS 43

Regiment from October 14th. Thus the 1st Double Company became A Company, and so on, and the platoons were numbered from one to sixteen throughout the Regiment.

Lewis gun lectures for British Officers were commenced in the 2nd Gurkha camp.

Orders having been received for the 36th Infantry Brigade to relieve us, the 62nd Punjabis sent word that they were marching at 7 a.m., on the 16th.

On October 16th at 7 a.m., an enemy plane came over the Pentagon; our anti-aircraft guns in the Sinn area quickly caused it to make off towards Kut, but for some time fragments of their shells were falling all over the Pentagon.

The Regiment fell in on their alarm posts at 7.30 a.m., and the 62nd Punjabis marched in at 8 a.m.; the relief was completed and, at 10 a.m., the Regiment fell back in artillery formation to their new camp, 500 yards west of Devizes Bridge. The Regiment had been quartered in the Pentagon since June 23rd, and had done fully 75 per cent. of the heavy labour of constructing and maintaining its defences at a very trying season of the year. All ranks were glad to get away to another area, and a change of occupation.

The 37th Infantry Brigade were all concentrated by October 17th, and on this day 2/Lieut. B. W. Murdoch, I.A.R.O., and 39 Indian Other Ranks proceeded to join the 37th Infantry Brigade Machine Gun Company, then in the process of formation.

The remainder of the month was a period of intensive training. Company training, together with bombing, Lewis gun training and gas drill, were usually carried out in the morning with Battalion drill in the afternoons. The Brigade worked together on three occasions, practising attack, retirement and night operations.

On October 10th the Commander-in-Chief in India, General Sir C. C. Munro, inspected the Regiment informally in camp, and all British and Indian Officers were introduced to him.

A draft of sixty men joined the Regiment on this date. They had all been attached to 15th Sikhs in France, and were a splendid body of men. They left Peshawar on September 16th, so joined up quicker than previous drafts. The river transport was improving since the Force was taken over by the War Office.

Lieut. and Adjutant G. H. Atkinson rejoined from sick leave in India on the 25th.

On the 30th Brigade sports were held. They were very successful, and brought all ranks and many old friends together.

The official strength of the Regiment on October 31st, was 14 British Officers and 828 Indian Other Ranks, but was probably 650 odd owing to sickness.

November. From the 1st to 12th the Regiment was in camp 500 yards west of Devizes Bridge, during which time we carried out six tactical exercises, the remainder of the time being occupied by company training and digging communication trenches in the vicinity. On the 5th our Indian ranks who had been attached to the 37th Infantry Brigade Machine Gun Company, returned, as with the exception of drivers, machine gun companies were to be entirely British. On the same date Captain R. A. Macausland was appointed staff captain, 37th Infantry Brigade. On the 6th Captain R. Rainsford Hannay had to replace him as acting 2nd-in-command 36th Sikhs.

On November 12th we were ordered to take over the river line near Magasis Fort from the 36th Sikhs and the Commanding Officer went to visit it.

Map No. 2. The Regiment took over the 26th Punjabis camp, near K.I. 37.A. on November 13th.

D Company took over the line Nasafieh Canal—Magasis Fort at 4 p.m., finding posts at Nasafieh and Magasis pumping stations; there was also an observation post in Magasis Fort with telephonic communication to Regimental Headquarters. A certain amount of day and night sniping went on, and there were T heads along the whole trench line for listening posts. The position commanded the Magasis Peninsula.

"D" Company, Lieut.-Colonel H. B. Rattray, D.S.O., moved to a separate camp N.W. of One Ball Bridge on November 14th in order to be able to reinforce the river line more easily if required, and two platoons "B" Company took over the Sector S.P.1, exclusive, to Magasis Fort, inclusive. On this day we had to send guards amounting to two Indian

HISTORY OF THE 45TH RATTRAY'S SIKHS 45

officers and 85 I.O.R.'s to the 3rd I.A. Corps, 14th Division and 37th Infantry Brigade.

On November 15th, Lieut.-Colonel F. T. Stewart, Commandant, was appointed to command No. 2 Sector of the line of communication defences, Amarah, with orders to report there at an early date, and on November 16th, left by the early morning train for Shaikh Saad, and only the British Officers knew he had gone for good. He had served in the 45th for 25 years and all ranks viewed his departure with the greatest regret. Lieut.-Colonel H. B. Rattray, D.S.O., assumed command of the Regiment, and on this day our new Corps Commander, Lieut.-General W. R. Marshall, inspected our camp and the river line.

Reports from the river line were normal for the remainder of the month, and the Regiment dug two new strong posts on the river line, S.P.6 and 7, and greatly improved the existing communication and fire trenches, also putting up wire in certain localities.

Work was also carried out in other areas which entailed a lot of digging.

Company training, however, continued when possible, and a good deal of field firing was carried out at Dead Calf Pond.

On November 30th, Lieut. G. H. Atkinson, and 15 regimental scouts proceeded to Imam-Ali-Mansur for work of a secret nature under the direct orders of the G.O.C. 14th Division. A rumour was in the air that an advance was imminent, and that major operations would shortly commence.

At the end of November the official strength of the Regiment was 14 British Officers and 771 I.O.R.'s.

On December 2nd all spare kits were transferred to a *December.* Brigade dump in the Sinn area, and on the 3rd we were relieved by the 3rd Brahmans. Companies marched independently to the new camp between Calf's Head and Calf's Hump. Map No. 2, 37 C.

Lieut. G. H. Atkinson and the Regimental scouts returned from Imam-Ali-Mansur on the 4th, and on the 5th the following message was received from the 14th Division : " G.O.C. would like to thank . . . and Lieut. G. H. Atkinson, 45th Sikhs, for their recent work which he considers excellent."

On the 6th it rained all day, on the 7th a Brigade tactical

exercise was held, during which a hostile plane came over whilst the Brigade was in mass, causing some anxious moments until it shook out into artillery formation.

On the 8th it rained all day again, but the ground could stand a great deal.

On the 9th there was battalion parade in the morning for practise in putting out two lines of strong posts at 350 yards interval, and 150 yards distance, the support line being opposite the gaps in the front line.

In the evening the 36th Sikhs, 45th Sikhs, and 128th Pioneers practised the same scheme, and put out a line of strong posts from S.P.5 to Dead Calf Pond, and then along Double Canals for 1,800 yards.

On the 10th, parades under picquet commanders were held for practise in laying out picquets.

On the 11th, a Day practice was carried out under the Brigade Commander as on the 9th, the 36th Sikhs, 45th Sikhs, and 128th Pioneers put out a line of picquets from S.P. 6 to Calf's Hump and thence along the Double Canal.

A night reconnaissance was carried out by Lieut. G. H. Atkinson and the Regimental scouts.

On the 12th, the day was spent in looking into details for the coming advance.

CHAPTER III

OPERATIONS, DECEMBER 13TH, 1916, TO FEBRUARY 19th, 1917.

THE situation at this time was as follows :—   *1916.*

The Turkish Army on the Tigris front numbered about 20,000 men with 70 guns, out of which 25 guns were believed to be on the right bank. They had bridges over the Tigris at the eastern side of the Shumran Bend, and one over the River Hai one mile S.W. of Kut.   *December 13th.*

Maps No. 2 and 3.

Our Army on the Tigris, under the command of Lieut.-General Sir F. S. Maude, K.C.M.G., C.B., D.S.O., was distributed as follows : 1st I.A. Corps (less 3rd Indian Division) holding the Sannayat position. The 3rd Indian Division was on the right bank of the river between Arab Village and Twin Canals.

The 3rd I.A. Corps, Major-General W. R. Marshall, C.B., 13th and 14th Indian Divisions were concentrated in the Sinn Area, whilst the Cavalry Division arrived this day after dark at Sinn Abtar.

The Infantry Brigades of the 13th Division, an all British Division, were numbered 38th, 39th and 40th, and the composition and numbers of the Infantry Brigades of the 14th Indian Division were as under :—

35th Infantry Brigade.—1/5th Buffs.
                2/4th Gurkha Rifles.
                37th Dogras.
                102nd Grenadiers.
36th Infantry Brigade.—1/4th Hants.
                26th Punjabis.
                62nd Punjabis.
                82nd Punjabis.

48 HISTORY OF THE 45TH RATTRAY'S SIKHS

37th Infantry Brigade.—1/4th Devons.
1/2nd K.E.O. Gurkha Rifles.
36th Sikhs.
45th Rattray's Sikhs.

The greatest secrecy for the coming operations had been maintained by the Higher Command, and, beyond the fact that a big move was on foot, little was known in battalions prior to December 12th.

The 3rd Corps operation order was issued at 11 p.m. on December 11th, and that of the 14th Division was issued to Brigades at 2.30 p.m. on December 12th.

The Army Commander's first intention was to move forward on the 14th, and secure an entrenched position on the River Hai. This was to be carried out by the 3rd Corps and Cavalry Division.

Corps order. (a) The 13th Division were to occupy Atab (47.d.8/25) at 5.45 a.m. on the 14th, and thereafter the line R.8 (exclusive)— —R.9—47.d.2/0—Old Encampment—Maharijah—58.b.10/55 —AA.5 (exclusive) as early as possible.

(b) 14th Division were to secure the line Calf's Head—P.4 by 5.45 a.m. on the 14th and thence to R.8 as early as possible.

(c) The Cavalry Division were to reach Basrugiyeh by daybreak, and thence to operate N.W. towards Shumran Bridge.

14th Division order. The 14th Division orders for the Infantry Brigades were as follows :—

(1) 35th Infantry Brigade would continue to hold the line Nasafiyeh Canal (exclusive) to S.P.H. (37.C.2/2) inclusive. Battle positions to be occupied by 5.45 a.m. on 14th.

(2) 37th Infantry Brigade (less two battalions) and 128th Pioneers, were to secure the line S.P.H. (37.C.2/2) exclusive to P.4 by 5.45 a.m. on December 14th and thence on to R.8 (inclusive) as early as possible.

Two battalions (1/4th Devons and 1/2nd Gurkha Rifles) were to form the Corps Reserve at Imam-Ali-Mansur.

(3) 36th Infantry Brigade were to occupy the old Turkish position between the Dujailah Redoubt (inclusive) and AA5 (inclusive) by 6 a.m. on the 14th.

These movements commenced on the night of the 13th/14th December. To follow the fortunes of the 37th Brigade, the 36th Sikhs and 45th Sikhs with the 128th Pioneers, paraded

HISTORY OF THE 45TH RATTRAY'S SIKHS 49

in two columns at 7.30 p.m. at their camp near Calfs Head, picquet line on the right, and support line on the left, and marched for S.P.H. (37.C.2/2) at 8.30 p.m. This point was reached about 10.30 p.m., and a halt was made here until 2.35 a.m. The column then advanced, laying out picquets alternately from the picquet and support lines (128th Pioneers leading off). Captain Cusins, R.E., led the column on the right, and Captain Goad, 128th Pioneers, the column on the left, assisted by Lieut. and Adjutant G. H. Atkinson, 45th Sikhs. The picquets were placed in two lines at intervals of 350 yards and distances of 150 yards filling in the gaps. After reaching P.4 a single line of picquets was laid at intervals of 100 yards along the nullah running north and south from P.4 to Q.5—R.8.

December 13th.

December 14th.

The 128th Pioneers held the line for 1,200 yards from S.P.H. 36th Sikhs (less two companies), from thence to P.4, and the 45th Sikhs from P.4 to R.8, where touch was obtained with the 13th Division.

37th Brigade Headquarters with two companies 36th Sikhs and one section Machine Gun Company, were situated 800 yards S.E. of P.4.

The picquets were all in position by 5.45 a.m., work was well under way by dawn, and completed by daylight. Our line was not shelled.

Captain R. Rainsford Hannay rejoined the Regiment from duty with the 36th Sikhs just before these operations commenced.

The 13th Division occupied Atab by 5.45 a.m. and worked up the River Hai on both banks maintaining touch with the 45th as the left battalion of the 14th Division.

The Cavalry Division crossed the Hai at Basrugiyeh by dawn according to plan.

During the morning patrols were pushed out towards Kut, and no great opposition encountered. To create a demonstration to assist the 13th Division in their advance up the east bank of the River Hai, the scouts of the 36th Sikhs and 45th Sikhs (Lieut. G. Mitchell) under command of Captain Bunbury, 36th Sikhs, supported by one company 36th Sikhs and one section Machine Gun Company, advanced against N.10 and N.15 under orders from Corps.

The 35th Infantry Brigade on our right made a similar demonstration against P.8 and P.9 for a similar purpose.

Lieut. G. Mitchell, with 25 scouts, proceeded to P.12, and placed himself under the command of Captain Bunbury, 36th Sikhs, at noon.

Lieut. Mitchell advanced through the ruins at 47.B towards N.15, whilst the 36th Sikhs' scouts advanced on his right on N.10. They were supported by one company 36th Sikhs and one section Machine Gun Corps, under Captain Bunbury, 36th Sikhs, at the Ruins. The scouts' orders were to fire as much as possible and on no account to get closely engaged.

The scouts advanced some 600 yards beyond the ruins, small parties of Turks retreating before them to their wire.

The scouts in turn came under both shell and rifle fire, but kept up a brisk long range fire on the Turks till sunset, when the retirement was ordered.

We sustained no casualties, and were lucky in escaping some.

Lieut. Mitchell reported that his scouts worked splendidly and especially mentioned the good work of No. 402 Sepoy Mangal Singh, " B " Company.

Sappers and miners wired in our part of the line by nightfall, and a quiet night was spent.

December 15th.

The situation is shown by a 3rd Corps operation order despatched 8.45 p.m. "Third Corps is ordered to move at 9 a.m., so as to throw its left forward along the line Pentagon —N.6—Q.8—R.17, strong patrols supported as necessary being pushed forward all along line to ascertain how far the Turkish trenches from J.9 to P.15 are occupied. Cavalry Division is ordered to move at 9 a.m. on Kala Haji Fahan. 13th and 14th Divisions will move at 9 a.m. to line indicated. Road and watercourse running N.N.W. from R.8 inclusive is right of 13th Division."

On receipt of above order, 14th Division ordered :—

(1) " 35th Infantry Brigade will throw their left flank forward, and construct a line of S.P.'s from Pentagon to 36.D.7/4 inclusive sending out strong patrols on line J.9 to N.8.

(2) 37th Infantry Brigade (less two battalions) will continue their new line from 36.D.7/4 exclusive to 47.A.8/6 exclusive

HISTORY OF THE 45TH RATTRAY'S SIKHS 51

sending out strong patrols on line N.8.N.14. 37th Infantry Brigade will hold their new line with 36th and 45th Sikhs, while 128th Pioneers are used for consolidating purposes only."

About 8 a.m. a hostile plane flew over the 37th Infantry Brigade dropping bombs without damage.

About 9.30 a.m., a Brigade of the 13th Division on our left advanced in artillery formation under shell fire towards the line P.11—P.6, and our men were much impressed by the orderliness and steadiness of their advance.

The 45th received the order to advance at 11 a.m., with the 36th Sikhs on their right. This move was carried out under considerable shell fire in artillery formation, and the Regiment behaved with the utmost steadiness. This was the first occasion on which the Regiment had ever advanced under enemy shell fire. " D " Company (Lieut. J. W. Guise) and " C " Company (Captain J. G. Wilson) came in for more attention than the right wing. Subadar Narain Singh and five other ranks of " C " Company were all knocked out by one H.E. shell, which also killed two British machine gunners (attached), and wounded a third.

The Regiment took up a final line some 2,000 yards in length roughly between P. 6 and N.6. Picquet and support lines were dug, and communication established with the 13th Division on our left, and the 36th Sikhs on our right.

A strong patrol of " A " Company under Lieut. A. C. Curtis, M.C., reached N.12 and got valuable information about the siting of some enemy batteries on the Kut Peninsula.

At 8.32 p.m., the 13th Division reported their right at 47.A. 8/8, but not in touch with the 14th Division. The 37th Infantry Brigade were therefore ordered to fill up gap and get in touch.

Enemy continued to shell our line with H.E. without casualties.

December 16th.

At 11 a.m., in obedience to orders, we advanced our line 400 yards so as to get into close touch with the 13th Division on our left. At the same time the 36th Sikhs on our right also moved forward to conform. " D " and " C " Companies again came in for shelling and rifle fire at long range. One Sepoy was killed, and Jemadar Labh Singh was severely wounded with one other rank. One Company 128th Pioneers assisted in consolidating the new line.

At 12.42 p.m., a Brigade message was received ordering the Regiment to be prepared for an advance on the enemy trenches at any moment. This attack failed to come off, but the orders caused anxiety as the enemy trenches were wired, and the wire was absolutely intact.

A Divisional operation order issued at 12.45 p.m. read: " 1st Corps are taking over line Pentagon inclusive on our right flank. 3rd Corps have been ordered to take up following line and secure it. K.4 exclusive—M.3—P.6—Pointed Ruin —Kala Haji Fahan—R.21—S.16—Old Encampment—A.A.5 —No. 4 Redoubt—Imam-Dujailah inclusive. 13th Division have been ordered to take from P.6 inclusive to the B of Nahr Bassouia. 14th Division from K.4 exclusive to P.6 inclusive, and from the B of Nahr Bassouia exclusive to Dujailah inclusive. 35th Infantry Brigade will take over the line K.4 exclusive to P.6 inclusive at once. Troops occupying the line Nasafiyeh Canal—K.4 will, however, not be moved until relieved by 1st Corps. 128th Pioneers and the two battalions 37th Brigade now in Divisional Reserve are put at the disposal of the 35th Brigade for consolidating this line. The latter two battalions will rejoin their Brigade by 6 a.m. to-morrow.

" 37th Infantry Brigade (less two battalions) will on relief by 35th Brigade withdraw to P.4 and be in Divisional Reserve.

" 35th Infantry Brigade (less two platoons) will secure the line from B of Nahr Bassouia exclusive to Dujailah inclusive."

During the afternoon a heavy bombardment was opened by our guns on the Hai Bridge Defences. The fire was observed by " D " Company, and reports sent in to the Batteries throughout from Battalion Headquarters. The wire appeared to be very little damaged.

In accordance with the above Divisional Order, the Regiment were relieved by the 1/5th Buffs, and joined the 37th Infantry Brigade at P.4 as Divisional Reserve after dark.

December 17th.
The Regiment with the 37th Brigade remained in Divisional Reserve at P.4, and held a line of picquets at P.11, P.12, S.12, P.13, S.13.

The day was spent in the improvement of communications

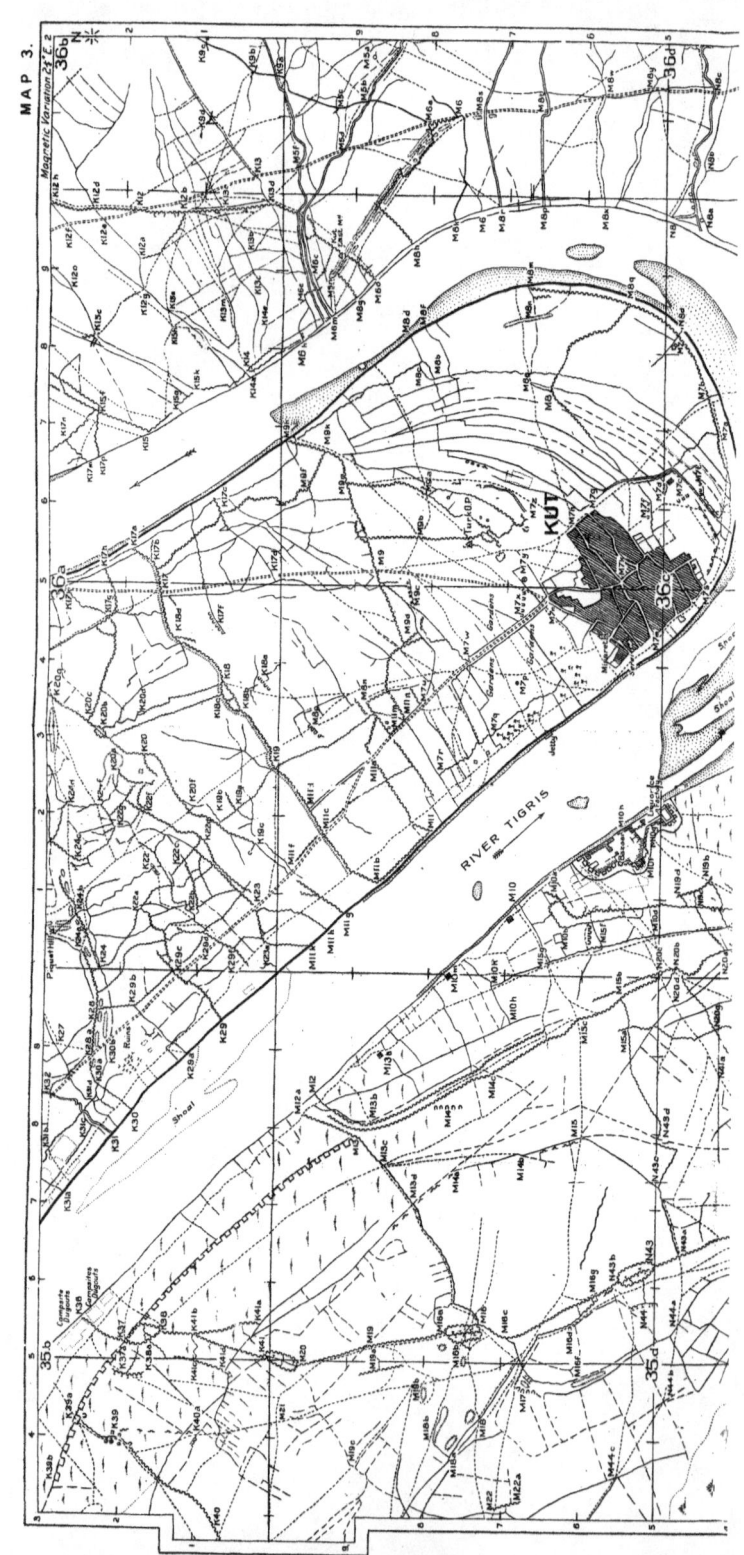

MAP 3.

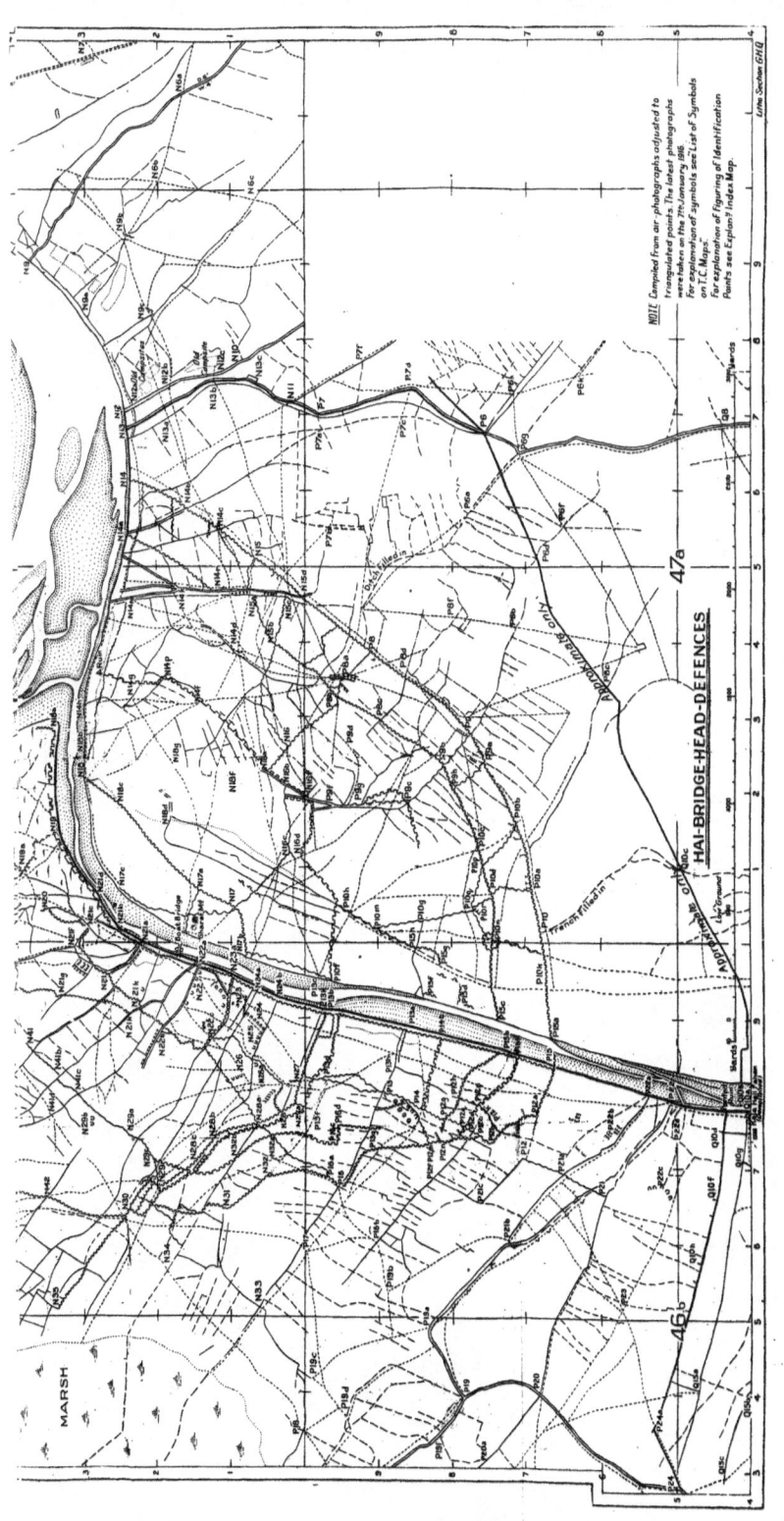

by all formations, and bridging operations over the River Hai. Also wiring of new front line.

Extracts from a 14th Divisional operation order, despatched 4.35 p.m., explain the situation : " The Army Commander intends to contain enemy at and East of Kut, and move westwards against his communications. 1st Corps is to prolong its left to 36.D.0/1 to-day, and is also to hold the Dujailah Redoubt. 13th Division is to secure the following line by 6 a.m. to-morrow, 36.D.0/1—P.6—Pointed Ruin— P.24—P.27—Q.23—Q.28—46.C.1/9 inclusive. 14th Division is to secure the following line by 6 a.m. to-morrow, 46.C.1/9 exclusive—AA.43—S.16—AA.5—Imam. In accordance with above, 35th Infantry Brigade will hand over their line from K.4 to 36. D.0/1 inclusive to 1st Corps and thence to P.6 to 13th Division. After relief the Brigade with 128th Pioneers will move via P.4—R.8 over the Hai at S.9 to Bassouia by 6 a.m., to-morrow, when they will become Divisional Reserve. 37th Infantry Brigade will move after dark via the Ummassaad Ford to the vicinity of 46.D.2/6, and secure the line 46.D.1/9 exclusive to AA.43 by 6 a.m. to-morrow. 36th Infantry Brigade will hand over their line from Dujailah Redoubt to No. 3 Redoubt inclusive to 1st Corps and secure the line Imam No. 4 Redoubt—AA.5— S.16—AA.43 by 6 a.m. to-morrow."

In accordance with the above orders the 45th with the 37th Brigade paraded at 5.30 p.m., and marched after dark to the Hai. This was reached about midnight, and we suddenly dipped into a deep depression with steep banks on either side. This was the Unmassaad Ford, dry at this season except for a few pools. From this point we marched on a compass bearing to the vicinity of 46.D.2/6 and took up a line facing west from 46.D.1/9 to AA.43. 36th Sikhs on right and 45th Sikhs left. Brigade Headquarters and the other two battalions in reserve being located at S.19. We were 12 hours under arms, and dug in by dawn.

December 18th.

At 2.30 p.m., we were ordered to advance our line in conjunction with the 40th Infantry Brigade (13th Division) and take up an advanced line from 45.C.5/8 to AA.43. The 45th, therefore, took up 1,800 yards of line, with the 1/2nd Gurkha Rifles on their left and the 40th Brigade on their right.

54   HISTORY OF THE 45TH RATTRAY'S SIKHS

No firing took place during the day. The cavalry division reconnoitred towards Shumran and returned at dusk.

December 19th.

Orders had been received during the evening of the 18th for the relief of the 37th Infantry Brigade by the 36th Brigade in the outpost line, and its concentration near S.21, S.28.

These orders were, however, cancelled, and the concentration ordered at S.18.

This move was completed by 2.30 a.m., and the Regiment joined up with its Second Line Transport for the first time since the 13th. The Officers had a meal in the open in mess to their great content, in spite of the lateness of the hour.

At 4.30 p.m., the Brigade again fell in in mass, marched to the vicinity of S.19 and bivouacked for the night.

3rd Corps operation order No. 12 was received at 4.55 p.m. by the 14th Division. Extracts of it give the moves for the 20th.

"Tigris defences are to take over the portion of our line from Imam to AA.5 inclusive this evening. Present garrison (*i.e.*, two Battalions 36th Infantry Brigade) will rejoin its unit after relief.

2. "Our line will be re-adjusted at once and held as follows : 13th Division, less troops mentioned below 36.D.0/1—Pointed Ruin—P.27—Q.28—46.C.1/9 inclusive. 14th Division, less troops mentioned below, 46.C.1/9 exclusive—AA.43—AA.5 inclusive.

3. "The following will be concentrated in the low ground about S.18 by 5.30 p.m. :

(*a*) Crockers Force. One 18-pr. Battery R.F.A., and one Infantry Brigade from 13th Division and No. 2 Bridging Train. To be joined by Cavalry Brigade. This force is to be ready to move west early to-morrow morning.

(*b*) Covering Force. Two Batteries R.F.A., and one Infantry Brigade from 14th Division, to be joined by one Cavalry Brigade.

(*c*) One Infantry Brigade from 14th Division."

and in continuation a further order received by 14th Division at 7.19 p.m. : "Crockers' Column is to move from vicinity of S.18 at 6 a.m. Column is to move due west until north of Tel Bismai, when it will turn almost due north and march on Brick-kilns. Crossing is then to be secured quickly,

HISTORY OF THE 45TH RATTRAY'S SIKHS 55

covering parties thrown out, and bridgeheads constructed on both banks. Covering force (35th Infantry Brigade) is to move from vicinity of S.18 at 7 a.m., to shell bridge at J.93, and any shipping in that neighbourhood, and to cover the withdrawal of Crockers' Force transport from the brick-kilns."

Thus it will be seen that a crossing or possibly a feint crossing was intended for the 20th.

Shortly after dawn, Crockers' Force passed the 37th Infantry Brigade bivouac at S.19 moving west, followed an hour after by the Covering Force. *December 20th.*

The 37th Infantry Brigade was detailed as the Brigade in paragraph three (c) of 3rd Corps operation order No. 12 (*ante* December 19th) as reserve to Crockers' Force and the Covering Force.

The Brigade order to move was issued at 12.4 p.m., and, shortly after, the Brigade marched in a westerly direction. Two companies 45th did advanced guard, and Headquarters and the remaining two companies moved at the head of the main body. After marching for three miles, a halt was ordered to await the arrival of Major-General R. G. Egerton, Commanding 14th Division, who had been detailed to command the covering force and our Brigade in reserve.

Major-General Egerton arrived, and at 4 p.m., we received information that Crockers' Force had been held up at the Brick-kilns, and had been unable to effect a crossing. The crossing could hardly have been effected in daylight against opposition, and sufficient opposition there proved to be.

The 37th Infantry Brigade then advanced two miles further west to try and effect a junction with Crockers' Force. This was not effected, owing to darkness, and after leaving the 1/2nd Gurkha Rifles to guard the brigade transport, a further advance of about a mile was made. The Brigade then halted and bivouacked for the night, which was bitterly cold as the temperature fell below zero.

At 7 a.m., the 37th Infantry Brigade made an advance of two miles due north, in order to cover the retirement of Crockers' Force, and to guard his left flank. The Brigade moved in two lines with the 1/4th Devons and the 45th Sikhs in the front line; formation: two lines of companies at 400 yards interval and 50 yards distance. *December 21st.*

Lieut.-Colonel H. B. Rattray, D.S.O., commanded the front line.

After marching two miles, the Brigade halted and remained in observation of Shumran. The Turks fired one round of H.E. only, which just missed the 45th Transport. At 8 a.m., Crockers' Force was seen retiring, and at 11 a.m., the Brigade retired in the same formation in which it had advanced. The Turkish artillery did not open fire, and the retirement was only followed up by hostile Arab cavalry, who, however, made no attempt to close.

Our old bivouac S.18 was reached at 3 p.m., and the 37th Infantry Brigade again went into bivouac there. They remained there for the next three days, and all ranks were able to obtain a much-needed rest. The men revelled in the waters of the lake, and toll was taken of the numerous duck and geese on it with every kind of weapon including the Lewis gun.

December 25th. The 37th Infantry Brigade moved into close bivouac at R.22. The Brigade was in support of the outpost line west of the lake held by the 36th Infantry Brigade, and were required to fall in at very short notice on Brigade Alarm Post in case of necessity.

Captain R. H. Anderson marched in in the afternoon, with a draft of 58 men from India. The Christmas dinner was taken at a trench table roofed over with reeds by the men, and Lord Curzon's gift of champagne to the officers of the whole force was much appreciated.

December 26th to 29th were taken up with heavy working parties on a new S.P. line facing west, every available man in the Battalion and Brigade taking part. There was a good deal of rain during these days, but the men cut reeds from the lake and put up very good waterproof reed shelters. All ranks were very fit and happy. On the 29th our tents and surplus kits arrived from the dump at Sinn, and were deeply appreciated, as the Brigade had been in bivouac in all weathers since the 13th.

Extracts from the following 37th Infantry Brigade messages dated the 27th December, explain the new situation :

(*a*) " 14th Division wire begins. In supercession of all previous orders owing to wet weather our defensive line

HISTORY OF THE 45TH RATTRAY'S SIKHS 57

western front is to be withdrawn to the intermediate position now being prepared along the line Pointed Ruin—P.24—Q.17—R.21—S. 16—B. of Nahr Bassouia and thence through M. of Mahairijah to AA.5. R.21 is inclusive to 13th Division. Withdrawal to new line will commence at 8 a.m., on the 29th. The 37th Infantry Brigade will occupy new line from R.21 exclusive to B of Nahr Bassouia, and take over the rest of the existing line from the latter point to AA.5 during that day. By the evening of the 29th the 36th Infantry Brigade will be concentrated in the vicinity of 46.D.9/6.

37th Infantry Brigade less battalions holding the new line will be concentrated about 46.D.6/5."

(b) " Continuation above message—45th Sikhs will occupy the new line from R.21 (exclusive) to B of Nahr Bassouia inclusive by 8 a.m., on the 29th.

2. " 1/2nd Gurkha Rifles will occupy line from B in Nahr Bassouia exclusive to AA.5 on 29th. This line is 8,000 yards long and will be held by 21 picquets.

3. " Brigade Headquarters will be at a point just north of S.13 and will consist of 1/4th Devons, 36th Sikhs and two Sections No. 187 M.G. Company.

4. " An O.P. of one platoon will be furnished by the 1/4th Devons and 36th Sikhs on alternate days, and will move out, escorted by remainder of company from which furnished, to AA.43 at 6 a.m. daily, returning before dark."

The move on the 29th was cancelled as the line was not ready.

The Regiment moved into the new line R.21 to B of Nahr Bassouia by 8 a.m. The line consisted of four redoubts, and each of these were connected by communication trenches to two lunettes, thrown out about 200 yards on either flank. Our redoubts numbered from north to south were 13, 14, 15 and 16, and lunettes 24—25, 26—27, 28—29 and 30—31, occupied by " A," " B," " C," and " D " Companies respectively. (See Map 2.) *December 30th.*

Each lunette was occupied by a half-platoon with Lewis gun, the remaining half-platoons acting as inlying picquets and sleeping fully accoutred in the redoubt. The remaining two platoons were in support in the redoubt. Standing patrols were kept out by day from redoubts 7 and 10, " A " and

58   HISTORY OF THE 45TH RATTRAY'S SIKHS

" D " Companies, and listening posts at night from all four redoubts.

Battalion Headquarters was some 400 yards east of No. 14 redoubt, behind the high bund of a water cut. Tents were pitched here. In the redoubts the men constructed reed roofs to the dugouts, and were comfortable enough.

The Regiment had just been through 14 days of hard campaigning with few casualties, and had always done excellently. Our chief enemy during the summer of 1916 was sickness, quite 75 per cent of which was scurvy, which had caused the Regiment 555 other ranks invalided out of the country in 1916. This was due to hard work and exposure with insufficient rations in a desert country. Since September, however, there had been a marked improvement in rations and weather, and consequently a marked reduction in sickness.

1917.

The Regiment started the New Year of 1917 with a strength of ten British Officers, 18 Indian Officers and 669 Other Ranks. The British Officers were :—

January.

Lieut.-Colonel H. B. Rattray, D.S.O., Commandant.
Captain   R. H. Anderson, " D " Company, 2nd in Command.
    ,,   R. Rainsford Hannay, " B " Company.
    ,,   J. G. Wilson, " C " Company.
Lieut.   G. H. Atkinson, Adjutant.
    ,,   A. C. Curtis, M.C., " A " Company.
    ,,   J. W. Guise, " D " Company.
2/Lieut.   G. Mitchell, " B " Company, Scouts Officer.
    ,,   K. H. Preston, Quartermaster.
             A. C. Stone, " C " Company.
T/Lieut.   V. M. Kaikini, I.M.S., Medical Officer.

Before the advance across the River Hai in December, the Regiment had drawn well-fitting thick serge clothing. They were exceedingly well turned out, smart and cheerful. They were also well known as an excellent digging unit.

When other duties permitted practice trench attacks, bombing and Lewis gun firing were carried out during the month.

The Regiment remained in its redoubt line up to January 22nd, when the following events took place day by day.

January 1st.

Owing to a week's rain, the bad roads and the temporary breakdown of the Shaikh Saad—Atab light railway, considerable difficulty had been experienced in getting up rations. The weather took a turn for the better this day, and was now very cold and dry. Two enemy planes were over our line all the morning.

January 2nd. The 36th Infantry Brigade moved out after dark to destroy an Arab fort some miles west of Shooters Hill. "A" Company had to send out a party at midnight to put up two lights on Shooters Hill to guide them in. The Brigade returned *3rd.* at 7 a.m., having completed their mission without casualties.

The sappers and miners demolished an Arab fort with two towers (Fort Pitt) in front of "D" Company's redoubt, leaving only one tower. This was henceforth used as an observation post.

4th. "D" Company completed a well in the Nahr Bassouia, and found sweet water. They also completed a small detached post, to hold one N.C.O. and twelve men, at a bend in the Nahr Bassouia and commanding it for use at night.

The scouts under 2/Lieut. G. Mitchell proceeded out to Shooters Hill and beyond, under orders from Brigade at 9.30 a.m. They returned at 3 p.m., after seeing many Arab flocks, and having a long range duel with their Arab guards without incurring any casualties.

5th. The scouts under 2/Lieut. G. Mitchell moved out at 3.30 a.m., with the 36th Sikhs' scouts and one company 36th Sikhs to Fox Hill, then moved along towards Shooters Hill, and remained in observation till dawn. About fifty Arabs were encountered, and one of them was wounded.

A considerable amount of firing took place on the east bank of the River Hai.

6th. A party of about fifty Arabs approached "D" Company's detached post on the Nahr Bassouia at 7 p.m. The night was very dark, and the N.C.O. in command did not wait till they were close enough to throw bombs, but opened rapid fire with the result that they all got away. After this an R.E. searchlight was established behind this detached post, but the Arabs never gave us another chance.

7th. We provided strong working parties to work on communication trenches between Redoubts 15 and 16.

Heavy bombardments were carried out against the Hai Bridge defences, and the trenches in the Mohomed Abdul

Hassan Bend. The River Hai rose considerably, and the pontoon bridges at R.17 and Atab had to be reconstructed.

8th. The River Hai continued to rise.

From 9 to 9.15 a.m., a heavy bombardment of the Hai Bridge and Mohomed Abdul Hassan trenches took place. The Turks replied leisurely with 5.9 howitzers, and were considerably helped by two aeroplanes, which flew with impunity over the whole of our positions, with every available gun in Mesopotamia firing at them.

Orders were received for our scouts to put a B.B. lamp facing west on Shooters Hill at 12 midnight, to guide in the 35th and 36th Infantry Brigades, who were to make a demonstration against Old Pump (Shumran Bend). Lieut. Mitchell left camp with our scouts at 9 p.m.

The Cavalry Division which were to have made a demonstration towards Bgailah returned before 10 p.m., owing to dense fog.

9th. "D" Company, Captain R. H. Anderson, proceeded as escort to No. 8 Battery, R.F.A., on Fox Hill. This move was to keep the flank of the Cavalry Division and Infantry Brigades protected on their return.

The Company met the Battery at L.34 in dense fog at 6 a.m., and marched to Fox Hill reaching this point at 7 a.m. The left flank guard was sniped by Arabs a good deal, but no men were hit. The Regimental scouts were met here returning to camp. A chain of posts was put out round the Battery in the fog, and about 9 a.m., one Sepoy was dangerously wounded in the abdomen whilst patrolling.

The mist remained very dense till 12.30 p.m., when Arab horsemen and Arabs on foot were seen. The guns got into these at 1,200 yards, and followed them up to about 3,500 yards. There were certainly some casualties amongst the Arabs, but the ground was very broken.

Subadar Ram Singh took a platoon forward some 1,000 yards to search the ground but found nothing. The Battery retired at 1.30 p.m., no enemy being in sight, and "D" Company got in about 2.30 p.m.

At midnight an intense rifle and artillery fire broke out on the left bank of the River Hai between both sides, and this continued until dawn.

The mess was dug down to five feet. The Turks were in the habit of searching for Division Headquarters near R.17 every evening with 5.9 howitzers, and the mess and Battalion Headquarters' tents were just as close.

10th. Lieut.-General W. R. Marshall, commanding the 3rd Corps, visited "D" Company in their redoubt about 2 p.m. He expressed his approval of the trenches dug by the 45th. Colonel Rattray and he had served in the Sherwood Foresters as subalterns some twenty-five years previously.

One Sepoy in "D" Company was accidentally wounded, and No. 590/B Sepoy Baj Singh, who was wounded on the 9th, succumbed to his wounds.

11th–13th. Working parties proceeded to various localities, and often came under fire.

Companies were sent down to the lake daily to get fish. "C" Company caught by various methods sixty good fish on the 11th. The Malwa Companies took great interest in the fishing, but the Manjha Companies displayed little enthusiasm. Though guns and ammunition were short, officers managed to get some duck and geese off the lake.

14th. There was an air fight over Kut, in the early morning, and the planes of both sides were forced to descend.

2/Lieut. G. Mitchell, and the regimental scouts, reinforced by one platoon, proceeded as escort to a survey party west of the lake. They reached the western edge of the lake at 9.30 a.m., and there the platoon took up a position at 9.30 a.m.

At 11.15 a.m., a small patrol of one N.C.O. and 16 men were sent out to see what was in front, as a slight rise in the ground about 1,000 yards away obscured the view. After the patrol had proceeded about half-a-mile, they noticed an Arab vedette about 800 yards away. They proceeded to stalk him through the grass, about two feet high. On reaching the edge of the long grass, the leading scout fired, breaking the pony's leg, and the rest of the patrol opened fire on the Arab who ran for his life, apparently with success.

Lieut. Mitchell then brought up some more scouts, caught the pony and shot it, and brought in the saddle, saddle bags and their contents. Some dozen Arab horsemen galloped round to try and intercept the party, who easily kept them off by fire. The survey party completed their work by 12.30

p.m., and the scouts returned to camp by 2 p.m., bringing their loot with them.

The saddle bags contained a large variety of articles amongst them being a revolver, a Russian Cross of St. George, Arab jewellery, telephone cable, dental forceps, false teeth, etc.

15th. "A" and "B" Companies carried out field practices with rifle and Lewis gun sections.

16th. A draft of 105 men marched into camp at 2 p.m. 65 were our own men who had been attached to the 15th Sikhs, and 40 men from the 15th Sikhs. As they were being inspected by the Commanding Officer, prior to joining their companies, an enemy aeroplane flew low over them, and the whole parade was ordered to take to trenches dug for security against aeroplanes.

This draft brought the strength of the Regiment up to about 794 Indian ranks.

A General Headquarters communiqué dated 15th informed us that the 3rd Division was making good progress against the Mohomed Abdul Hassan Bend, that two hostile planes had been driven to ground by our planes on the 14th, and that the Cavalry Division had returned from Hai Town on the 14th, with large supplies of cattle and sheep.

17th–20th. We provided large working parties on the 14th Division Advanced Report Centre near our Brigade Headquarters and on strong posts farther north of our line.

For the past week there had been heavy fighting in the Mohomed Abdul Hassan Bend, and we had seen heavy bombardments in that direction daily. The bend was finally cleared by the 3rd Division on the 19th.

All our Companies carried out field practices.

On the 20th, Lieut. J. W. Guise took out 20 rifles to try and ambush Arabs at dawn but without success.

21st. We received intimation that we were to be relieved by the 105th Mahratta L.I. on the 23rd. The C.O. and Adjutant of this Battalion rode over and went over our line. They had suffered heavy casualties in the Mohomed Abdul Hassan Bend fighting, and gave us many points to look out for.

Three enemy planes flew over our line with impunity most of the afternoon, and no guns out of the many firing were able to hit them.

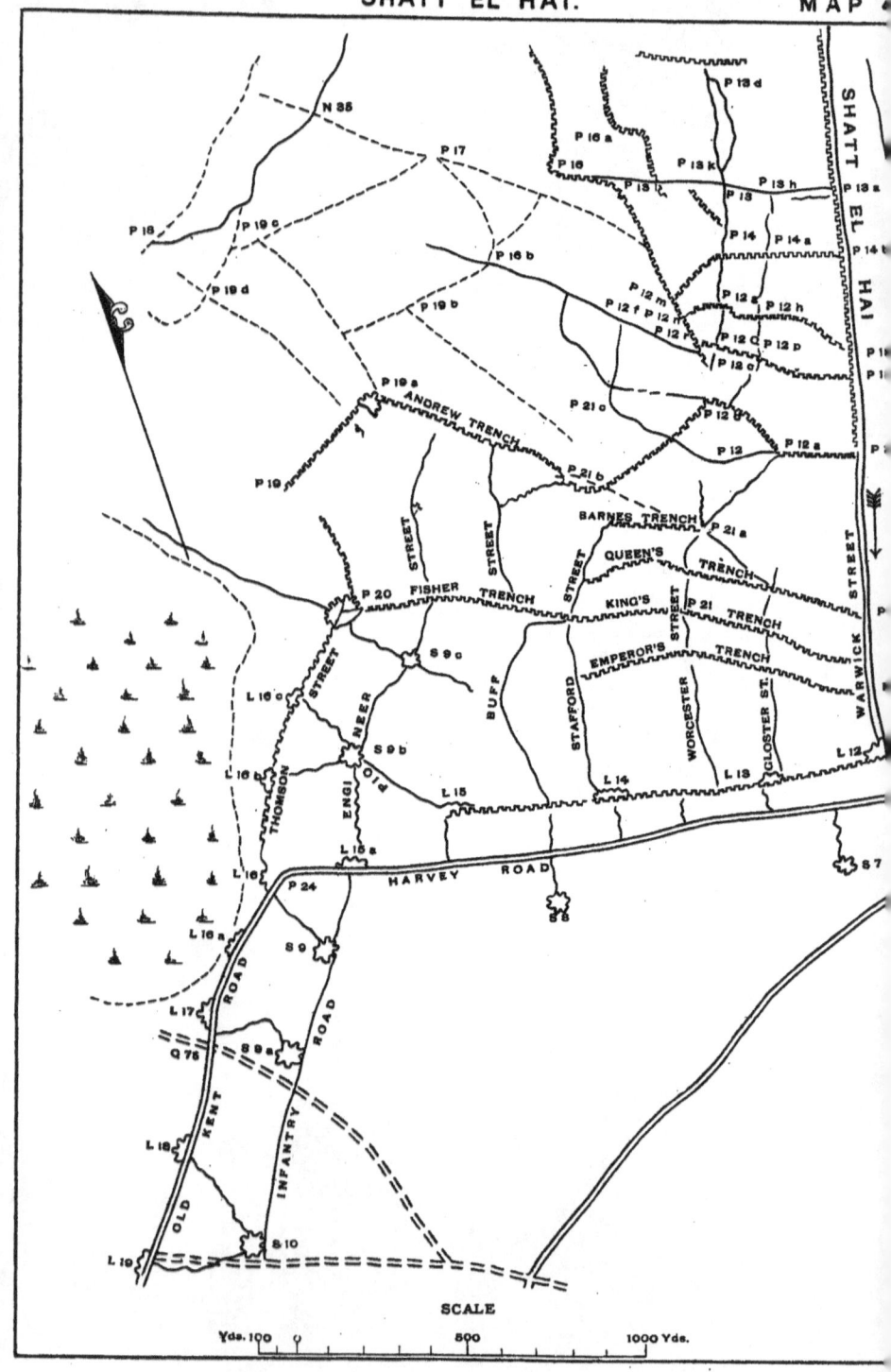

HISTORY OF THE 45TH RATTRAY'S SIKHS 63

We carried out the usual working parties, and "D" *22nd.*
Company carried out field firing.

"B," "C," and "D" Companies were relieved by the *23rd.*
105th Mahratta L.I., and "A" Company by the 1/2nd
Gurkha Rifles. The relief was completed by 1.15 a.m., and
the Regiment moved into a perimeter bivouac about 400
yards east of our old Regimental Headquarters.

The 3rd Corps, 13th and 14th Divisions, were now about
to commence operations against the Hai Salient on both
banks of the Hai. The 7th Division were still in front of the
Sannaiyat position, and the 3rd Division were holding the
right bank of the River Tigris from Sannaiyat to Kut.

Operations against the Hai Salient were to have commenced *24th.*
this day, but were postponed 24 hours.

37th Infantry Brigade Operation Order No. 1 was issued *See Maps 2 and 3.*
at 4 p.m. on the 22nd and gave us the following main information.

(1) That the enemy force on our front and left flank was
estimated to be 300 sabres, 51 guns and 20 Battalions (11,800
rifles) of which three were in the Hai Triangle R.B., and three
in the Hai Triangle L.B.

(2) That the 3rd Corps was to reduce the trenches in the
area N.14—P.15—N.43.

(3) The first stage of the operations would be that after
artillery preparation and with artillery support the enemy
front line trenches P.10.a—P.15—P.12.a—P.12.b would be
assaulted at 9.40 a.m. on the 24th by the 40th Infantry
Brigade on the east bank of the Hai, and by the 39th Infantry
Brigade on the west bank. Both Brigades on a frontage of
900 yards.

(4) That the 37th Infantry Brigade would remain in
Divisional reserve.

(5) That units were to be ready to move at short notice
after 9.30 a.m. on the 24th, with waterbottles and pakhals
filled, equipment ready to put on, first line mules ready to
be saddled and all loads tied up.

The Regiment remained in camp ready to move at a *25th.*
moment's notice. The artillery bombardment started early
and the 39th Infantry Brigade went over at 9.40 a.m. They
quickly captured the line P.12.b to P.15. They were heavily

counter-attacked three times during the day, beat off two of them most gallantly, but the third time in the afternoon they were driven back to their old line with heavy casualties.

On the right bank of the Hai things went well, and the 40th Infantry Brigade captured all their objectives with moderate loss. By the end of the day their line was extended to P.9.b and P.9.

The Corps Reserve, 36th Infantry Brigade—14th Division, moved up to the line P.24—Pointed Ruin (henceforward known as Harvey Road) passing our bivouac about 3 p.m. (See Maps 4 and 5.)

26th. They relieved the 39th Infantry Brigade the same evening. The 37th Infantry Brigade were still in divisional reserve, and the Regiment remained in bivouac ready for instant action. Our men spent the time in playing the most friendly football with the 2nd Gurkha Rifles.

27th. The 36th Infantry Brigade took up the attack, and went over with artillery support at 10.40 a.m. The 82nd Punjabis retook the Turkish front line from P.12.a to P.15, and bombed up to P.15.b. They held this ground against all counter-attacks.

The 26th Punjabis, on their left, missed their objective, and reached P.16, where they were partially surrounded. They maintained their isolated position very gallantly, however, with a good deal of loss and extricated themselves by the evening.

The 36th Infantry Brigade gained some more ground by bombing attacks up communication trenches.

The Regiment still remained in camp ready to move at a moment's notice, and the continued uncertainty and tension of waiting was rather trying to all ranks.

About 4 p.m., No. 753 Sepoy Dulla Singh, "B" Company, saved a number of casualties by his presence of mind. Someone dropped a bomb outside the quarter guard, the pin came out and the fuse began to burn. He at once picked it up, threw it over a small "Bund" and called on all to lie down. It exploded and, fortunately, only wounded one man.

28th. The Brigade received orders to move up to the front line in the afternoon. In the morning, therefore, the Commanding Officer and Company Commanders went up to the line to

SHATT EL HAI.

MAP 5.

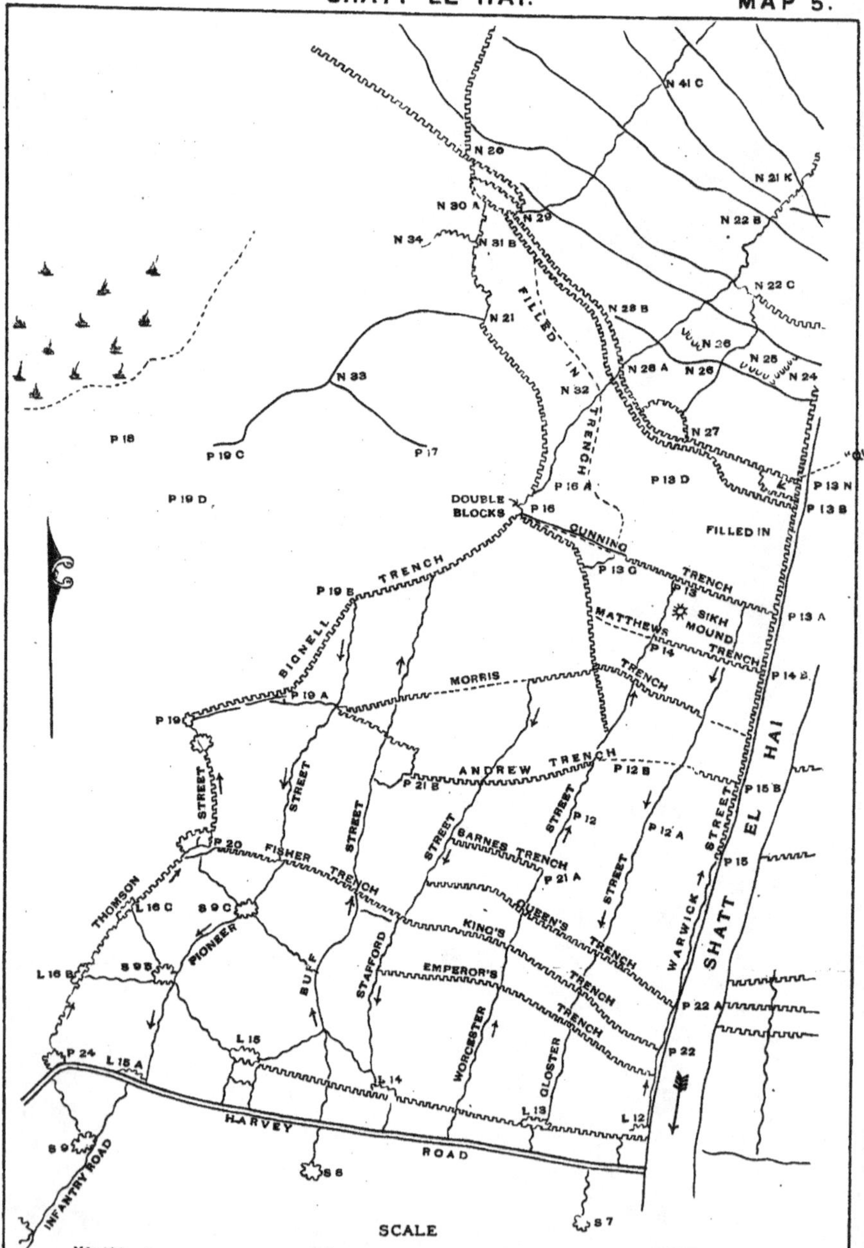

HISTORY OF THE 45TH RATTRAY'S SIKHS 65

see the trenches they were to take over, returning to bivouac by 1 p.m.

Lieut.-Colonel H. B. Rattray, D.S.O., issued the following regimental order : " The Commanding Officer relies on all ranks to maintain to the best of their ability the good name of the Sikh."

In accordance with orders, the 45th moved up to Harvey Road by Companies. " D " Company led off at 2.15 p.m., in artillery formation, followed by the other Companies at 15 minute intervals. *Map No. 4.*

The Battalion formed up in Harvey Road between L.13 and L.12 by 4.30 p.m., only the last company having been shelled by a noisy Camel gun on their way up. While we were in Harvey Road, a deep nullah, the Turkish guns opened on our guns in the vicinity with 5.9 howitzers, and several shells landed fairly adjacent to us. We moved up to the front line at 5.30 p.m., up Warwick Street, and took over from the 62nd Punjabis. " A " and " B " Companies, the front line. P.14.a to P.14.b, " C " Company the second line P.12.h to P.15.b, and " D " Company the third line P.12.p to P.15.k. The 36th Sikhs were on our left in three lines and the 1/4th Devons and 1/2nd Gurkhas in support.

Progress up to the line was very slow and we did not finish taking over from the 62nd Punjabis till about 9 p.m. *Map No. 5.*

After we had taken over the line, with a view to the eventual consolidation of the line P.16—P.13.a, " A " and " B " Companies under Lieut. A. C. Curtis and Captain R. Rainsford Hannay moved out to P.13.h and P.13.a respectively, with a working party and a covering party of fifty rifles each to establish themselves at these points. Heavy sniping was going on at the time, and as the parties were moving out the enemy opened heavy machine gun fire on them, which, fortunately, for the most part went high. " B " Company managed to establish a picquet at P.13.a and dug in, but " A " Company's attempt failed owing to a heavy bombing attack.

The 36th Sikhs on our left established picquets and dug in in the same way at P.16 and just west of P.16.C.

Our casualties this night were slight, only amounting to three other ranks wounded. The night was very dark, and the enemy were shooting high.

E

66 HISTORY OF THE 45TH RATTRAY'S SIKHS

29th.

The morning was spent in improving our trenches. The day was quiet except for the usual sniping.

About noon an operation order was received regarding the consolidation of the line P.13.a—P.16, from Lieut.-Colonel O. G. Gunning, 36th Sikhs, who was in command of the front line for this night. On receipt of this 45th Sikhs operation order No. 2 was issued to companies this day at 4.20 p.m., and was to the following effect:

"In order to secure a line of picquets at P.13.a—P.13.h—P.13—P.13.g—P.16, and one other between P.16 and P.13.g, also at P.13.k, the artillery will bombard the high ground, roughly from P.13.g to P.13.h, from 5.45 p.m., to 6.5 p.m.

The picquets at P.13.k, P.13 and P.13.h, will be furnished by the 45th Sikhs, and that at P.13.g, by the 36th Sikhs. Each picquet will consist of 50 men.

2. "At 5.45 p.m., before bombardment commences, the following precautionary measures will be taken. The present picquet held by the 36th Sikhs between P.16 and P.13.g, will be withdrawn to P.16. Both double blocks at P.14 held by 36th and 45th will be withdrawn to our front line trench.

3. "The 36th and 45th will have the necessary picquets waiting at the points at which they will issue out of the front line at 5.45 p.m.

"The parties will provide themselves with the necessary entrenching tools, water, sandbags and ammunition.

"Immediately the bombardment stops at 6.5 p.m., the picquets will at once move out of the trench preceded by organized bombing parties, and will take up the positions allotted to them. The picquets will at once dig themselves in in lunettes bearing in mind that these lunettes will eventually be joined up by a continuous fire trench.

"The picquet of the 36th Sikhs which has withdrawn during bombardment will resume its former position between P.16 and P.13.g, after bombardment. It must be remembered that all nullahs and communication trenches running to lunettes must be double-blocked.

"Watches will be synchronized at 36th Sikhs Headquarters, at 5 p.m.

4. "Captain R. Rainsford Hannay will arrange for two

HISTORY OF THE 45TH RATTRAY'S SIKHS

bombing parties from 'B' Company, and 50 men for P.13.h, from 'B' Company.

"50 men from 'D' Company with picks and shovels will report to Lieut. Stone at P.13.a at 6 p.m.

"One platoon 'D' Company will report to Captain Hannay at P.14.b. at 5.30 p.m.

"Lieut. Curtis will arrange for three bombing parties (two to be found from 'A' Company and one from 'C' Company), 50 men for P.13 from "A" Company, and 50 men from 'D' Company at 5.30 p.m., for the new communication trench. Lieut. Curtis will take over the line up to P.14 from 36th Sikhs by 5 p.m."

At 5.45 p.m., the bombardment opened, which immediately produced a heavy machine gun fire from the Turkish side. At 6.5 p.m., our guns stopped, and the bombing parties from "B" and "A" Companies, followed by the working parties of 50 men for P.13.h ("B" Company) and P.13 and P.13.k ("A" Company), immediately advanced with the 36th Sikhs party on their left. In spite of heavy machine gun fire they dug in and consolidated the required picquets by 8.15 p.m., except for a gap of some 160 yards between P.13.h and P.13.a.

During the consolidation, Lieut. A. C. Curtis was very severely hit, and was got back to our front line with difficulty owing to the sniping about midnight.

In addition to Lieut. Curtis, we had the following casualties during this operation :—

Indian Officers.

Subadar Wariam Singh, severely wounded.
Subadar Jiwa Singh, B.M.P., severely wounded.
Subadar Major Sundar Singh, slightly wounded. Remained at duty.
Subadar Lehna Singh, slightly wounded. Remained at duty.

Other Ranks.

Killed 3.
Wounded 35.

Severe sniping continued throughout the night with occasional bursts of machine gun fire. No flashes were observed as usual. After the evacuation of Lieut. A. C. Curtis, Lieut. G. Mitchell took over the command of "A" Company.

Amongst some of the messages received during the action, O.C. "A" Company reported: "Subadar Major Sundar Singh's party missed the objective and charged, cheering wildly, 200 yards forward of our present position into our barrage. They were got back, and fell back on our present line in magnificent order under very heavy fire of all sorts. Lewis gun section under No. 180 Havildar Sarup Singh was last to fall back, and came in in perfect order."

The O.C. "B" Company, in describing the share of "B" Company reported "that the advance to P.13.h, and the consolidation of the position were carried out without loss, but that the covering party of his left front suffered somewhat severely from the fire of patrols and snipers concealed in the broken ground."

He brought to notice the following I.O.'s, and N.C.O.'s.

Subadar Wariam Singh who gave him able support during the consolidation of the line.

Subadar Thaman Singh who throughout showed great ability and coolness.

No. 77 Naick Bagga Singh who was in command of the covering bombing party and was wounded. "He and his party remained out, and kept off a much stronger body of enemy snipers and patrols while the line was being consolidated. His party suffered a loss of 66 per cent. without being in any way shaken."

No. 325 Naick Kaka Singh in charge of a covering party. "He advanced with great coolness under a heavy fire, and took up a position in the open. He subsequently showed great judgment and restraint in not opening fire indiscriminately on invisible snipers, who were firing at him at short range. He covered the work efficiently and finally withdrew without loss."

Lieut.-Colonel H. B. Rattray, D.S.O., the Commanding Officer, sent in the following report to the 37th Infantry Brigade on the 30th :—

"The following is a brief report of the part played by the 45th in the action last night. The advance to P.13.h by 'B' Company was carried out and the position consolidated

HISTORY OF THE 45TH RATTRAY'S SIKHS 69

without loss, though the covering party to the left flank suffered severely from enemy patrols and snipers concealed in broken ground. It is impossible to locate the Turkish snipers at night, as their rifles give no flash. I have drawn attention to this fact before, but I do so again because it does give them a very great advantage.

"The ground in front in this part of the line is rough, broken and covered with scattered bushes and patches of grass. It found an ideal terrain for snipers, and one with which they are thoroughly acquainted. Every effort is being made to gain superiority of fire. The enemy made some attempts to advance on P.13.a along the river during the night, but was each time driven off by bombs.

"The advance to P.13 and P.13.k was also carried out with very few casualties by 'A' Company, but during consolidation and ever since there has been a heavy stream of casualties. The enemy bombers who gave us trouble on the night of the 28th/29th were found to be in occupation of a small redoubt near P.13. They came out during the advance, hurled their bombs and retired. There were some Turkish corpses lying about killed by the bombardment. Our casualties amounted to killed, 3; missing, 1; wounded, 41."

At the conclusion of the report he brought to notice the names of the Indian ranks mentioned by the Officers commanding "A" and "B" Companies.

The day was spent in the consolidation of the line P.13.a—P.13.k. It was a tolerably quiet day, and the Turks shelled Gunning Trench (as the line P.13.a—P.16 was now called) for about half-an-hour with 5.9 howitzers at 5 p.m., without causing any damage.

"C" and "D" Companies relieved "A" and "B" Companies in the front line that night under the following instructions by the C.O. :—

"1. 'A' and 'B' Companies will be relieved by 'C' and 'D' Companies in the front line beginning at 6.30 p.m., to-day.

2. All oddments who may be in the front line will rejoin their companies at the same time.

3. 'D' Company will occupy the trenches connected with P.13.a and P.13.h. 'C' Company, P.13 and P.13.k

(Gunning Trench). ' B ' Company will occupy the line P.14.b westwards as far as convenient (Mathews' Trench).

' A ' Company from P.15.b westward (Morris Trench).

4. Regimental Headquarters will be near the entrance of Gloster Street with Mathews' Trench.

5. Regimental Aid Post will be at the junction of Gloster Street and Morris Trench.

6. The gap between P.13.h and P.13 will be consolidated and occupied to-night."

The relief of the front line trenches was postponed to a much later hour than 6.30 p.m., owing to harassing machine gun fire. The relief was completed by 11 p.m., and the consolidation of the 160 yards between P.13.h and P.13 was carried out by " C " and " D " Companies without casualties, though the enemy sniping was very heavy, and two or three enemy machine guns kept enfilading them with bursts of fire at uncertain intervals.

The casualties on the 30th were four other ranks killed, and 11 wounded.

31st.

There was a very heavy thunderstorm from 3–6 a.m., which made the trenches very uncomfortable, and rendered any offensive action by either side impossible. The day was spent in the final consolidation of the front line, Gunning Trench, and the improvement of the communication trenches running up to it. Our guns, which had moved up closer during the night, did a lot of registering, and the Turkish guns had their turn in the afternoon about 5 p.m.

At 5.45 p.m., the orders for the next day's attack were received, and were explained in detail to all ranks.

37th Infantry Brigade Order No. 3 is herewith given in full.

"1. The enemy's force on our front and left flank is estimated to be 310 sabres, 52 guns and 19 battalions (7,200 rifles).

Of these, 11 battalions (3,500 rifles) are on the Hai triangle, right bank.

2. The 3rd Corps is to continue the reduction of the enemy's trenches in the Hai Triangle.

3. The enemy's position will be attacked on both sides of the Hai on February 1st.

4. From 9.30 a.m. to 9.33 a.m. there will be a dummy intense bombardment of the front P.13.n to N.28.a.

5. On the east bank the 13th Division will assault at 9.50 a.m. the trench N.16.a to N.16.f to N.16.d.

6. The 37th Infantry Brigade will co-operate in these operations with machine gun fire on the enemy trenches N.17.a to N.17—N.17.b and Gharaf Mound.

N.B.—Preliminary paragraphs 1 to 6 dealing with enemy dispositions, and operations to be carried out to-morrow by troops other than 14th Division will be forwarded later.

7. The 37th Brigade is to capture the double line of trenches between P.13.m to P.13.b to P.13.n and N.28.a, and the "Bank" immediately behind them.

8. The assault will actually be delivered by the 45th Sikhs and 36th Sikhs, who will be assembled in their present first and second line trenches by 8 a.m. to-morrow as follows :—

45th Sikhs on the right on front of 260 yards from P.13.a.

36th Sikhs on left of 45th Sikhs on front of 200 yards. At 12.10 p.m. the assault will be delivered on the enemy trenches P.13.m to N.27.a.

The right of the 36th Sikhs will direct.

Magnetic bearing of attack is 10 degrees. Each regiment will advance in 8 waves with 50 yards distance between waves.

After the double line of trenches P.13.m to P.13.b to P.13.n, has been captured, the 36th Sikhs will bomb along the trenches running N.W. from N.27.a towards N.28.a, and the 45th Sikhs along the trench from P.13.b towards N.24.b.

A party of sappers and miners will accompany the 36th Sikhs to assist in blocking trenches, and will join the 36th Sikhs by 8 a.m. to-morrow.

At 12.10 p.m., when the 36th and 45th Sikhs advance to the assault, the 1/4th Devons and 1/2nd Gurkhas will occupy Gunning Trench and Mathew Trench.

The 1/2nd Gurkhas will be on the right to Worcester Street exclusive, and the 1/4th Devons on the left from Worcester Street inclusive.

9. The 35th Infantry Brigade will, at 12.10 p.m., send forward a bombing attack from P.16 via P.16.a to N.32.a. This attack will keep pace with the attack of the 37th Infantry Brigade.

10. The Artillery on the west bank, assisted by the artillery on the east bank, will continue wire cutting and bombardment of enemy's position on west bank from 7.30 a.m. to 12 noon to-morrow.

At 12 noon to 12.20 p.m., intense bombardment on the west bank to assist the assault.

The bombardment will lift from the front trenches P.13.m to 35.d.76/05 and P.13.n to N.20 at 12.14½ p.m.

From 12.20 p.m. to 12.40 p.m. general bombardment and barrage.

From 12.40 p.m. artillery will be held in readiness to deal with counter-attacks.

11. The line P.13.n to N.28.a to N.32.a to P.16.a to P.16 will be consolidated, and all forward trenches and nullahs will be blocked until it has been made good.

The dividing line between 37th and 35th Brigades on this line will be the junction of nala and trench at 35.D.76/05. The 37th Brigade take up to the latter point inclusive.

As soon as the above line has been made good, bombing patrols will be pushed up all communications leading to the enemy's position, and will establish blocks close up to it.

Preparations will be made for a further advance to be carried with artillery support.

12. The 36th Brigade are in Divisional Reserve, and will send one Battalion to King's Trench by 12 noon. Remainder of Brigade to be ready to move at short notice.

13. Black flags with yellow cross in centre will be employed by our Infantry to indicate to our Artillery that their fire is interfering with their progress.

14. Main dressing station at Redoubt S.8.

15. All units will send an officer to the Brigade Signal Office at 8 a.m. to-morrow to check watches.

16. Brigade Headquarters will be at the junction of Queen's Trench and Worcester Street."

The night was a quiet one, except for the usual sniping. Our casualties on the 31st were one other rank killed and five wounded.

February 1st. The morning broke very misty, but cleared into a gloriously fine day, so much so that about 11 a.m. Kut stood out very clearly and the inhabitants could be plainly seen sitting on the

HISTORY OF THE 45TH RATTRAY'S SIKHS 73

roofs of the houses watching events on the plain on which we were operating.

About 8 a.m., a patrol sent out by "D" Company under Jemadar Kehar Singh II, crept up to the Turkish wire under cover of the mist and found it cut.

At 9.50 a.m., the 13th Division on the Right Bank attacked and successfully captured the trenches N.16.a.—N.16.f—N.16.d.

The orders for our attack were again carefully explained to all ranks, who were exceedingly happy and cheerful. They then had their food, and tied their Safas afresh, and before the attack looked as if they were turned out for a guard mounting parade. They were full of confidence.

Our Attack. In strict accordance with the orders issued overnight, the 45th, under the command of Lieut.-Colonel H. B. Rattray, D.S.O. (strength: 8 British Officers, 17 Indian Officers, and 562 Other Ranks) advanced to the attack at 12.10 p.m. on a frontage of 260 yards, under cover of a terrific artillery bombardment, with their right on the River Hai, and the 36th Sikhs on their left.

They advanced in eight lines of double platoons at 50 yards distance. "C" and "D" Companies were in the front line, ("D" Company on right) and "B" and "A" Companies in the second line.

"C" and "D" Companies went over from Gunning Trench and 'B" and "A" Companies from Mathews' Trench. Both lines got out of their respective trenches simultaneously to get the distance of 50 yards correct.

As the Regiment went over, they shook out into perfect lines at once, and moved forward as steadily as if on an ordinary parade.

The leading line found the wire in front of the first Turkish trench completely demolished, and arrived there with slight loss. Lieut. J. W. Guise was at this junction severely hit in the arm in two places. The bombardment, which was timed to rest on the Turkish front line for $4\frac{1}{2}$ minutes after the Regiment went over, had not finished, and Captain J. G. Wilson, ordered the front line to lie down until the barrage had lifted.

When this occurred, the first four lines immediately advanced, slightly closed up owing to the halt. The first

Turkish line was but lightly held, and the few live Turks in it were bayonetted. "C" and "D" Companies then advanced on the second line as ordered. This was found to contain many Turkish dead and wounded. Having gained possession of this, "C" and "D" Companies at once made for the "Bank" (P.13.n westwards) which was the final objective in attack orders. It was just before reaching this Bank that Captain J. G. Wilson was killed, after being wounded in two places, setting a magnificent example to his men.

This "Bank" turned out to be a deep nullah full of Turks, and it was here that the Turks were found in large numbers. 2/Lieut. A. C. Stone was killed about this time.

Practically no rifle ammunition was expended, except from Lewis guns, and the men threw many bombs. Every man went over with three on his person, and many of them had more. The bayonet was also freely used.

2. "D" Company's bombers, half in the trench and half outside, managed to bomb up the continuation of Warwick Street, and keep up with the advance, Jemadar Kehar Singh, II, leading them with great gallantry. This gallant Indian Officer was finally killed, and his whole party either killed or wounded in trying to erect their "double block" in the nullah as ordered.

The bombers of "B" and "C" Companies had been previously detailed to clear the "Quadrilateral" (P.13.b. P.13.n). Captain R. Rainsford Hannay was with them. They accomplished their task, and advanced to assist the leading companies on the "Bank." It was here that the intrepid Captain Rainsford Hannay was killed, setting a grand example.

3. The last four waves, "B" and "A" Companies, suffered considerably from the machine gun fire that enfiladed the 36th Sikhs on our left, whilst they were crossing the ground between Mathews' and Gunning Trenches. They pressed on, however, to the "Bank." 2/Lieut. G. Mitchell, "A" Company, was killed whilst crossing "No man's land."

4. At this period the fighting was all hand-to-hand, and the Turkish counter-attacks began to come down the flanks of both lines of trenches. A bombing counter-attack down the trenches from N.28, and across the open from the mounds

HISTORY OF THE 45TH RATTRAY'S SIKHS 75

between N.28 and N.26.a, about 200-300 yards away. Parties (largely " B " Company) were seen from the East Bank to go out and meet bayonet with bayonet, and some of our men came into our own barrage. Some of our dead were found some 100 yards ahead of the " Bank " after the successful attack on the 3rd.

The 45th were at this time isolated owing to the very heavy casualties sustained by the 36th Sikhs during their advance, from machine gun fire on their flank and from the vicinity of N.29. Consequently but few got up on our flank and some got mixed up with our men. All efforts were then concentrated in trying to keep off the counter-attacks on our left flank, which, however, proved unavailing owing to heavy casualties, lack of support and the superior numbers of the enemy. One party got back to our front line about 2 p.m. mostly along the river bank.

A small party of about 60, with whom were Lieut.-Colonel H. B. Rattray, and Captain G. H. Atkinson, the Adjutant, were surrounded in the " Quadrilateral." These two Officers the last two remaining alive, behaved with the most desperate gallantry, and set a magnificent example. They fought on, alas, until both were killed, and nearly all the party were also killed or wounded.

Subadar Thaman Singh, and 39 Other Ranks (almost all wounded), were taken prisoners. All this party's fate remained uncertain for six weeks, when five of our wounded were found in a Turkish hospital in Baghdad, on our entry into the city, and later four others escaped from near Mosul.

5. About 3 p.m., orders were issued through the Brigade Major that the 45th were to be collected in Morris Trench. Captain R. H. Anderson and Subadar Major Sundar Singh, who had been kept in Reserve this day, collected 122 of all ranks by about 3.30 p.m., and this little party marched down to Queen's Trench for the night.

The Regiment's casualties this day were :—

British Officers.—Killed in action   6
                  Wounded   1
Indian Officers.—Killed in action   7
                  Missing   1
                  Wounded   7

Other Ranks.—Killed in action 128
Missing 39
Died of wounds 13
Wounded 280

Our casualties in the previous four days had been :—
Captain Curtis, wounded ; four Indian Officers wounded
(two remained at duty), eight Other Ranks killed in action and
fifty-four wounded.

The Regiment left Queen's Trench at 4 a.m., leaving the
Medical Officer and stretcher-bearers to continue the search
for any of our wounded. They reached a camp at S.19 in
such a dense fog that it took three hours to do four miles,
and the total strength of the Battalion was found to be
three British Officers (Major R. H. Anderson, Lieut. K. H.
Preston, 2/Lieut. E. Hopkins, I.A.R.O.), three Indian Officers
(Subadar Major Sundar Singh, Jemadar Ishar Singh and
Jemadar Wattan Singh), and 280 other ranks (including the
slightly wounded).

The 45th had indeed been through a hard time, and the
Turk knew what it was to come up against a Sikh Regiment ;
the Turkish losses on the 1st, from bomb and bayonet had
been very heavy. We had lost many brilliant officers.
Lieut.-Colonel H. B. Rattray, D.S.O., the son of Colonel
Thomas Rattray, C.B., C.S.I., who had raised the Regiment
in 1856, had been killed in action; also Captains R. Rainsford
Hannay, J. G. Wilson, and G. H. Atkinson, officers of the
finest stamp who knew the men intimately, and also two
young Officers, 2/Lieut.'s G. Mitchell, and A. C. Stone who
had done very good work.

Of a splendid body of Indian Officers seven had been killed
in action, seven wounded and one missing. It may be
invidious to mention names, but the loss of Indian Officers
like Subadars Lehna Singh, Ram Singh, and Thaman Singh
was not to be easily replaced.

In spite of their heavy losses, the fatigue of five days'
incessant work and fighting, and the grievous loss of many
comrades, all ranks were as ever smart and cheerful, and
were ready after a day's rest to carry out any duty they
might be called upon to perform.

A note was received by the Commanding Officer this day

from the G.O.C. 37th Infantry Brigade which read :—
"My dear Anderson,

Just a line to thank your regiment for the more than magnificent effort of yesterday. That it was not successful was the fortune of war, but it was a day that should be as glorious in tradition as any victory. I dare say you know how much I regret the losses in a regiment that I looked on as my personal friends, and the great friends of my own regiment.   Yours sincerely,
                                       (sd.) O. W. C."

The other two battalions of the 37th Infantry Brigade, the 3rd. 1/4th Devons and the 1/2nd Gurkha Rifles, closely supported by the 36th Infantry Brigade, attacked the same objectives as we had attacked on the 1st February, with an artillery bombardment altered in the light of experience gained on the 1st; they gallantly captured the line P.13.m to N.27 with less severe casualties than our attack. The line was pushed forward some 300 yards during the day, and our guns heavily punished no less than five counter-attacks before evening.

This day the Regiment received the following message from the Division : " 3rd Corps wire 3rd begins M.S. 8 Army Commander wires as follows AAA Please convey to 36th and 45th Sikhs my warm appreciation of gallantry and stubborn qualities displayed by them in fighting February 1st AAA Both regiments appear to have dealt enemy heavy blow as regards casualties, ends for communication to all ranks please, addressed 37th Brigade repeated 36th and 45th Sikhs."

The Regiment remained at S.19 until February 18th, and was for the most part daily employed on salvage and burial work. On the dates mentioned below special incidents as described took place.

Lieut. C. W. W. Ford, rejoined the Regiment from Shaikh 6th. Saad, where he had been detained on duty, and took over the duties of Adjutant.

The Regiment was inspected by Major-General Sir R. 7th. Egerton, K.C.I.E., commanding the 14th Division, who complimented them on their recent fine performance. He also gave us the first intimation that we, and the 36th Sikhs, were to proceed down the line of communication to reform at an early date as a purely temporary measure, when we had been replaced by another unit.

In the evening the Brigade Commander summoned the C.O.'s of the 36th and 45th to a conference at his Headquarters, and told them that Army Headquarters India were sending them drafts of P.M.'s and Jats to replace casualties, and asked for suggestions. The O.C. 45th Sikhs mentioned the Sikhs of a certain Imperial Service Unit he was acquainted with instead of these reinforcements. The request was forwarded through the proper channel, but instead of Jats we eventually received Rajputs.

8th.

The G.O.C. 3rd Corps asked for a special guard from the 36th and 45th Sikhs, and the 45th sent 31 rifles under the command of No. 4885 Havildar Rawel Singh.

The following is a copy of a report dated February 8th from the 37th Infantry Brigade regarding the operations during the first week of February.

" Reference your telegram of date. I consider the following units to have particularly distinguished themselves during the recent operations :—

        36th Sikhs.
        45th Sikhs.
        1/4th Devons.
        1/2nd Gurkha Rifles.
        62nd Punjabis.

" The 36th and 45th Sikhs made a most determined and gallant assault against the Turkish positions on the west bank of the Hai on February 1st. The two Regiments advanced under a heavy enfilade fire from guns and machine guns from flanks, and though many men fell as they left our trenches, each succeeding wave pressed on until they finally gained the enemy's position. They were, unfortunately, unable to maintain themselves and had to fall back, but the spirit of the survivors was in no way impaired, and reflects the greatest credit on these two Regiments.

" The 1/4th Devonshire Regiment, the 1/2nd Gurkhas and the 62nd Punjabis attacked the same Turkish positions on February 3rd. These three regiments, in spite of the fact that the 1/4th Devons and 1/2nd Gurkha Rifles had seen their trenches full of wounded Sikhs two days before, attacked with great gallantry and determination. They captured three lines of enemy trenches, and maintained themselves there all day against several counter-attacks. When withdrawn next day they were still ready to continue the offensive.

"The severity of the fighting during these two attacks may be judged by the casualties suffered, the losses being over 50 per cent. of the total strength of the regiments engaged."

A 4.5 howitzer took off the complete top and verandah of *9th.* the minaret in Kut, and completely altered the landscape we had been used to for so long. This minaret formed an excellent observation post.

The Regiment received definite information that they *12th.* were, with the 36th Sikhs and 1/4th Devons, to proceed to Amara to reform when relieved. Also that a reinforcement of Jats had actually left India to reinforce them. The whole of the Dahra Bend was occupied by our troops, and picquetted *15th.* by the 35th Infantry Brigade. The 36th Infantry Brigade returned to S.7, and the 37th Infantry Brigade were ordered to be ready to move up to the line at short notice.

Orders were received for the 36th and 45th Sikhs to march *16th.* to Shaikh Saad on the 17th, on relief by the 2/9th Gurkhas and 2/67th Punjabis respectively. At 5.30 p.m., however, a heavy thunderstorm broke, followed by five hours of hail and a hurricane of wind, and our move was postponed.

We woke up to find the country completely flooded, looking *17th.* like a lake.

Our 60-pounders in the morning bombarded the Turks sitting on their trenches in the Kut peninsula. In retaliation a Turkish plane, flying very low, came over and dropped eight bombs in our vicinity, which luckily caused no damage, as all the trenches were full of water, and there was no cover.

We received orders to march to Shaikh Saad via Sinn on the 18th.

The Regiment left S.13, and the 14th Division, at 7.30 *18th.* a.m. Strength: four B.O.'s, two I.O.'s, and 274 Other Ranks (31 rifles were left behind as a personal guard to the General Officer Commanding 3rd Corps). Atab was reached at 10 a.m., and transport was changed over with the 2/67th

Punjabis. On reaching Imam-Ali-Mansur the Regiment took over Turkish prisoners-of-war (three officers and 248 other ranks) for escort to Shaikh Saad. Marching on to Sinn, they halted for the night, and received detailed orders for their inspection on the morrow, together with the 36th Sikhs, by the Army Commander, Lieut.-General Sir F. S. Maude, K.C.B.

19th. The 36th and 45th Sikhs together with their prisoners-of-war paraded on the now green plain outside Advanced General Headquarters at 9 a.m.

The two regiments were drawn up in line, with their prisoners-of-war in rear of them. The day was perfect, still and cold. After the general salute, the Army Commander distributed immediate rewards for gallantry to the two Regiments.

For the 45th, No. 525 Naick Chanan Singh received the I.O.M. 2nd Class. The Army Commander then went round the ranks of both regiments, and after the inspection made the following speech in English, which he desired Commanding Officers to pass on to the Indian ranks.

"Major Macdonald, Major Anderson and all ranks of the 36th and 45th Sikhs.

"It is a matter of very real regret to me that I have not been able to see these two fine regiments before this. Under ordinary circumstances I should have gone down to see you immediately after the recent action in which you gained such honourable distinction. But, as you will understand, things have been somewhat busy lately, and I have found that it was not possible for me to spare the time from my other duties to enable me to do so. Consequently I have come here to-day to express to you my admiration at the magnificent fighting qualities you displayed on February 1st. On that date you not only took with splendid dash the first line of Turkish trenches, but you pushed on and captured the second and third lines also. These you held on to for a considerable time beating off repeated counter-attacks, and it was not until the evening, when a very weighty counter-attack was pushed in by the enemy, that you were compelled to give ground, not, however, without inflicting very severe losses on the Turks. The deeds accomplished by you on that day are such that any regiment may be proud of, and they bear testimony to the heroism and well-known fighting spirit of the Sikh soldier.

"I regret very sincerely the heavy casualties suffered by both regiments on that occasion : but you have at least this consolation in mourning your comrades—that you inflicted far heavier losses on the enemy, and your stubborn courage and magnificent behaviour paved the way for the successful capture of these trenches by another brigade. Indeed, it is not too much to say that this fine beginning on your part was the means of bringing about the culminating blow which fell on the 15th, when over 2,000 prisoners surrendered to our forces.

"You are now going down to obtain a well-earned rest, and I want you clearly to understand that you are going there in order to enable you to reform and refill your ranks, and to have a much-needed rest. We shall all look forward to your rejoining us in a very short time at the front, for both these Regiments are of a stamp such as we can ill spare when serious fighting is in progress.

"I thank you all for your magnificent services."

The two Regiments, after a final general salute, marched off with many fatehs together with their prisoners-of-war to Twin Canals, where they camped for the night.

CHAPTER IV

FEBRUARY 20TH, 1917, TO SEPTEMBER 30TH, 1918

1917
February 21st

The 45th marched into Shaikh Saad (the advanced base) on February 10th, and there handed over their prisoners-of-war into the cage. Together with the 36th Sikhs they took over two lines of tents in the rest camp.

Information was received that the Regiment would sail at very short notice for Amara with prisoners-of-war. But our fate was destined to be otherwise, for the 36th Sikhs sailed on the 22nd, and the 1/4th Devons in the steamer that had been allotted to us. The 45th voluntarily loaded their kit for them, and gave the whole Regiment tea. Both acts were much appreciated.

On February 21st and 22nd terrific bombardments were observed at Sannaiyat (some seven miles away). The 3rd Corps crossed the River Tigris at the Shumran Bend, whilst the 7th Division assaulted and captured the Sannaiyat position. The Turks were retreating on Baghdad, with the whole army in pursuit.

From having been treated in the front line as a fighting unit, the 45th saw the 36th and 1/4th Devons depart for Amara, and stayed in Shaikh Saad until March 9th. They became "hewers of wood and drawers of water," and did innumerable fatigues and guard duties.

Before leaving Shaikh Saad information was received that a draft of one company of Jats from the 10th Jats were leaving India on February 25th to be attached until such time as the Regiment was up to strength in Sikhs. The Regiment was to keep its organization of four companies Sikhs, and further that it was not possible to utilize the Imperial Service troops asked for.

HISTORY OF THE 45TH RATTRAY'S SIKHS 83

March 9th. The Regiment was ordered to embark on the P.16 on the 10th leaving one B.O. (Lieut. K. H. Preston) and 90 Other Ranks for garrison duty at Shaikh Saad out of the small strength of the Regiment.

10th. After a good deal of unnecessary work, we embarked on the P.16 at 7 a.m., and sailed at 11 a.m. Strength : three British Officers and 200 Other Ranks under command of Major R. H. Anderson. We had a very comfortable journey, tying up for the night, and arrived at Amara at 9 a.m., in pouring rain on the 11th.

Having disembarked, we marched to a huge camp of E.P. tents pitched at the southern end of the town on the left bank. This camp was contracted into a perimeter camp with mess and Officers' tents in the centre. Amara was a bad place for rifle thieves in spite of the whole town being blockhoused and wired in, but during our three-and-a-half months' stay we had no trouble.

12th. We received news of the capture of Baghdad in the evening.

Lieut. K. H. Preston and the 90 Other Ranks we had left behind in Shaikh Saad arrived with 900 Turkish prisoners-of-war. These they handed over, and joined the Regiment, whose strength was now five B.O.'s and 400 Other Ranks. A small draft of 70 odd from our own depot had been waiting for us in Amara and joined on our arrival.

18th. No. 18 Havildar Ude Singh, No. 1121 Sepoy Puran Singh, I.D.S.M., No 1488 Sepoy Tara Singh and No. 1251/15 Sepoy Wazir Singh arrived in hospital in Amara by hospital ship, followed four days later by No. 1287/15 Sepoy Thaman Singh. These men had been found in a Turkish hospital in Baghdad on the entry of our army into Baghdad, and had all been wounded and taken prisoners in the attack on February 1st. The Turks had forcibly cut the hair and shaved all of them, which fact was duly reported to General Headquarters. Their arrival confirmed the deaths in action of Lieut.-Colonel H. B. Rattray and Captain G. H. Atkinson, and the missing were duly identified as prisoners-of-war, and missing—killed in action.

26th. Intimation was received through Tigris defences that the outside reinforcements for the 45th were to be six platoons

84 HISTORY OF THE 45TH RATTRAY'S SIKHS

29th. of Rajputs (two each from the 2nd, 8th and 11th Rajputs) and one company P.M.'s (25th Punjabis).

These all arrived this day, with the exception of two platoons 11th Rajputs, who arrived three days later. The following British Officers joined: Captain W. R. Boswell, 28th Punjabis; Lieuts. J. G. Kilpin and R. K. Henson, 25th Punjabis; and Lieut. G. L. Watson, I.A.R.O. These Officers all came with the P.M. Company of the 25th Punjabis, and strangely enough not a single British Officer came with over 300 Rajputs.

About this time the Regiment received orders to hold a line of some 14 blockhouses from our camp, across the Chahala Canal, linking up with the 36th Sikhs, and to camp half the Regiment at the north end of the line. These reinforcements therefore, occupied this camp under the new Officers who had arrived, and our men called it the 2/45th camp. The P.M. Company were an excellent lot. The Rajputs were very handicapped by having no officer with them who knew their ways and habits.

The P.M.'s were called " E " Company, and the Rajputs " F " Company.

On the 30th, 2/Lieut. E. Hopkins, I.A.R.O., proceeded to join the Political Department.

April. The month was occupied in quiet training and re-organization for the 45th, and intensive training under our own drill instructors for the Rajputs, who were improving, but frequently going sick.

On the 19th two rifles were stolen at night from the Rajput tents, and their camp was heavily wired in in addition to the blockhouse wire close to it.

On the 25th the P.M. Company of the 25th were ordered to join the 28th Punjabis up the line, but without British Officers. The bulk of them sailed on the 26th. On this date No. 799 Sepoy Ujagar Singh, who was wounded and taken prisoner on February 1st, and who escaped from the Turks beyond Samarra rejoined the Regiment.

Towards the end of the month drafts from our depot joined up. Two I.O.'s (Jemadar Mehar Singh, I.D.S.M., and Jemadar Lal Singh) and 255 Other Ranks.

On April 30 the strength of the 45th (without Rajputs) was :—five B.O.'s—10 I.O.'s—709 Other Ranks.

On May 1st the remainder of the P.M. Company proceeded up river to join the 28th Punjabis. Lieuts. R. K. Henson and G. L. Watson were left with the Rajput Company, and Captain W. R. Boswell and Lieut. J. G. Kilpin came across to the Regiment.

May.

The Regiment was now getting well up to strength, and steady training in all branches was carried out. They were as smart and cheerful as ever. Their health was excellent, and football was played by all. The Regiment just missed winning the Amara Football League.

No. 325 Naick Kaka Singh, No. 461 Naick Naranjan Singh and No. 1355/15 Sepoy Wazir Singh, who were all wounded and captured on February 1st and had escaped from the Turks near Mosul, rejoined the Regiment on May 14th, after undergoing terrible hardships. Their experiences are related in a later chapter.

Naick Kaka Singh afterwards received the I.D.S.M. for gallantry, and the Army Commander rewarded all of them with four months' pay and allowances, as well as to No. 799 Sepoy Ujagar Singh who rejoined in April.

The guard of 30 rifles to the G.O.C. 3rd I.A. Corps rejoined the Regiment on May 22nd.

The following officers joined the Regiment during the month :—

Lieut. G. D. Pybus 14th K.G.O. Sikhs (12th); Lieut. J. E. Hughes, I.A.R.O., 15th Sikhs (17th); and Captain M. Saunders, 36th Sikhs (29th).

The strength of the Regiment on May 31st (exclusive of Rajputs) was :—B.O.'s, 11; I.O.'s, 13; I.O.R.'s, 726.

Training in all its branches was carried on. Our only duties were to occupy seven blockhouses by night, and one by day. We could not have been sent to a better place to get together.

June.

Lieut. R. B. Ramsbotham, I.A.R.O., 35th Sikhs, joined the Regiment on June 5th, but was at once taken away for a line of communication billet.

On June 13th Major D. A. D. McVean, D.S.O., rejoined the Regiment from staff employ in India, and assumed command vice Major R. H. Anderson.

On June 18th we received orders that the Regiment would move to Bgailah at very short notice, with one company to be located in Kut. On the 24th, after many orders and counter orders, we received orders to embark on the 25th.

We struck our camp early on the 25th, and sent all kits, tentage, etc., to be loaded on a barge, due at 10 a.m., but which did not appear till 6 p.m. After sitting in the open all day in a tearing dust storm, we embarked very expeditiously and quietly on the P.91, a very large and roomy Brahmaputra river steamer, at 6.15 p.m. The whole Regiment got into the ship with ease and were very comfortable.

We left Amara at 7 a.m. on the 26th, and passing the old landmarks of Shaikh Saad, Kut and the much-fought-over country along the banks, arrived at Bgailah at 5 a.m., on the 29th.

We at once disembarked and went into camp. The 119th Infantry, whom we relieved, sailed up river in the afternoon.

Besides ourselves the garrison of Bgailah contained the 96th Infantry and one section 18-pounders. It was the Headquarters of a section of the line of communication.

On the 30th, a leave party of three I.O.'s and 40 I.O.R.'s left for one month's leave in India.

July.

The month of July was unusually hot, and day after day very high temperatures prevailed. 127 degrees in the men's E.P. tents and 113 degrees in the officers' Mess dugout were registered on several days.

The month was mostly devoted to musketry, and the whole Regiment fired a special course of 10 practices.

The whole Regiment also took to the river like ducks every evening.

Two leave parties totalling one I.O., and 63 Other Ranks left for one month's leave in India on the 2nd and 6th.

We had to send the following detachments away :—

(a) On the 7th, two I.O.'s and 98 I.O.R.'s from "A" Company under Lieut. J. G. Kilpin to Imam Mahdi (five miles down stream).

(b) On the 13th, "C" Company (150 rifles) under Captain W. R. Boswell to Kut. This was in addition to "E" Company (Rajput) who had proceeded to Wadi from Amara, and were now in Kut under Lieut. R. K. Henson.

The 14th Sikhs arrived in Bgailah for up the line on the night of the 13th, and the two Regiments fraternized tremendously until 10 a.m. on the 14th, when their steamer sailed amidst round after round of fatehs.

The water in the river at this season of the year was very low, and many steamers used to stick for hours in the reach above Bgailah. At one time there were eleven.

On July 22nd the 96th Infantry took us on at sports, and we won every event and every place. After the sports, at which the G.O.C. Tigris Defences was present, we received the information that we should very shortly move up to Baghdad.

On July 27th, Arrah Day was celebrated with a service in the Gurdwara and a platoon sack football tournament in the morning. In the afternoon, aquatic sports were held, amongst other events was a "Guffa" race for teams of four, B.O.'s, I.O.'s and I.O.R.'s. The B.O.'s and O.R.'s' teams arrived at the finishing point almost neck to neck, the B.O.'s won by two lengths, about twelve feet. Both teams got on shore, and discovered that the I.O.'s were still spinning round and round in circles at the starting point, as they had not discovered the art of propelling a "Guffa." The "Guffa" by the way is the oldest form of boat in the world, and is a coracle of varying dimensions, in the use of which the river Arabs are very skilful.

On the 30th, news was received from our depot that Army Headquarters, India, had ordered Sikh Regiments to enlist P.M.'s, which were not to be extra to the establishment.

August. The heat continued to be very great, but the nights got cooler. Musketry and bombing was carried on.

The detachment at Imam Mahdi was relieved on the 7th.

On August 8th, news came from our Depot that our August draft of sixty recruits were ordered by Army Headquarters to reinforce the 14th Sikhs, who were already overstrength and all Sikh!

On August 15th, we received news that our relief was the 126th Baluchistan Infantry from India, and that they had actually sailed from Basra.

On the 17th "C" Company, Captain W. R. Boswell, returned to Headquarters from duty at Kut.

On the 20th the 126th Infantry arrived at Bgailah and at once disembarked. The Regiment (less " C " Company and part of " A " Company) embarked at once and sailed.

" C " Company and part of " A " Company under Captain W. R. Boswell, with Lieut. J. G. Kilpin, were to come up later, owing, it was said, to lack of room.

" E " Company (Rajputs) remained in Kut under Lieut. R. K. Henson.

After a very slow passage owing to the low water, the ship having to drag herself along by her anchors on several occasions, we arrived at Hinaidi (four-and-half miles south of Baghdad) at 10 a.m., on August 23rd.

No staff officer met us, and no one seemed to know anything about us, so we dumped ourselves on the shore, and pitched camp. We remained there in splendid isolation till the end of the month, and received orders to move on September 1st to Karradah (two-and-a-half miles) and camp on the camping ground of the 34th Infantry Brigade. We were to belong to the 52nd Infantry Brigade, 15th Division, which was in process of formation.

September. On the 1st we marched to our new camp at Karradah, and got settled down by noon in great heat. The other battalions of the 52nd Infantry Brigade had not arrived, but were on their way up river. They were the 1/6th Hants, 84th Punjabis, and 113th Infantry.

On September 2nd " C " and part of " A " Company under Captain W. R. Boswell arrived from Bgailah, and rejoined.

In the evening we were visited by Major-General H. T. Brooking, C.B., C.M.G., commanding the 15th Division and his staff.

On the 6th, " E " Company (Rajputs) arrived from Kut quite unexpectedly under Lieut. R. K. Henson. They camped with the Regiment for the first time since their arrival in the country on March 29th.

On the 7th the Regiment marched into the Citadel, Baghdad, to draw H.V. rifles, and " E " Company drew theirs on the 8th. We were all much disappointed in the " City of the Caliphs." It looks enchanting from afar, but does not bear looking into at close quarters.

Lieut.-Colonel D. A. D. McVean, D.S.O., had an interview with the A.G.'s Branch General Headquarters about getting rid of the Rajput Company in accordance with promises received. It was decided that the Rajput Company was to remain " owing to the question of maintenance."

As this company was composed of men of three different units, it was very strongly represented that they might be broken up, and one platoon put into each of our Companies. On the 20th verbal sanction was accorded to this measure, which on the whole worked very well.

Thus the fourth platoon in each company became Rajput as a temporary measure.

We had one more promise as to our ultimate composition, for on a representation dated August, 1917, from our late Commandant the reply was received from Army Headquarters, India, that " the introduction of an outside class into the 45th Sikhs is a temporary measure, only until such time as the Regiment is able to complete with Sikhs, and has a reserve for maintenance."

Steady regimental training was carried out during the month. All the new units of the new 52nd Infantry Brigade had now arrived, and our Brigade Commander was Brigadier-General F. A. Andrew, D.S.O. (late 128th Pioneers).

On October 1st we heard of the victory of Ramadie by the 15th Division and a cavalry Brigade. The troops engaged had very recently been encamped in our area. *October.*

On the 2nd the Regiment, with the 52nd Infantry Brigade, was transferred to the newly-formed 17th Indian Division, commanded by Major-General Webb Gilman, C.B., C.M.G., D.S.O.

At this time there was a great deal of talk of a Turkish army under Field-Marshall Von Falkenhayn coming to retake Baghdad, and to drive the British armies out of Mesopotamia. Consequently the 17th and 18th Indian Divisions were formed from troops on the line of communication and from India.

On the 6th the honours and mentions for the fighting last winter were received.

They consisted of six I.O.M.'s and one I.D.S.M. and

"Mentions in Despatches" for five British Officers, two Indian Officers and nine I.O.R.'s. (See Appendix Honours and Rewards.)

On the 7th written permission from General Headquarters to break up the Rajput Company was received in the following letter:—"It is understood that the Officer Commanding 45th Sikhs prefers that his battalion should be organized into four mixed companies of class platoons. There is no objection to this."

On the 12th a party of three I.O.'s and 45 I.O.R.'s under Major R. H. Anderson went to attend a "Jormela" and sports given by the 47th Sikhs at Istabulat on the 13th. We won the obstacle race and one mile race, and were second in the relay race, encountering severe competition. There must have been 4,000 Sikhs at the "Jormela" and sports, mostly from the 3rd and 7th Divisions. The party returned to Baghdad on the 14th.

On the 21st Major B. W. Shuttleworth joined the Regiment from staff employ in India, and took over the duties of 2nd-in-command and command of "B" Company.

There also arrived on this date from the base, where they had been kept for a long time, to our great joy, Subadar Nidhan Singh and 228 of our own men. They were followed at intervals by about 30 more.

On October 26th, Lieut. B. W. Key arrived from the Depot, and took over the duties of Adjutant.

On the 30th there was some rain, and the winter arrived with great suddenness. The summer had been a very hot one, much above the average, and stayed very late.

The month was taken up with much training, mostly Brigade, with a fair amount of night operations.

The strength of the Indian ranks of the Regiment on October 31st was:—

Sikhs   18 I.O.'s and 869 Other Ranks.
Rajputs 5   ,,   ,, 228   ,,   attached.

We all felt that it would not be very long before we were all Sikh again.

November. By a Force order, Indian ranks, who had been in Turkish hands as prisoners-of-war, were ordered to return to India.

On November 1st, under this order the following N.C.O.'s and men left for India, though most unwillingly :—

    No. 325 Havildar Kaka Singh.
    No. 461 Naick Naranjan Singh.
    No. 799 L/Nk. Ujagar Singh.
    No. 1488 Sepoy Tara Singh.
    No. 1355/15 Sepoy Wazir Singh.

In March, 1917, the Commanding Officer had written in an official complaint regarding five wounded prisoners-of-war of the Regiment being forcibly shaved and their Kés cut in a Turkish hospital. The following letter was sent by the Foreign Office, London, to H.M.'s Minister at the Hague for communication to the Turkish Government under date, August 7th, 1917 :—

" His Majesty's Government have learnt that certain wounded Sikh prisoners-of-war at Baghdad, were, after their capture, forcibly shaved and their hair cut on the orders of a Turkish medical officer, a procedure which, as was clearly explained to the medical officer, constituted a violation of the Sikh religion.

" The Turkish Government has from time to time, professed concern for the spiritual welfare of the Turkish prisoners-of-war in British hands, and it might therefore have been that they would show respect for the religious scruples of the British prisoners-of-war captured by them. Many baseless complaints have been made by the Turkish Government respecting the treatment of Turkish prisoners-of-war, but it has never at any time been so much asserted that these prisoners had been forced, or even invited, to do anything contrary to the Mohammedan religion.

" It is therefore with surprise that His Majesty's Government have learnt of this outrageous treatment inflicted on the Sikh prisoners above mentioned, and they desire to record the strongest possible protest against it."

On the 5th news was received of the capture of Tekrit by the 1st Corps, and on the 6th of the capture of Gaza by General Allenby's Army.

On the 8th, Headquarters and the right wing marched over to a new camp at Iron Bridge (Tigris right bank), followed on the 9th by the left wing. The whole 52nd Infantry Brigade was now concentrated there, just to the north of the Iron Bridge over the Khirr Canal.

On the 14th we held the most successful sports, to which a very large number of Officers came. The most unique event was a relay race in gas masks for three British and two Indian Officers per company.

From the 16th to the 20th, the Brigade dug a complete system of trenches about a mile from camp, and trench warfare was much practiced.

Within three-quarters of a mile of the camp was a large expanse of water known as Lake Akakuf. This year it was very large owing to deliberate flooding on the part of the Turks on our entry into Baghdad. At this time it was very cold, and geese and duck swarmed on it. On November 18th, a Brigade shoot was arranged to try and make a bag. Forty-five guns took post round the western end, but the shoot was not a success owing to the expanse of water and absence of cover, and all told the bag was only 50 birds.

On this day we heard that the Army Commander Lieut.-General Sir. F. S. Maude, K.C.B., was dangerously ill. At 11 a.m., the men held a service in the Gurdwara, to which British Officers were invited, praying for his speedy recovery. To the intense regret of all ranks we heard about noon that the Army Commander had died of cholera during the night. It was a very dark, gloomy day, and about 1 p.m. a Turkish aeroplane flew over Baghdad from the north with every anti-aircraft gun firing at him, which sounded very like minute guns. He dropped no bombs, however, and flew away unhurt towards Feluja.

The funeral of Lieut.-General Sir Stanley Maude, K.C.B., took place in the cemetery north of the cavalry barracks at 4 p.m. It was a very simple and most impressive ceremony. His death cast the deepest gloom over the whole Force, who had the most profound confidence in him. He was succeeded in command by Lieut.-General W. R. Marshall, C.B., C.M.G., commanding the 3rd Corps.

November 28th was the birthday of Guru Govind Singh. The men were given half-a-day's holiday, and the following message from the president of the Chief Khalsa Dewan,

HISTORY OF THE 45TH RATTRAY'S SIKHS 93

Amritsar, was received by the Regiment and all Sikhs in the Force.

" To our most dear brothers now serving the benign King-Emperor. The Chief Khalsa Dewan tenders hearty and sincere greetings on the auspicious guru gurb of the first Guru. You are upholding the name and fame of Gurpura. Our hearts are with you, and our prayers are that Satguru and Akalpurth may ever be with you, and lead you to victory and return home safe after vanquishing the King-Emperor's foes, with honours and flying colours."

There were persistent rumours towards the end of the month that we were shortly to proceed down the River Euphrates in the Babylon direction, and these proved not to be far wrong.

Brigade training was carried out on eight occasions from the time we arrived at Iron Bridge to the end of the month.

The first half of the month was spent in Regimental and Brigade training.

December.

On the 5th, Lieut.-Colonel D. A. D. McVean, D.S.O., and another Commanding Officer in the Brigade went down to Hillah in Ford vanettes on special duty.

On the 10th the weather turned intensely cold, eight degrees of frost being registered for some weeks in Baghdad.

On the 12th we received information that the Regiment was very shortly to be broken up into several detachments. On the 13th the exodus began, when Nos. 11 and 12 platoons of " C " Company marched out and took over the small posts of Akarkuf and Daudiyah.

On December 15th, the following detachments marched for the places named in the undermentioned table. Only Headquarters, " A " Company and spare men remained at Iron Bridge.

1. Hindiyah Barrage Musaiyib	" B " Company B.O.'s .. .. 3 I.O.'s .. .. 4 I.O.R.'s .. 223	Major B. W. Shuttleworth, Lieut. R. B. Ramsbotham, Lieut. Santokh Singh, I.M.S. The Company marched at 8.30 a.m., as under. *1st Day*, Mahmudiyah. *2nd Day*, Khanhiswah. *3rd Day*, Musaiyib. *4th Day*, Hindiyah Barrage. (2 platoons.)

94 HISTORY OF THE 45TH RATTRAY'S SIKHS

2.	Khan Nuqtah	" C " Company less 1½ platoons. B.O.'s .. .. 2 I.O.'s .. .. 1 I.O.R.'s .. 57	Captain W. R. Boswell, Lieut. G. L. Watson. (These posts were on the Baghdad-Feluja Railway.)
	Gharib	I.O.'s .. .. 1 I.O.R.'s .. 57	
	Mohomed Saiyid	½ No. 12 Platoon from Daudiyah.	
3.	Mufraz	" D " Company less 1 platoon. B.O.'s .. .. 2 I.O.'s .. .. 3 I.O.R.'s .. 171	Major R. H. Anderson, Lieut. C. W. W. Ford. (A march of 23 miles across the desert.)
	(railhead)	No. 16 Platoon I.O.'s .. .. 1 I.O.R.'s .. 57	This Platoon was to remain at railhead until completion of railway.

On December 18th, Captain W. R. Boswell proceeded to join his own regiment, the 28th Punjabis. Lieut. C. W. W. Ford took over the command of " C " Company, and Lieut. G. D. Pybus joined " D " Company at Mufraz.

On December 19th and 20th there was very heavy rain, which turned the so-called roads into quagmires. On the 21st orders were received for Headquarters and " A " Company to march to Musaiyib on the 23rd. A dump of heavy kit and a small Depot only were to be left at Iron Bridge.

On the 23rd, Headquarters and " A " Company, strength : five B.O.'s, six I.O.'s, 253 I.O.R.'s, marched out of Iron Bridge for Mahmudiyah, 19 miles. The road was in a terrible condition owing to the rain, and the carts had consequently to be manhandled a large part of the way. They arrived at Mahmudiyah at 4 p.m., and billetted in the " Serai " after a very hard day.

On the 24th before the march it was raining heavily, and continued to pour for 10 hours, so this detachment remained at Mahmudiyah. The road was reconnoitred, at the Musaiyib end also, and found to be absolutely impassable. Accordingly, a telegraphic report was sent to the 52nd Infantry Brigade, and five days' rations asked for.

On the 25th, Christmas day, 125 pack mules were sent out from Baghdad, which brought orders that Musaiyib was to be reached at all costs. So Headquarters and " A " Company marched on the 26th at 8.30 a.m., and reached Musaiyib after a very hard march late in the afternoon, for the carts had to be manhandled most of the last nine miles. On arrival the detachment went into billets in three different caravanserais.

On the 28th they all went into a very damp camp south of the big " Serai." The Commanding Officer rode over to see the Barrage (six miles), built and actually completed by Sir John Jackson after the outbreak of war, where half " B " Company were found to be very comfortable in huts and E.P. tents.

On the 30th, " B " Company (Major B. W. Shuttleworth) took over the Barrage, whilst Battalion Headquarters and " A " Company (Captain M. Saunders, D.S.O.) remained in Musaiyib.

JANUARY, 1918

The strength of the Regiment on the New Year was :—

British Officers .. 13
Sikhs .. .. 17 I.O.'s. 898 I.O.R.'s.
Rajputs .. .. 5 I.O.'s. 231 I.O.R.'s (attached).

and it was greatly hoped that the outside class would disappear as soon as we had completed to 1,000 Sikhs.

The Regiment was split up into nine detachments.

On January 2nd, Major-General G. A. J. Leslie, C.B., C.M.G., who had taken over the command of the 17th Division in December, 1917, inspected Musaiyib ; on the 3rd he proceeded to visit the sacred Shiah shrine of Kerbela, Lieut.-Colonel D. A. D. McVean accompanied him ; and on the 4th he inspected " B " Company at the Barrage.

On the 6th, official intimation was received that Lieut.-Colonel D. A. D. McVean, D.S.O., had been appointed Commandant of the Regiment from July 28th, 1917, vice Lieut.-Colonel F. T. Stewart, vacated.

On the 9th, " C " Company, Lieut. C. W. W. Ford, arrived at Iron Bridge from posts on the Feluja Railway, and No. 16 platoon from Feluja Railhead arrived at Musaiyib from Iron Bridge as escort to a survey party.

On the 10th, " D " Company, Major R. H. Anderson,

arrived at Iron Bridge from Mufraz, after a hard waterless march of 23 miles.

"D" Company had a very pleasant three weeks in Mufraz. The inhabitants here had murdered a British Officer in April, 1917, and had very guilty consciences. Bad weather only prevented their carrying out the execution of the actual murderers on the site of their crime, and they were hung in Baghdad instead.

They had good huts in this post, which was evacuated as the toy railway was pulled up, and all material which could not be got away was burnt before evacuation.

On the 17th Lieut. C. W. W. Ford left the Regiment on appointment to a new battalion in India, and on the 18th, Captain M. Saunders, D.S.O., left to take up his appointment as G.S.O. 3, Dunster Force.

The loss of all these Officers was much regretted.

On January 20th, the left wing marched from Iron Bridge for Kufa under Major R. H. Anderson with Lieut. R. K. Henson. There was trouble at that place, and the holy city of Nejf, and a show of force was necessary. They marched with an Echelon consisting of Brigade Headquarters (the G.O.C. commanded the force and had gone on by motor) together with the Brigade signal section and S.A.A.S., and the 1/113th Infantry. (For movements of the left wing see February, 1918.)

On the 21st, "A" Company, Lieut. R. B. Ramsbotham, relieved "B" Company at the Barrage, and "B" Company returned to Musaiyib.

February.

On the 1st, Commemoration Services were held at 12.10 p.m. at Musaiyib, the Barrage and Kufa. This was the hour of the attack on February 1st, 1917.

On the 3rd the G.O.C. 53rd Infantry Brigade (18th Division) arrived at Musaiyib, and from him we learnt that we would be relieved by the 1/3rd Gurkhas at that place in a few days.

This regiment marched into Musaiyib on the morning of the 6th having been delayed by rain, and took over all duties at that place and the Barrage.

On the 7th, Headquarters and the right wing, less certain escorts down the river, marched from Musaiyib at 10 a.m., and camped at Iskandriyah by 1 p.m. Helio communication

HISTORY OF THE 45TH RATTRAY'S SIKHS 97

was at once established with the left wing at Khan Haswan, whence it had just arrived on its march up from Kufa. It rained a lot in the night, but, fortunately, a tearing gale helped to dry the road and make it passable.

On the 8th the Regiment (Headquarters and right wing) marched at 8.30 a.m., and met the left wing at the junction of the Musaiyib, and Hillah roads. The whole Regiment after a halt marched on together, having been split up since December 15th, and camped by the canal at Mahmudiyah by 1.15 p.m. The remainder of the Echelon arrived at 3 p.m., and Lieut.-Colonel D. A. D. McVean, D.S.O., became O.C. Echelon.

At this point it is interesting to follow the movements of the left wing to Nejf and back, since they left Baghdad on January 20th until February 8th. *Narrative of the Left Wing from Iron Bridge to Kufa.*

January 20th. "C" and "D" Companies, under Major R. H. Anderson, marched to Mahmudiyah, 19 miles, as part of the 2nd Echelon of the 52nd Infantry Brigade. Strength: B.O.'s, 3; I.O.'s, 8; I.O.R.'s, 448. No. 16 platoon, away on escort duty, was replaced by a composite Sikh platoon. We had no men fall out, and did not bother the field ambulance.

21st. Marched to Khan Haswan, 14 miles.

22nd. Marched to Khan Mahawil, 14½ miles.

23rd. Marched to Hillah, 14 miles. No. 12 platoon was left at this place as a guard on the barracks.

24th. Marched to Kifl, 23 miles. The men marched extremely well. Camped on the left bank. This place is noted for the possession of the tomb of the prophet Ezekiel, situated in an old world church with a gallery at the western end.

25th. The Echelon crossed over to the right bank by means of a flying ferry made of mahelas. The men had a very hard day, as they worked for over 12 hours taking Brigade stores and ammunition over.

One hundred rifles under Subadar Wattan Singh escorted the brigade transport carts and signal section into Kufa, marching about 2 p.m.

26th. Leaving No. 14 platoon as a garrison over the ferry in a blockhouse, the left wing (less two platoons), marched into Kufa, 15 miles, alone. The remainder of the Echelon were given a day's rest. The men marched in splendidly, and we were allotted a Turkish police post, half way between Kufa and Nejf on the tramway, one mile away from the remainder of the force, now known as Andrew's Column.

January 27th to February 2nd. We remained camped on the tramway, and built a very strong post of sandstone round the police post. Nejf, three miles away, stood out ever so clearly at sunset and sunrise. No troops were allowed to approach nearer to the city than two miles, as it has the reputation of being very fanatical. The show of force, however, proved sufficient, for the inhabitants paid up the fine inflicted on them, and handed in 500 rifles. The force departed within three days. Two months later they murdered the Political Officer, and had to be more severely dealt with by another column from the 18th Division.

February 3rd. The left wing, with the 1/6th Hants, marched to Kifl. We picked up our platoon and crossed over to the left bank.

4th. Was spent quietly at Kifl. 1/6th Hants crossed over. Heavy rain came down in the evening, with much wind.

5th. Woke up to find it raining heavily. As the road to Hillah lay mostly through a swamp, the O.C. Echelon decided to halt. Peremptory orders were received from the Brigade at 10 a.m. to march whatever the weather. We got off at 11 a.m. We got into Hillah at 6.30 p.m., the men covered the 23 miles splendidly in seven-and-a-half hours, and billetted for the night. The Hants arrived much later.

6th. Marched to Khan Mahawil. A very bad place for rifle and other thieves; we lost nothing.

7th. Marched to Khan Haswan where we got into helio communication with Battalion Headquarters at Iskandriyah at 1 p.m.

8th. Marched to Mahmudiyah, joining up with Headquarters and right wing, at junction of Hillah and Musaiyib Roads, having marched 200 miles since January 20th.

The Regiment marched into their old camp at Iron Bridge *February 9th.*
getting some rain on the road. On arrival we found that our
depot and dump had been moved to Beled by rail the night
before, and that we ourselves should also move there by
rail very shortly, but that our transport would march up.

We received orders to entrain for Beled from the advanced *10th.*
base, right bank, at 7 a.m. on the 11th. So at 4 p.m., we
marched to the advanced base and camped in the rest camp,
close to the station.

Entraining commenced at 7 a.m., and was finished by *11th.*
8 a.m. We arrived at Beled at 1.15 p.m., and at once went
into camp.

The country about Beled changes from the flat monotonous
country found south of Baghdad. From here northwards
the river runs through cliffs, and the bed of the river is gravelly.
The country on either side is a plateau much intersected by
wadis or nullahs. Trees except in a few places are conspicuous by their absence.

Our transport had been left behind to march up to Beled
with a brigade echelon at a later date.

Spent in clearing up and settling into camp. Funk pits *12th.*
were dug, as Turkish planes often came over. News came
of a Baghdad Week in the near future; we entered a team,
and started hockey with vigour.

Our transport and horses arrived with the road *15th.*
echelon.

Spring races were held at Akab on the 21st and 23rd under
the auspices of the 17th Division. It was a very good, well-run race meeting. The Regiment entered some horses, and
Captain B. W. Key on "Xerxes" came in second in one
race.

2/Lieut. R. V. Fox joined the Regiment from the Depot. *23rd.*

The Regiment was informally inspected by Lieut.-General *24th.*
Sir A. Cobb, V.C., etc., commanding the 1st Corps.

We were drawn against the 14th Sikhs in the Baghdad
Hockey Tournament, the game to be played off locally. The
14th won the toss, and decided to play at Istabulat. So on
February 21st a party of five I.O.'s and 240 Other Ranks left
by train for Istabulat to stay with the 14th Sikhs and see
the match.

100 HISTORY OF THE 45TH RATTRAY'S SIKHS

28th — Every available officer went to Istabulat in cars to see the match, and stay the night. The game commenced at 3.30 p.m., before a very large crowd on a perfect afternoon. At half-time the game was 1—0 in favour of the 14th. In the second half we equalized. After an extra ten minutes each way the 14th Sikhs won by 3—1, after a very exciting and clean game of hockey.

Teams and spectators returned to Beled on March 31st. Although the month seems to have been occupied in racing and hockey, training was not given up. An interesting feature of the month was the constant effort made to get Sikhs to wear the steel helmet. The efforts failed.

March 3rd. — Lieut. J. G. Kilpin, 25th Punjabis proceeded to join his own unit.

See Map No. 11 — On the 5th, Lieut.-Colonel D. A. D. McVean and Major B. W. Shuttleworth with a party of Officers from the Brigade went to Samarra to see the defences. They were expected back in a week.

On the 7th at 10.30 p.m., orders were received for the 52nd Infantry Brigade to march to Samarra at 10 a.m. on the 8th at war establishment. All ranks in excess were to remain at Beled as a reserve company.

Consequently the Brigade marched at 10 a.m. for Istabulat, 16 miles, with the 45th leading. Our strength was : B.O.'s, eight ; I.O.'s, 18 ; and 917 Other Ranks. It was a hot day, and marching in serge was trying. On arrival at Istabulat the units of the Brigade went into the various camps of the 51st Infantry Brigade. The 45th into the 14th late camp.

On the 9th, the Brigade marched to Samarra—eighteen miles—with the 45th again leading. The Brigade Commander complimented the Regiment on its march the previous day. Only one man had fallen out.

On arrival at Samarra, we went into camp on the Plateau, less than a mile from the 47th Sikhs. A great fraternization took place between the two Regiments. We played them at hockey on the 10th, but were beaten 5—1.

On the 11th, we took over stores, etc., from the unit of 9th Infantry Brigade at Alajik whom we were to relieve, and on the 12th took over a standing camp from the 1st/1st

Gurkha Rifles. The short march was carried out over roads waterlogged by rain.

At this time all fear of Von Falkenhayn's "Yilderim" Army recapturing Baghdad had vanished. The 3rd and 7th Indian Divisions were leaving for another theatre of war—Palestine—and all movements took place under cover of darkness.

The 17th and 18th Divisions were taking their places in the 1st Corps, of which the Commander and staff remained behind.

Whilst we were in Samarra we had one company on duty in our sector of the defensive position every night. The Turks were some 40 miles away at Tekrit.

On the 13th, the Reserve Company under Lieut. R. K. Henson, and the dump, arrived by train from Beled.

On the 16th, it poured with rain. Orders came for the 11th Rajputs attached to proceed to India when train accommodation became available. On the 17th, a special guard of sixty other ranks proceeded to 1st Corps Headquarters under Subadar Nidhan Singh.

On the 19th, torrents of rain fell, and on the 20th the 11th Rajputs attached marched for the railway station and India. Thus "D" Company were the first company to become all Sikh again.

This day we received orders that the Battalion would proceed to join the Moveable Column at Daur on the 21st, strength W.E.

The surplus were to stay at Alajik and take over all duties.

This move was almost immediately postponed to the 23rd. On the 21st, our look-outs blew up two mines on the Tigris. The Turks were continually sending mines down the river to try and blow up our bridge of boats. They never succeeded.

We also had a visit from two enemy planes flying very high; these flew southward right over our aerodrome.

On the 23rd, the 52nd Infantry Brigade (less 1/113th Infantry, already at Daur) marched at 9 a.m. for Daur, fifteen miles. It was a hot march and the men were still wearing serge. On arrival we at once went into bivouac. It became known that the 17th Division were going to carry out manœuvres.

On the 24th at 3 p.m., our Brigade took up the same defensive line taken up by the Turks the previous November.

The 34th and 51st Infantry Brigades made a night march from Samarra, and attacked us in the early hours of the 25th. We carried out a retirement for five miles, and the whole force bivouacked by the river.

After dark on the 26th, the entire Division assembled at a position of assembly three miles inland. This was marked by two most elaborate circles of light facing south. The three Infantry Brigades were in mass with the Field Artillery Brigades on the flanks, and Medium Artillery in the rear. Having assembled, the Division lay down and slept till 1 a.m. At 1.45 a.m., the advance began, and the objective was the old line of Turkish trenches at Tekrit, captured at considerable loss by the 1st Corps the previous November, some six miles distant.

After the attack we bivouacked by the river near Tekrit Town about noon.

On the 28th, the 34th Infantry Brigade carried out a reconnaissance northwards, the 51st returned to Daur to take up a defensive position, and we remained at rest.

On the 29th, the 34th and 52nd Infantry Brigades marched to Daur, and attacked the 51st Infantry Brigade in position, afterwards going into bivouac by the river.

On the 30th, the whole Division concentrated at Jubur, from which place they were to have attacked the Samarra defences on the 31st.

Heavy rain at night, however, and very threatening weather altered all plans, the attack was cancelled, and the 52nd Infantry Brigade marched independently straight into Samarra, the Regiment arrived in its old camp at Alajik at 1 p.m. in pouring rain. We had taken part in a strenuous week's "manœuvres" in the face of the Turk, whose planes were up daily, so he knew all our movements. A part of the Force therefore always kept a watchful eye on the north.

April.

The month opened with very wild weather. For about five days it rained continuously, and there was a gale of wind. Many tents were blown into shreds, and a good deal of damage was done to tentage generally.

On the 6th, "A" Company, Lieut. R. B. Ramsbotham,

relieved a company of another battalion at Hawaisilat. This was a small hill about five miles north of Alajik, which was held as an outpost.

After the recent heavy rains, the country was covered with high and luscious grass, and all our mules were sent out to " A " Company to graze. Gradually grazing camps for the animals of all units in the Division were established at various places, covered by the detachments at Daur and Hawaisilat.

On the 12th, a Turkish plane paid us one of his periodical visits. He was fired at by every anti-aircraft gun in the place, but proceeded south untouched. He dropped no bombs.

On the 16th and 17th, there was great activity in " Gas " training, and all ranks were put through a gas chamber.

Orders were received that the 52nd Infantry Brigade would move up to Telmuhaijir on the 19th, 20th and 21st instants to take up a line of outposts. The 45th (less " A " Company at Hawaisilat) marched at 9 a.m. on the 21st, and arrived at Telmuhaijir at 1.45 p.m. A Turkish plane passed over us on the march, but was pursued and brought down by one of our planes an hour later.

The Regiment stayed at Telmuhaijir until the end of the month, and worked on strong posts and trenches daily. On the 26th, owing to a sudden rise of the River Tigris, our camp was flooded out, and we had to move it.

On the 27th, at 7.45 p.m., a report was received that " six Kelleks (rafts) with 150 Turks on each and six guns had arrived just north of Tekrit." Precautionary measures were taken, but this and other rumours of attack did not materialize.

On the 28th, we sent two men and a Lewis gun in a Ford car as escort to a political officer to reconnoitre north of Tekrit. They were fired on by Turkish picquets, and the cars hit several times.

The last two days of the month were spent in hay making ; the work went on all day in reliefs of fifty men.

During the month, Major R. H. Anderson, Lieut. R. K. Henson, Subadar Wattan Singh and forty Other Ranks proceeded to India on one month's leave.

Owing to the heavy and frequent rain, the weather remained very cool all the month.

104 HISTORY OF THE 45TH RATTRAY'S SIKHS

May.

The Regiment commenced the month with a strength of Indian ranks : Sikhs, 883 ; Rajputs (attached), 185.

On the 3rd, "A" Company, Lieut. R. B. Ramsbotham, rejoined the Regiment from Hawaisilat. All work on defences and hay making, was suspended, which indicated another move. This came sure enough on the 4th, when orders were received for the following force to march to Tekrit on the 5th :—

1 Squadron 32nd Lancers
1 Section No. 258 M.G. Company
45th Sikhs
} Under Command of Lieut.-Col. D. A. D. McVean, D.S.O.

On May 5th, this column marched at 4 a.m., camping one mile north of Tekrit by 10.30 a.m. An advanced aerodrome was established in our camp, and a similar force from the 18th Division was in position on the left bank.

The following were the orders for the guidance of the Column Commander, Lieut.-Col. D. A. D. McVean, D.S.O. "The troops at Tekrit are for the purpose of protecting new aerodrome under construction, and R.A.F. dump.

"In case of attack, force at Tekrit will not fall back, but will be reinforced by remainder of Brigade."

This forward move by the 1st Corps up the Tigris was made to divert the attention of the enemy from offensive operations being carried out at this time by the 3rd Corps in the Kirkuk direction. From now onwards Tekrit was held, and work on the extension of the railway from Samarra was shortly commenced by the troops of the 17th Division, and completed by the end of September.

On the 6th, our morning patrols brought in two Turkish deserters and six Armenians.

On the 7th, there was heavy rain again. On the 8th, the whole 52nd Infantry Brigade arrived at Tekrit. The Regiment moved camp one-and-a-half miles to the west, from which they took up an outpost line covering the Brigade, and suffered a good deal from lack of water in being so far away from the river.

On this day also two platoons " B " Company, under Lieut. R. V. Fox, accompanied by a squadron of the 32nd Lancers, marched to Aburajash, fifteen miles, to make the road fit for armoured cars.

On the completion of the work, the two platoons retired seven miles and bivouacked for the night, returning to Tekrit the next day, whilst the Squadron proceeded straight into Tekrit. No enemy were met with.

May 12th was an eventful day for the Battalion. At 7 p.m., orders came in that the Commanding Officer was to choose a whole company (less any Rajputs) for despatch to India the next day to join the newly raised 151st Sikh Infantry in India. The company was to leave at full war establishment strength, plus fifteen per cent. This was a great bombshell, and a difficult matter. " C " Company were chosen under Lieut. K. H. Preston with 2/Lieut. C. Eastmead, and certain adjustments in Indian Officers were made to suit prevailing conditions.

On the 13th, eleven hours later, "C" Company : strength, two British Officers, four Indian Officers, 228 Other Ranks and ten followers, marched for Telmuhaijir, and the Base, at 6 a.m. They were a very fine Company indeed, and the blow was as sudden to them as it was to the Battalion.

A new " C " Company had to be formed a day or two later by transfers from other companies, and later reinforced by recruits from the Depot. But it took years to get the Company an all-Malwa Company again.

On May 15th, all work was stopped, indicating an early move, which came on the 16th, when the 52nd Infantry Brigade marched to Telmuhaijir at 4.30 a.m., arriving there at 8.15 p.m. They halted from 12 noon to 4 p.m., the hottest part of the day, and it was now very hot. Shortly after the Brigade left Tekrit, enemy planes dropped bombs on our old camp without effect.

The 45th remained at Telmuhaijir for one day, and on the 18th, marched to Alajik, and went into the old camp. The remainder of the Brigade remained at Telmuhaijir.

The next day the second leave party left for a month's leave in India. Strength : Lieut. G. L. Watson, two Indian Officers and thirty-nine Other Ranks.

On the 21st, the Regiment marched at 6 a.m. and took over the 31st Punjabis camp on the Plateau near the 17th Divisional Headquarters. It was a good camp, but four miles from the river. Although a pipe line was laid to it, the pumping engine frequently went out of gear, with the result that the four months we were in this camp, the hottest months of the year, we were often troubled with a shortage of water. On the other hand we were little troubled by sandflies, which were rather a scourge to troops quartered near the river. Duties were always extremely heavy whilst we were in this camp.

On the 16th, Captain R. B. Ramsbotham and sixteen Other Ranks proceeded on a month's leave to India, and Major B. W. Shuttleworth proceeded to Tekrit to run the 17th Division School for Platoon Commanders.

On the 29th, a hostile aeroplane came over and dropped several bombs round Alajik, but caused no damage.

June.

On the 2nd, we received a draft of twenty-eight Other Ranks from the Depot, which brought us up to 729 Sikhs, present and on leave in India.

On the 4th we had to provide working parties of 150 men daily for an eight-hour task on the extension of the railway just being commenced by the 17th Division, from Samarra to Tekrit.

Our task lay on the embankment between Samarra station and Alajik; we, as was usual, finished our thirty-two hour task on the 11th in eighteen hours' work.

On the 9th, Subadar Nidhan Singh proceeded to India to become Subadar Major of some new unit. This fortunately never materialized, and we got him back in 1920. Also a further eighteen Other Ranks proceeded on a month's leave to India.

On the 14th the 2nd Rajputs attached marched out of camp to rejoin their own unit, and so only about 90 odd Rajputs remained. These were all put into the new "C" Company as No. 12 platoon.

On the 16th one more party of fifteen Other Ranks proceeded to India on one month's leave.

On the 22nd, Captain R. K. Henson rejoined from a month's leave in India. A day later, Major B. W. Shuttleworth returned from duty with the Platoon Commanders' School, and assumed command of the Battalion, vice Lieut.-Col. D. A. D. McVean, D.S.O., who proceeded on a month's leave to India.

On the 24th, the following Officers joined the Regiment for duty :—
Captain A. L. Butcher, 2/35th Sikhs ; Lieut. G. W. Benton, I.A.R.O., 45th Sikhs ; and Lieut. Kelly, 2/35th Sikhs.

Owing to the very heavy duties and working parties we were only able to carry out specialist training during the month.

On the 1st, Major R. H. Anderson rejoined from short leave *July.* in India, and brought with him, picked up at Baghdad, a very welcome draft of 134 Other Ranks from the Depot. They were mostly young recruits, but were a good lot, and as the majority belonged to " C " Company, they went to swell the numbers of that company.

Our strength this day went up to 892 Sikhs, present and on leave, plus ninety-five Rajputs attached.

On the 5th, Major B. W. Shuttleworth, proceeded on short leave to India, the command devolving on Major R. H. Anderson.

The new draft were struck off all duties, and commenced an intensive course of training, including a short course of musketry and bombing. The heat was severe, but all ranks remained very healthy.

On the 18th we sent two platoons for duty at Samarra Camp, and the duties increased until one night in bed was the rule. On the 23rd, a further duty was allotted us, and four Lewis gun sections from "A" Company proceeded to Samarra Station for escort duty on trains running on the new line towards Tekrit.

On July 27th, Arrah Day, a service was held in the Gurdwara in the morning, but sports could not be held owing to the severe duties, and they were postponed till a quieter time.

On this day Lieut.-Col. F. S. Keen, D.S.O., was appointed G.S.O.I. of the 17th Division.

The only training carried on during the month was that of the new draft, and they were coming on very rapidly, as they were struck off all duties.

On the 28th, Captain R. B. Ramsbotham and twenty-seven Other Ranks rejoined the Regiment from short leave in India.

The first part of August was very hot, but we got in some *August.* of our detachments, and our duties were reduced. So on

108 HISTORY OF THE 45TH RATTRAY'S SIKHS

August 17th, the postponed Arrah Day sports were held, and were a great success. They were attended by the Divisional Commander and Lieut.-Col. F. S. Keen, D.S.O., G.S.O.I.

On the 19th a severe form of fever broke out, but the men stuck it well, and very few were evacuated. This turned out to be influenza, and it was very prevalent in the Division. Our isolated camp undoubtedly helped to keep the epidemic within bounds.

On the 25th, the second leave party, one Indian Officer and twenty-one Other Ranks, rejoined from short leave in India, and one platoon "B" Company, under Subadar Bishan Singh, proceeded to the Platoon School at Tekrit as a Demonstration Platoon.

During the month the Regiment carried out some Contact Patrol schemes with the R.A.F., whose aerodrome was only 1,000 yards from our camp.

The R.A.F. were much impressed with our signallers, who worked the Popham Panel admirably. The Regiment was informed by the R.A.F. that they had reported on our signallers as the best in the Corps!

September.

On the 1st, Lieut.-Col. D. A. D. McVean, D.S.O., and Major B. W. Shuttleworth, rejoined from a month's leave in India.

Also a small draft of fifteen Other Ranks under Subadar Narain Singh joined from the Depot. Our strength in Sikhs had now risen to 912, and we still had ninety-six Rajputs.

On the 2nd, the 52nd Infantry Brigade (less the Regiment) marched from Alajik to Jibin Wadi (two miles south of Tekrit). So we were now the only Battalion of the Brigade in the Samarra area, and came directly under the Division.

Major B. W. Shuttleworth left us to reopen the Platoon School at Tekrit on the 6th.

On the 10th, No. 1367 Sepoy Mela Singh, "A" Company, died in the Regimental Aid Post from burns received the night before.

At 8 p.m., on the 9th, this Sepoy went to the oil trench outside the Quartermaster's Store tent, and was in the act of filling a hurricane lantern, whilst it was still alight. The lamp exploded, setting fire to all the oil with a loud explosion and to the unfortunate man himself. Maddened by pain he ran round the camp enveloped in flames, and finally made for two isolated transport tents. No. 1084 Sepoy Bhan Singh seized him and put out the flames before he could enter the tents, but he died before dawn. Sepoy Bhan Singh received, shortly afterwards, the Meritorious Service Medal for his prompt and plucky action.

On this day we received with great regret the official news that that fine and gallant Indian Officer, Subadar Thaman Singh, had died as a prisoner-of-war in Turkish hands.

On September 28th, Lieut.-Col. D. A. D. McVean, D.S.O., proceeded to Kut-el-Amara on special duty.

During the month one battalion from each Brigade of the 17th and 18th Divisions was taken away and sent away to an unknown destination, which afterwards turned out to be the Black Sea. All the Brigades, therefore, only contained three battalions. The 52nd Infantry Brigade lost the 84th Punjabis.

The composition of the other two in the 17th Division were :

34th Infantry Brigade.—1st Battalion Royal West Kent Regiment, 112th Infantry, 114th Mahrattas.

51st Infantry Brigade.—1st Battalion Highland Light Infantry, 14th K.G.O. Sikhs, 1/10th Gurkha Rifles.

CHAPTER V

OCTOBER 1ST TO DECEMBER 31ST, 1918.

(Including the operations on the River Tigris, the action of Fat-Hah and the Battle of Sherqat.)

October. STRENGTH at the beginning of the month : 917 Sikhs and ninety-five Rajputs.

On the 2nd, Captain A. C. Curtis rejoined the Regiment from duty with the Nabha I.S. Infantry, having been replaced there by Captain J. A. Finlay. He took over the duties of Adjutant, vice Captain B. W. Key, who assumed the Command of " B " Company.

An inter-Platoon football tournament was commenced, for which much practice had taken place, and very keen play was anticipated.

On the 3rd, Lieut. G. W. Benton proceeded to take over the duties of temporary Orderly Officer to Major-General G. A. J. Leslie, C.B., C.M.G., Commanding the 17th Division.

On the 4th, we received very sudden orders that the Regiment would move up to Tekrit by rail on the 6th, and be replaced by a battalion from the 18th Division.

On the 5th, we were busy moving kit all day to Samarra railway station, and formed a dump there. We were relieved by the 116th Mahrattas during the afternoon, and marched down to the station and bivouacked there for the night.

On the 6th, we entrained, with twenty pound kits, left Samarra at 10 a.m., and arrived at Tekrit at 2 p.m. Our horses and first line transport marched up under Lieut. G. D. Pybus and arrived on the 7th.

On arrival at Tekrit, we were informed that we should move on at operation scale of kits (10 lbs.) and at once set about forming another dump at Tekrit station. It now began to dawn on us that active operations were about to commence, but nothing definite was given out to units.

On the 7th, the Regiment was very busy on fatigues, dumping tents and other odd jobs in the Brigade area. In the afternoon, Major B. W. Shuttleworth and the two platoons of the Regiment from the Platoon School, rejoined.

In the evening we received Brigade orders for the march to Abu Rajash the next day.

The general situation at this time was that the Turks who had been completely overwhelmed by General Allenby's Force in Palestine and Syria, were on the verge of giving in. It was considered imperative to strike a decisive blow against their last remaining Army in the field, viz. the VIth Army in the Tigris. These operations were now about to commence.

October 8th. As rear Battalion in the Brigade (strength British Officers ten, Indian Officers fourteen, and Other Ranks 776) the Regiment passed the starting point at 05.45 hours, leaving one platoon as rear guard. We received seven carts short of our allotment, which caused confusion, and some of "A" Company's kits had to be left behind. The regiment arrived at 13.00 hours, and bivouacked under the cliffs on the lower Tekrit–Mosul road. Half-way the Jebel Hamrin Range became visible. The march was sixteen miles, the day hot and airless, so the march was a trying one. Our men as usual stood it well without any fall outs. The rear guard did not arrive in until 17.00 hours.

After dark, a Brigade Order was received for the following force to proceed next day to Jift, under the command of Major B. W. Shuttleworth, to take up a position to cover the formation of a forward supply and ordnance dump :—

    1 Squadron 32nd Lancers.
    45th Sikhs.
    1 Section No. 258 M.G. Company.
    1 Section C.F. Ambulance.

The squadron were already out with a company of the 114th Mahrattas, as escort to a Survey Party, and were to join on the road, the Mahrattas returning to join their unit in Tekrit.

October 9th. In accordance with orders the 45th moved out with the sections M.G.C. and C.F.A. at 06.45 hours, "D" Company—Major R. H. Anderson—forming the advanced guard. As the

112 HISTORY OF THE 45TH RATTRAY'S SIKHS

road ran along the low ground by the river, and was commanded by a plateau to the west, picquets were put out as in mountain warfare to protect the left flank. An hour after marching an enemy plane hovered over us for some time, but did not molest us. Half-way we received news that the enemy were occupying Jift Hill, but the squadron was able to turn them out unaided, and we entered Jift (ten miles) at 10.00 hours without opposition, though some firing was going on in front.

"A" and "B" Companies at once went out to take up an outpost line to cover the dump. This was difficult owing to the thick scrub in the river area ("A" Company). This Company was engaged for some hours in the scrub with small parties of enemy cavalry, without casualties. The line was made good by dark, and "C" and "D" Companies and the rest of the Column remained in reserve south of Jift Hill, which was a very full Arab cemetery. Lieut.-Col. D. A. D. McVean, D.S.O., arrived in the evening from Kut-el-Amara, and assumed Command.

At this period the following Officers were serving with the Regiment:—

      Lieut.-Col. D. A. D. McVean, D.S.O.
      Major B. W. Shuttleworth, 2nd-in-Command.
      Major R. H. Anderson, "D" Company.
      Captain A. C. Curtis, M.C., Adjutant.
      Captain B. W. Key, "B" Company.
      Captain R. B. Ramsbotham, "A" Company.
      Captain A. L. Butcher, "C" Company.
      Lieut. G. D. Pybus.
      Lieut. R. V. Fox.
      Lieut. B. W. Kelly, Quartermaster.
      T/Captain Santokh Singh, I.M.S., Medical Officer.

October 10th.
See Sketch of Jift Post, Map No. 6.

The 52nd Infantry Brigade Commander came over to see our dispositions, and it was decided that the line taken up on the previous day was too extended and too far out. A new line was selected nearer Jift Hill, and also an inner defensive line round Jift Hill itself. The outer line consisted of a series of strong posts giving all round fire, and the inner line of short lengths of trenches. The day was spent in digging

JIFT POST

the above. M.T. convoys commenced to arrive, and the reserve companies unloaded sixty-one tons of supplies.

The scrub on Laq-Laq Island was also fired to give a clearer field of view. Dense clouds of smoke resulted, which lasted for twenty-four hours, and the fire dislodged large numbers of pig, partridges and other game.

A similar Column to ours from the 18th Division took up a position opposite to us on the left bank, and we got into visual communication with them.

The day was spent in improving our defences and com- *October 11th.* munications, the Squadron acting as a screen. The usual fatigues for the supply dump shifted tons of supplies, and this continued daily for the companies in reserve.

The Battalion Scouts of the 1/6th Hants, and 113th Infantry came out and joined Jift Force, the name we were now known by.

Instructions for Jift Force received this day were :—

(1) In the event of attack to maintain its position until reinforced (from Abu Rajash).

(2) To endeavour by means of scouts and patrols to obtain all possible information regarding the country, roads and watering facilities north, west and north-east of Jift.

(3) To prevent the enemy from maintaining close observation of our camps and dumps at Jift.

A reconnaissance under Major B. W. Shuttleworth con- *October 12th.* sisting of one squadron 32nd Lancers, one section No. 258 M.G. Company, " C " Company, 45th Sikhs—Captain A. L. Butcher—and two armoured cars moved out at 07.00 hours to reconnoitre the ground N.W. of Jift Post. A party of enemy *See Map* cavalry were found in position on Pimple Hill (Map 8 *No. 8.* AM.85.A).

These Turks remained in position until the infantry got within 250 yards. When they retired the machine guns got into them from the right flank. The force followed them up for four miles, and reached camp at 15.00 hours. Our retirement was not followed up, and the Regiment had no casualties though some horses were hit in the squadron.

A survey party accompanied this reconnaissance, and with all reconnaissances that went out afterwards.

114 HISTORY OF THE 45TH RATTRAY'S SIKHS

October 13th. "C" Company, Captain A. L. Butcher, moved out of camp at 07.00 hours and relieved "A" Company in the right sector of the outpost line.

The Divisional Commander visited Jift.

October 14th. A reconnaissance under Major B. W. Shuttleworth (strength as on the 12th, but with "A" Company and without the armoured cars) moved out about five miles N.W. of Jift. The armoured cars had found the ground unsuitable on the 12th. A few mounted Turks opened ·fire from Pimple Hill and bolted when the infantry were 1,000 yards away. They subsequently fired at the Squadron on the left flank and hit some horses.

The little force reached camp about 15.00 hours, leaving Captain R. K. Henson and the Battalion scouts on Pimple Hill.

The enemy did not follow up, and the scouts returned to camp at dusk.

The Army Commander, Lieut.-General Sir W. R. Marshall, K.C.M.G., paid Jift a visit.

Jift Force was reinforced by one section R.F.A. (eighteen pounders) and two anti-aircraft guns, as the enemy planes were very active and interested in the formation of the dump.

October 15th. "D" Company—Major R. H. Anderson—relieved "B" Company in the left sector of the outpost line.

Lieut. R. K. Henson, with our own scouts, reinforced by those of the 1/113th Infantry, made a night reconnaissance of the Wadi Shuramiyah in the vicinity of the Khan or Post, leaving Jift at 21.00 hours. They completed their work, and retired on to Pimple Hill by dawn, having met with no parties of the enemy during the night.

October 16th. At 06.30 hours, a reconnaissance under Major R. H. Anderson, consisting of :—

    1 Squadron 32nd Lancers,
    1 Section 258 M.G. Company,
    "B" Company 45th Sikhs (Captain B. W. Key),

moved out of Jift to examine the approaches of the Khan Shuramiyah a mile west of the Turkish Post. Pimple Hill was occupied by the 45th scouts at dawn and held until the return of the reconnaissance.

The Force pushed on up to the Wadi, brushing aside some small opposition. Whilst the approaches were being examined the squadron formed a screen to the front and right flank. They were shelled from the lower slopes of the Jebel Makhul. At 11.30 hours, the withdrawal commenced, and was very half-heartedly followed up for a short distance. The Force reached camp at 15.30 hours without any casualties, having accomplished all they set out to do.

At 22.10 hours, a warning message was received from the Brigade for one squadron 32nd Lancers, section 258 M.G.C. and one company 45th Sikhs to be ready to move without tents on the morrow.

At 23.00 hours, the following Brigade Order was received by the Officer Commanding Jift Force—" You will establish to-morrow an outpost of one Company 45th Sikhs, one Squadron 32nd Lancers and Section 258 M.G.C. at Khan Shuramiyah—you may use any troops under your command including section 1068 Battery to assist in establishing this outpost. One Company 1/113th Infantry and Headquarters and one Section M.G. Company leave here to-morrow at 08.00 hours and will come under your orders. Report name of officer who will command. You will arrange visual communication between Jift and Shuramiyah."

" B " Company—Captain B. W. Key—was detailed as our company to hold Shuramiyah.

To carry out the foregoing order the following force moved *October 17th.* out of camp at 08.30 hours under the command of Lieut.-Colonel D. A. D. McVean, D.S.O.:—

1 Squadron 32nd Lancers.
1 Section 1068 Battery R.F.A.
1 Section 258 M.G. Company.
45th Sikhs (less " D " Company and two platoons " C " Company) under Major R. H. Anderson.
45th Sikhs Scouts.

Shuramiyah was some seven miles distant. The force first moved to Pimple Hill, near which the section of guns took up a position to cover the attack. Our two-and-a-half companies advanced straight on the objective in two lines with the Squadron out on the right flank. Owing to the number of observation ladders behind the Khan it was first thought

116 HISTORY OF THE 45TH RATTRAY'S SIKHS

to be strongly held. But to the surprise of all, we entered the place at 11.00 hours without a shot being fired. The cavalry put out a screen, and we all dug " B " Company securely in. The remainder of the 45th marched back to Jift at 18.30 hours, arriving after dark. In the afternoon we could plainly observe great movement of enemy troops in the Jebel Hamrin on the left bank, which was duly reported. The O.C. of the garrison this night was the O.C. Squadron, but Major B. W. Shuttleworth relieved him on the 18th. At 18.00 hours No. 2110 Sepoy Santa Singh, " B " Company, was severely wounded by a sniper whilst on escort duty with the animals watering.

Brigade orders directed that in case of attack, the Shuramiyah force would maintain its position, and be reinforced from Jift, and also that this detachment would be under the direct orders of Jift force. (Lieut.-Colonel D. A. D. McVean, D.S.O.)

The 18th Division also sent forward a detachment level with Shuramiyah on the left bank.

In the evening the Brigade required the following information through our scouts :—

(1) Position of enemy advanced trenches on south slopes of Jebel Makhul.

(2) Whether any barbed wire or other obstacles existed.

(3) Location of enemy's right (western flank).

(4) Nature of country in front. Cover, routes for night advance, recognizable land marks, nature of surface.

(5) Watering facilities for men and animals upstream of the Wadi Shuramiyah.

From Shuramiyah a most wonderful view of the hills in front about six to seven miles away presented itself, and also of the Fat-Hah Gorge. On the right bank the range runs N.W. from the river and is known as the Jebel Makhul. Whilst on the left bank its direction is slightly south of east, is known as the Jebel Hamrin and stretches as far as the Persian frontier. These ranges run up to 1,200–1,400 feet in height, are very steep and a formidable obstacle to operations.

October 18th. The day was quiet in our area. During the night of the

18th/19th Lieut. R. K. Henson was out with our scouts all night. He located the extreme right of the enemy's position and brought in a lot of other valuable information.

On this night also, an infantry column of the 18th Division by a night march seized the Darb-el-Khail and Ain Nakhaila Passes. The sappers improved the water supply, and a supply depot was formed at Ain Nakhaila for the use of the cavalry.

From previous reconnaissances, our left flank was found to be impossible for a turning movement on account of lack of water, so our right flank was selected for this purpose by the Higher Command. They were up against a very strong natural position, which the Turks had had ten months to make the most of. It is obvious, therefore, that a turning movement on one or both flanks was necessary.

At 15.55 hours the Officer Commanding Shuramiyah was warned that an artillery reconnaissance would take place on the line A.M.69.B.5/5 to A.M.70.A.3/1, and was ordered to cover the reconnaissance from 08.00 hours until its conclusion. *October 19th. Maps No. 7 and 8.*

During the afternoon patrols were sent out and the propsoed scene of the reconnaissance was found to be occupied by the enemy. This information was reported to the Brigade, and at 20.45 hours the Officer Commanding Shuramiyah received the following message from the 52nd Infantry Brigade : "Do not become seriously engaged in endeavour to expel enemy from forward line. If possible threaten his right flank with your cavalry and scouts. Policy is not to provoke serious engagement."

This was followed by the receipt at 23.00 hours of the following message from the 17th Division :—" Enemy cavalry are reported to be holding the line A.M.69.D.9/8 to A.M.68.B.3/5. In order to cover the reconnaissance Shuramiyah detachment will send forward patrols to this line at 07.00 hours 20th and squadron cavalry will move round enemy right flank. By arrangement with 18th Division, one battery eighteen pounders will be in position about Umm-Al-Laqlaq at 08.00 hours and will co-operate by shelling enemy's cavalry. Establish visual communication. Ground gained will not be held."

During their stay at Jift, the Regiment in addition to defence and reconnaissance duties shifted 1,365 tons of supplies into the dump, and also enormous quantities of gun and S.A. Ammunition.

October 20th. In accordance with the above instructions Major B. W. Shuttleworth moved out at 07.00 hours with the following force :—

1 Squadron 32nd Lancers.
" B ". Company 45th Sikhs (less 1 platoon)—Captain B. W. Key.
1 Section No. 258 M.G. Company.

Maps No. 7 and 8. to the line A.M.79.A.9/4 to A.M.79.A.3/8, and found enemy in position on line A.M.79.A.9/7—A.M.70.C.2/4, with infantry in trenches about A.M.70.A.3/2.

The force moved out with two platoons " B " Company in two waves, followed by the section M.G.C., with one platoon echeloned to the left flank on rising ground. The Cavalry were on the plateau to the left flank, but were soon forced to retire by the enemy gun fire.

At 11.00 hours the reconnaissance, composed of a large number of Gunner and Staff Officers, started. As the Senior Officer wished to go forward, " B " Company was ordered to advance to the line A.M.79.A.9/7—A.M.70.C.2/4, and the battery of the 18th Division on the left bank was asked to assist.

The advance commenced at 11.45 hours, when " B " Company at once came under shell fire, but reached their objective without casualties, the 18th Division battery assisting.

After reaching the objective, the Senior Artillery Officer gave permission to retire. The retirement had no sooner begun, when " B " Company were subjected to a heavy and continuous fire from the enemy guns, which continued until they were within 1,000 yards of Shuramiyah Khan, and out of range.

" B " Company's retirement under these sudden and trying conditions was carried out with the utmost steadiness, and evoked praise from all who witnessed it.

We suffered the following casualties. *Killed*, One Sepoy ; *Wounded*, Captain B. W. Key (who afterwards received the M.C. for his gallantry) and eight Sepoys out of a strength of

FAT-HAH POSITION.

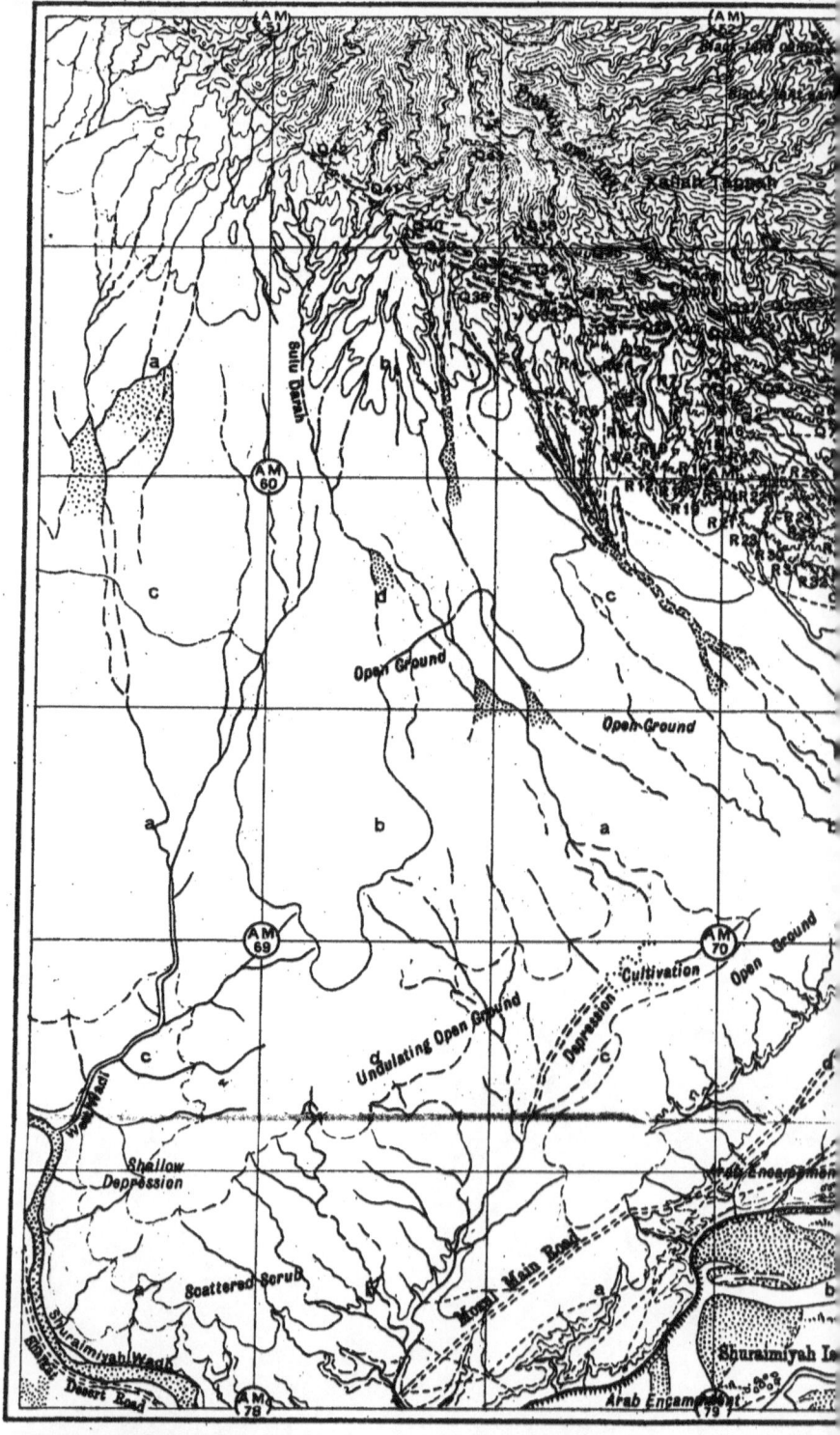

Form lines at roughly 50 feet intervals.
Intermediate lines broken.

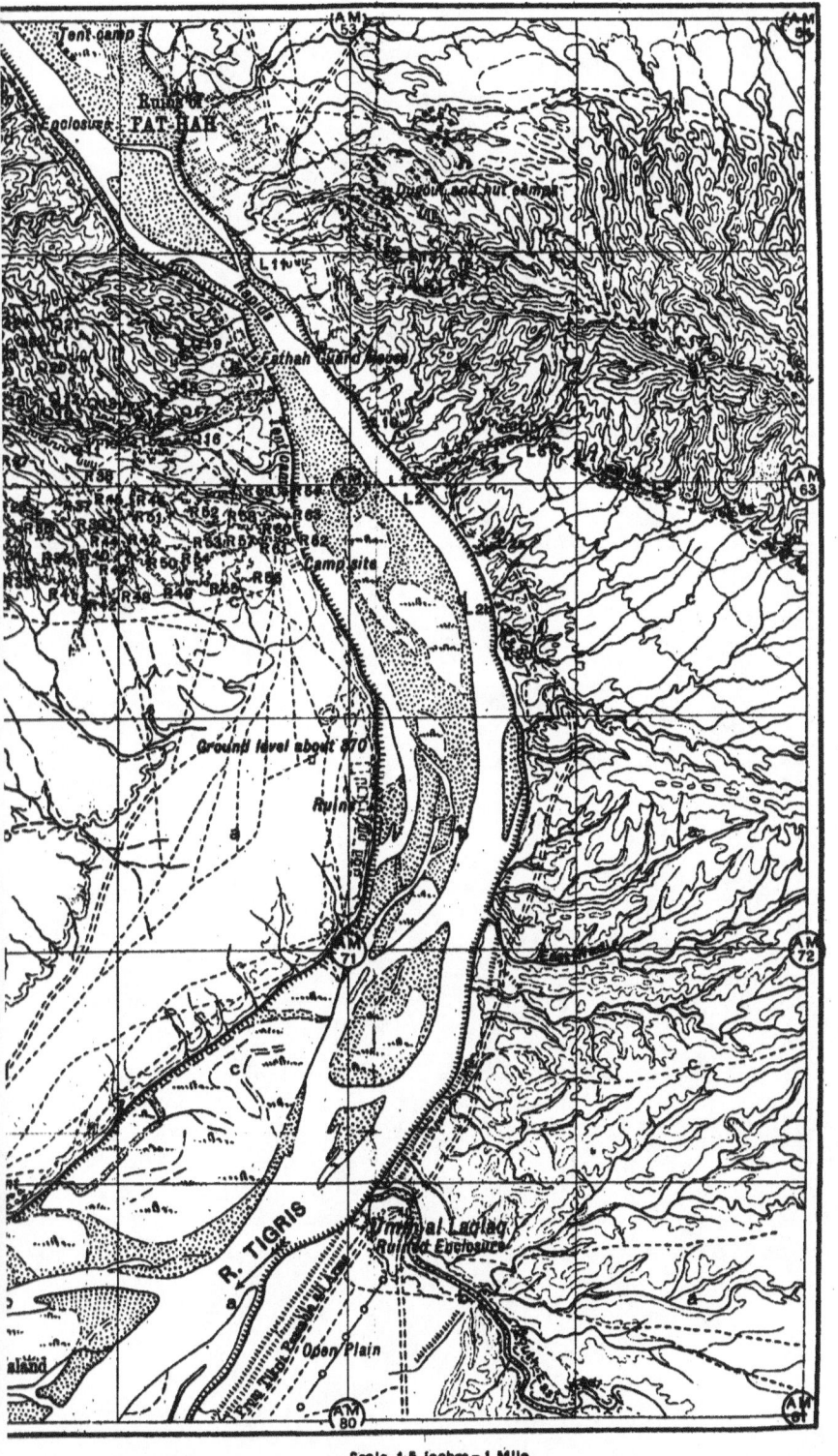

MAP 7.

92. One Lewis gun mule was killed and two wounded. Our leading line reported fifteen Turks hit at our furthest objective. On the whole we were lucky to get off as lightly.

The number of guns from the reconnaissance point of view was never disclosed to us, but Major Shuttleworth in his report on the action put them as "at least four heavy and one light gun."

At 14.30 hours a Brigade order was received ordering the Jift detachment to march for Shuramiyah at 18.30 hours without tentage.

Accordingly at that hour the 45th (Headquarters, "A," "C," and "D" Companies) marched and joined "B" Company in Shuramiyah Khan and the same night the 52nd Brigade and attached troops marched from Abu Rajash and bivouacked at A.M.78.C.7/3, *i.e.*, one-and-a-half miles south of us on the river bank.

The following message regarding the action of "B" Company was received from the 17th Division through Brigade :—

"Corps Commander wire G.246 begins. Please tell 45th Sikhs that I am very pleased at the way their company attained their objective this morning in the face of heavy shelling from enemy guns. The skill of their dispositions is shewn by their comparatively light casualties. They can be assured that on the next occasion the enemy guns will not be able to fire with impunity—ends."

In the M.E.F. the practice prevailed of a detached force *October 21st.* being called by the name of its commander, thus for the 21st and 22nd instants the 52nd Infantry Brigade and attached troops became Andrew's Column.

By Andrew's Column order No. 1 issued at 16.00 hours, the following moves took place this night to the north bank of the Wadi Shuramiyah. This had to be left clear by 23.00 hours, for by this hour the 51st Infantry Brigade was to arrive at Khan Shuramiyah from Abu Rajash.

(1) Andrew's Column (strength as below) moved from bivouac at A.M.78.C.7/3, for Khan Shuramiyah, the head of the main body passing the starting point at 19.00 hours.

    52nd Infantry Brigade.
    32nd Lancers (less two squadrons).

221st Brigade R.F.A. (less one battery).
34th M.B.R.G.A. (less one section).
35th C.F. Ambulance.

(2) On arrival at Khan Shuramiyah a line of outposts was taken up as follows on the line A.M.69.D.40/60, to A.M.68.D.40/50, both inclusive.

No. 1 Section (Right).
1/6th Hants and 1 Section No. 258 M.G. Company.

No. 2 Section (Left).
1/113th Infantry and 1 Section No. 258 M.G. Company.

(3) The 45th Sikhs and two sections M.G. Company maintained their position covering the Khan until the outposts were in position, and then moved to bivouac in vicinity of AM.68.D.7.1. Except for "D" Company—Major R. H. Anderson—and battalion transport and baggage which moved at dusk to this bivouac and put out a line of outposts facing west, linking up with the left of the 1/113th Infantry outpost line.

(4) The squadron bivouacked in square 78.C. a mile south of Khan.

On this date the 7th Cavalry Brigade marched from Tekrit to Ain Nakhaila, arriving there at 21.00 hours.

The advanced troops of the 18th Division on the left bank were in the vicinity of Umm-Al-Laqlaq.

Andrew's Column, Order No. 2. Andrew's Column order No. 2 was received by the 45th about 19.00 hours. Extracts are as follows:—

* * * * * *

(2) On the 22nd and 23rd Andrew's Column will drive in the enemy's advanced troops and establish outposts to cover artillery reconnaissance and move of artillery to selected positions. Objective the general line AM.61.D.2/6 to AM.60.B. 2/6. The line AM.60.A.2/3 to AM.69.A.46/99 must be secured before 17.00 hours on 22nd.

Map No. 7.

Distribution. (3) *Cavalry.* 32nd Lancers (less two squadrons) and No. 34 I.M.B. will protect the left flank moving from bivouac at 05.30 hours (22nd) and operate on the general line AM.68 Central to AM.59 Central.

(4) *Artillery.* 221st Brigade R.F.A. (less one battery) will support the attack from positions in AM.69.C.

HISTORY OF THE 45TH RATTRAY'S SIKHS 121

101st Brigade R.G.A. will be prepared to support the attack from positions in vicinity of AM.69.C.9/1.

18th Divisional artillery on left bank will co-operate by shelling enemy's advanced troops from 07.00 hours (22nd).

(5) On 22nd, advance will be carried out as follows :—

1/6th Hants on right, frontage 1,800 yards.

1/113th Infantry on left, frontage 1,800 yards.

The right of the 1/6th Hants will direct, moving on AM.61.D.2/6.

The frontage of the final objective is allotted as under :—

1/6th Hants, AM.61.D.2/6 to AM.61.A.2/1, both inclusive.

1/113th Infantry AM.61.A.2/1 exclusive to AM.60.B.2/6 inclusive.

In addition the 1/6th Hants will establish a strong post at AM.62.C.1/3. Strength at least one platoon.

The advance from the line occupied on night 21st/22nd will commence at 07.00 hours.

* * * * * *

(7) 45th Sikhs (and No. 258 M.G.C. less two sections) will be in Column Reserve, and will move from present bivouac at AM.78.D.7/1 to north bank of Wadi Shuramiyah at 07.00 hours 22nd instant.

(8) Officer Commanding No. 258 M.G.C. will place one section under each command of 1/6th Hants and 1/113th Infantry.

(9) 8th L.A.M.B. (less two sections) is to start at 06.00 hours on 22nd instant and patrol to AM.1.D on Shergat Desert Road.

* * * * * *

In accordance with the above order the Regiment moved up to the north bank of the Wadi by 07.00 hours in reserve. *October 22nd.*

The 1/6th Hants and 1/113th Infantry began their advance at 07.00 hours. Those who had seen the artillery reconnaissance on the 20th felt certain that these two battalions would suffer very heavily, as the Turks had range marks dotted about the plain. But they advanced to almost their objective before the enemy opened fire, and from 10.00 hours to dusk these two battalions were enveloped in smoke. The Hants managed to dig in, but the 113th, owing to more open ground could not. They both maintained their position till dusk, when two companies of the 32nd Pioneers went to assist them to dig in.

Their casualties were light. Hants 4, 1/113th Infantry 40.

At 06.00 hours in accordance with Andrew's Column Order No. 3, the 45th moved up in support, and dug in in two lines at AM.69.B.8/2. "C" Company and "D" Company (less two platoons) under Major R. H. Anderson, put out a line of outposts facing west from AM.69.B.5/5 to AM.78 Central. As this outpost line had to withdraw by dawn, the remaining two-and-a-half companies had to dig trenches for four, but they were ready and excellently dug down by dawn.

The 51st Infantry Brigade sent a strong Officer's patrol (1/10th Gurkha Rifles) this night to reconnoitre the crest of the Jebel. It was found to be quite impracticable for infantry.

The 34th Infantry Brigade concentrated at Khan Shuramiyah after dark. Thus the whole 17th Division was now complete in front of the right bank, Fat-Hah position. The fighting strength of the 45th this day was B.O.'s, 10 ; I.O.'s, 15 ; I.O.R.'s, 747.

October 23rd. Maps No. 7 and 8.
Our outpost line withdrew before break of day and the 45th remained all day in support, in their well-dug trenches at AM.69.B.8/2.

The enemy shell fire was much less violent, and our trenches were not shelled at all. Our sixty-pounders did a good deal of shooting.

A 52nd Infantry Brigade operation order giving the following information regarding the enemy and our own forces was issued at 18.00 hours.

Regarding 18th Division.
1. (*a*) The 18th Division is to attack the enemy position at Fat-Hah, left bank, at dawn on the 24th.

The 7th Cavalry Brigade at dawn on the 24th is to be at AM.85 Central.

[NOTE.—They seized Tarfawi to-day, and the 11th Cavalry Brigade marched from Tekrit to Ain Nakhaila arriving about midnight.]

Regarding 17th Division.
(*b*) The 17th Division is to be prepared to assault the right bank position on the 25th, and is to be prepared to advance at any time as the attack of the 18th Division progresses.

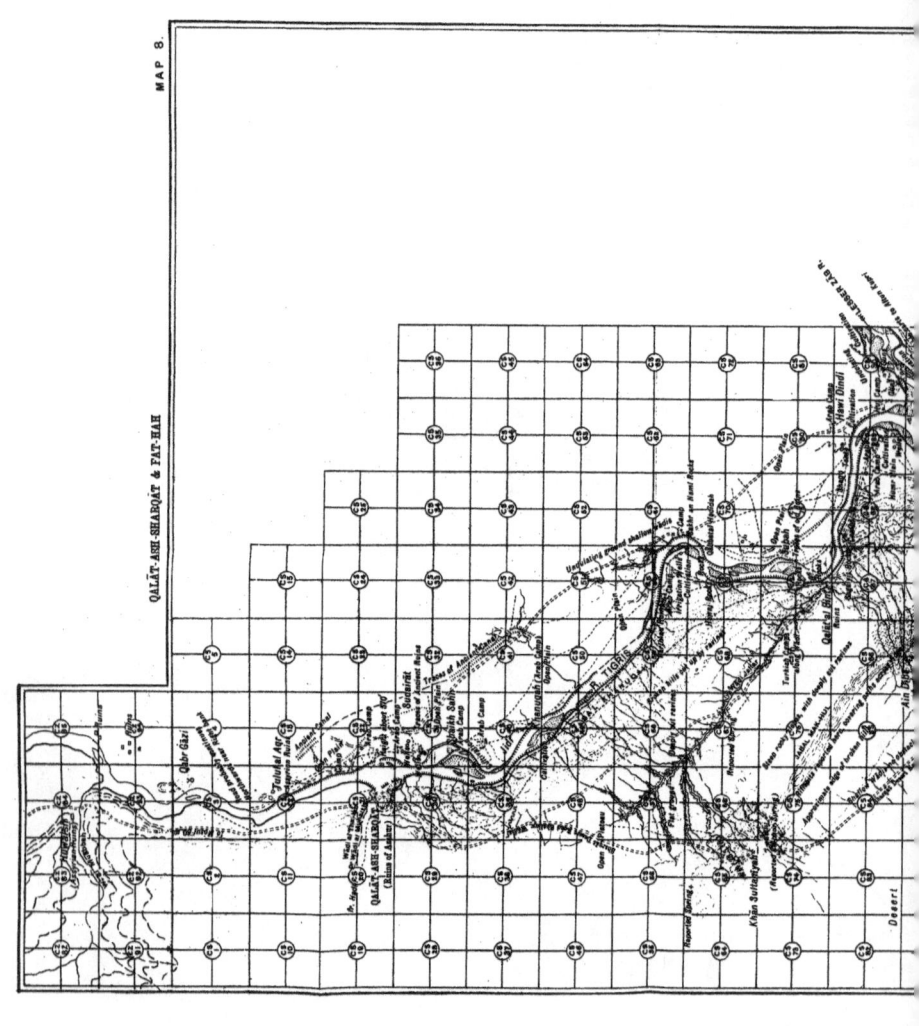

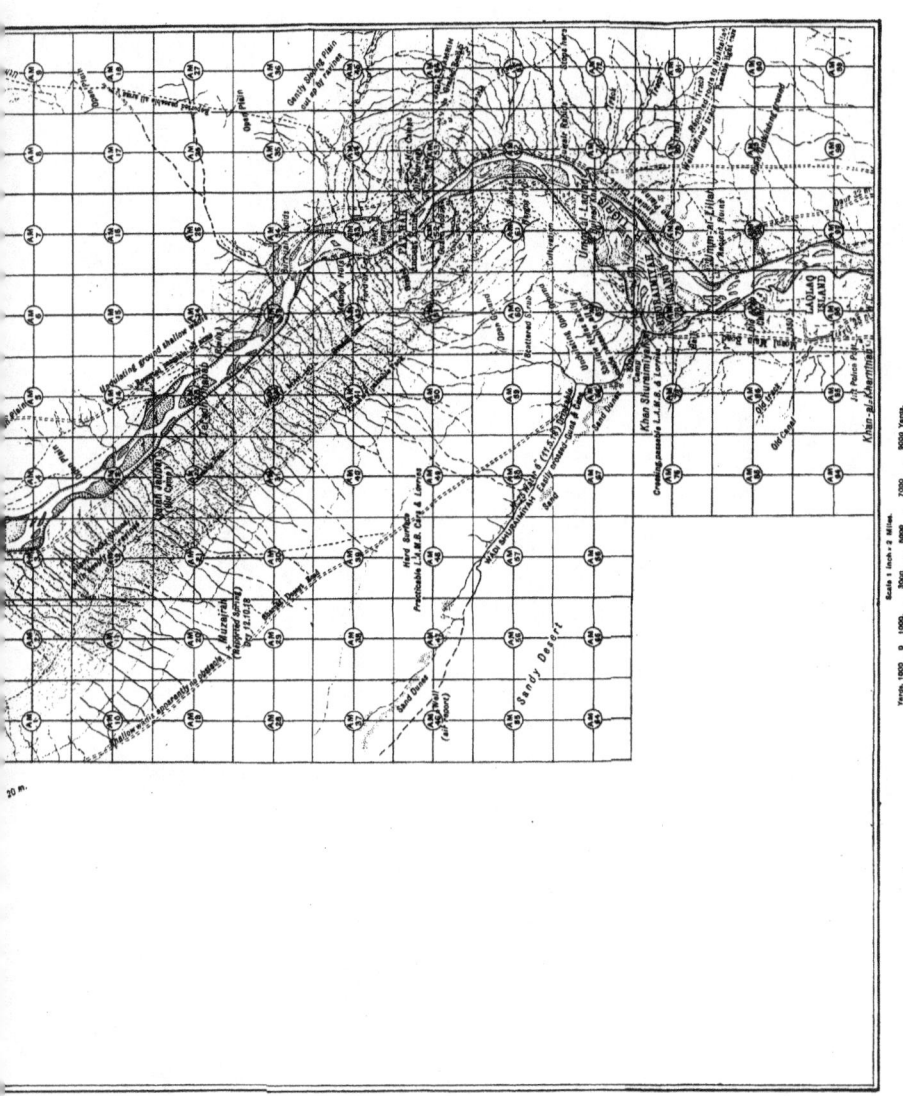

(c) 51st Infantry Brigade is to advance at 19.00 hours this evening, and occupy line AM.62.D.10/10 to AM.62. C.25/10.   *Map No. 7.*

(d) 336th, 220th and 221st Brigades R.F.A. are to occupy the general line AM.71.A.70/30 to AM.70.B.30/50, to-night.

(e) 32nd Lancers (less two squadrons) and one section No. 8 L.M.A.B. move at 06.30 (2 hours 4th) to vicinity AM.30 Central.

(f) 34th Infantry Brigade is to protect the left flank from AM.69.A.55/00 to Wadi crossing AM.68A.

(g) One squadron 32nd Lancers is to be located in AM.58.C. with a standing patrol night and day on the Shergat Desert Road.

In accordance with the same Brigade operation order the 52nd Infantry Brigade moved as follows:—   *Regarding 52nd Infantry Brigade.*

1/6th Hants and 1/113th Infantry moved at 19.00 hours and occupied line AM.62.C.25/10—AM.61.D.55/05 to AM. 61.C.70/45. Approximately 1,000 yards from the enemy front line trenches.

FRONTAGES.

1/6th Hants, with 276 M.G. Company and two sections No. 258 M.G.C. AM.62.C.25/10, to AM.61.D.55/05.

1/113th Infantry with No. 258 M.G. Company (less two sections) AM.61.D.55/05, to AM.61.C.70/45.

(Thus the right of the Hants linked up with the left of the 51st Infantry Brigade.)

The 45th remained in their existing trenches in support, and put out an outpost line AM.61.C.15/20 to AM.69.A.55/00.

Major R. H. Anderson put out this line after dark, with "A" Company and No. 13 platoon, and obtained touch with the 113rd Infantry at our end and the 114th Mahrattas at the other.

These outposts were to remain in position on the 24th unless the Brigade advanced.

All animals were to be north of the Wadi Shuramiyah after 05.30 hours on the 24th.

The 45th Scouts under Lieut. G. W. Benton, moved through the 1/113th Infantry line by orders of the Brigade to see if the enemy trenches were occupied. They were heavily fired

124 HISTORY OF THE 45TH RATTRAY'S SIKHS

on at 21.00 hours and brought in the information required.

October 24th. At 06.00 hours we awoke, expecting to hear a terrific bombardment, to see the 18th Division attacking, and to be attacking ourselves in a few hours. There was, however, no firing of any description. About 06.05 hours an enemy plane came leisurely over our trenches, and machine-gunned some targets in the 17th Divisional Area behind us, and flew away unharmed and unpursued.

At about 06.30 hours we heard that the enemy had retired from both banks of the Fat-Hah position, with very little loss to our army. The penetration of the passes on his left flank had made him give up a very strong natural position, which he had fortified for ten months, firing hardly a shot of S.A.A.

The enemy was followed up at once

(1) *By the 17th Division.* The 34th and 51st Infantry Brigades took up the advance about 10.00 hours along the river road, whilst a detached column 1/10th Gurkha Rifles and one Mountain battery under Colonel Coningham moved off along the crest of the Jebel Makhul against the enemy right flank (Coningham's Column).

(2) *By the 18th Division.* An infantry brigade and the 7th Cavalry Brigade moved to the junction of the Lesser Zab with the Tigris. The 11th Cavalry Brigade moved from Ain Nakhaila to the Zab, and established a bridgehead at Utmaniyah before midnight. Our Brigade was ordered into bivouac on the Tigris, AM.62.D.2/8. It was found impossible to move on with more than two brigades, owing to transport and supply difficulties, so we sat down with as good grace as possible for someone else to win the war.

A bridge of boats was established at Fat-Hah, which greatly facilitated the supply question.

October 25th. The 52nd Infantry Brigade remained in bivouac at Fat-Hah sending large working parties to repair the road through the Fat-Hah gorge, which the Turks had severely damaged before their retirement. This impeded the advance of the 17th Divisional artillery.

The 45th sent " A " and " C " Companies, and they were out at work for eight hours.

The 7th Cavalry Brigade supported by an infantry brigade

18th Division forced the passage of the Lesser Zab near its junction before nightfall.

The Turk withdrew all his force from the left bank by his pontoon bridge near Humr and burnt the bridge. So from now onwards the whole Turkish force was on the right bank, opposed to the 17th Division.

The 11th Cavalry Brigade spent this day at Utmaniyah, completing their crossing of the Lesser Zab.

About dusk, the advanced guard 1st H.L.I. of the 51st Infantry Brigade, which was advancing along the river road, advanced through a Turkish position skilfully chosen in dense jungle with the foot hills of the Jebel Makhul rising close to their left flank, beyond Mushaq. The head of the main body 1st H.L.I. was ambushed at very close quarters and suffered severely. They maintained their position for the night. "D" Company, Major R. H. Anderson, pro- *October 26th.* ceeded at 07.00 hours under orders from the Brigade to do salvage work on the Fat-Hah position, and recovered a lot of shell cases, timber, telephone wire, etc. It was realized by them how very strong this position was. At 11.30 hours, under Brigade orders, "A" Company (less one platoon)—Captain R. B. Ramsbotham—without Lewis guns, ammunition, bombs etc., proceeded to the masonry huts (Map No. 8 AM.43.A. and D.) to act as stretcher bearers, in country over which motor ambulances could not work. They had their work cut out, for many wounded from Mushaq came in during the afternoon and night, and were accommodated in the huts (till recently a Turkish hospital). At 16.00 hours, "D" Company returned to bivouac to find that the Regiment had been ordered to march at once to join Coningham's Column, which had been checked on the Jebel Makhul some twenty to twenty-five miles away.

The orders directed that 150 rounds S.A.A. and iron rations were to be carried on the man, and no kits, rations or bombs were to be taken. A minimum of first line transport was allowed, twenty-two mules only for the battalion. Also, that weak men unable to march were to be left at Fat-Hah. Ninety-three O.R.'s were therefore left with a dump.

"A" Company were to move on the 27th from the huts, pick up one day's rations from a supply dump, and join the

Battalion as best they could on the summit of the Jebel.

At 16.30 hours the 45th (less "A" (less one platoon) and "D" Companies) with two sections No. 258 M.G. Company, moved off straight up the Jebel through the Fat-Hah position and gained the track before dark.

"D" Company, Major R. H. Anderson, had a hasty meal, collected rations, discarded weak men and marched at 05.30 hours via Divisional Headquarters, where orders *re* rations were given verbally, and also orders for the 1/6th Hants (who had marched earlier to support Coningham's Column) to proceed to Qalat Jabbur.

After being put on the lower road by a British guide, "D" Company got on the crest by about 22.00 hours and followed in the wake of the Battalion.

Our destination in orders was A.M.1 but turned out to be A.M. 12, eighteen miles by the map, but actually twenty-six allowing for the turns and twists of the track.

The track was good in places, but in others a mere goat track, very stiff going for men and animals—a half-moon assisted us from midnight.

October 27th. After an all-night march, with short halts of ten minutes each hour, Headquarters and "B" and "C" Companies with the two sections No. 258 M.G. Company arrived at A.M.12 at 06.15 hours.

"D" Company, unhampered by so many animals, arrived at 08.30 hours. The dawn was a most perfect sight, with a very clear view up the Lesser Zab, and the Persian Mountains in the distance.

On "D" Company's arrival, the 45th was ordered to attack a cross ridge on which the 1/10th Gurkha Rifles had failed to dislodge the enemy the day before with severe casualties. As the Colonel was about to carry out a reconnaissance and settle the method of attack, the welcome news, to us, came in that the Gurkha patrols had found that the enemy had evacuated the position.

The 1/10th G.R. and the mountain battery marched at once for Ain Dibbs. The 45th were ordered to follow after a rest. The tea, milk and sugar invariably carried by our men in their packs came in very handy at times like these. In addition, many men were carrying "chaguls" of water, and we were able to send our pakhals and these down to the Tigris to be replenished.

Headquarters, " B," " C," and one platoon " A " Company pushed on at 11.00 hours, and " D " Company marched with the two sections 258 M.G.C. at noon. Both parties entered Aib Dibbs (eleven miles) at 16.00 hours, to find that Colonel Coningham had advanced towards Balalij, and had not yet got in touch with the Turk. The 10th G.R. had very kindly left four bags of Atta for us. Major Shuttleworth had been appointed Staff Officer to the Column by an aeroplane message dropped at 11.00 hours, and had ridden on and arranged this piece of " Q " work, so our men got a little much-needed food. Outposts were put out on the surrounding hills, and we spent an undisturbed night. " C " Company had to bivouac on the desert road to meet the heavy artillery and escort it on when met. It was expected at 06.00 hours (28th).

" A " Company (less No. 1 Platoon)—Captain R. B. Ramsbotham—marched from the masonry huts at 11.00 hours with orders to join the Regiment on the Jebel, near A.M.12.

He climbed up a rough track near Qalat Jubbar, reached A.M.12 at 13.00 hours (28th), where he found a small picquet we had left to assist him.

" A " Company reached Ain Dibbs at 04.45 hours, with *October 28th.* forty-four mules rations, and seventeen mules S.A.A. The Company was ordered to cook the rations and rest at Ain Dibbs, and to follow as early as possible, after leaving one platoon as garrison there. The ammunition we took on with us.

The Regiment less " A " Company (less one platoon) and " C " Company, on desert road to meet and escort heavy artillery, marched at 06.00 hours, and after watering the animals at the very brackish springs of Ain Dibbs reached Balalij (Map No. 8/C.S.74.B.8/8) at 11.00 hours, where the Column Commander's permission to halt for two hours was obtained by the C.O. who went on in a car with a Staff Officer.

The 10th G.R. had pushed on towards the junction of the river and desert roads; we could see them in the distance, and our signallers were in touch.

The following message was received from Headquarters Coningham's Column about 11.00 hours. " 11th Cavalry Brigade is established astride Mosul Road, right bank, Tigris, in touch with our Lamb Brigade. Battle position is Hawaish Gorge. Wauchope's and Coningham's Columns are to push on and attack enemy who is entrenching on line C.S.39.C.8/8—C.S.29.D.5/5—C.S.29.A.4/9. Please push on with all speed, the 1/10th G.R.'s are a weak battalion and more rifles are required for the attack."

Map No. 8.

Information about our Cavalry.

This was the first intimation the 45th had that a cavalry brigade was astride the enemy's communications. As a matter of fact the 11th Cavalry Brigade arrived opposite Hawaish on the 26th, and part of this force got across that night.

Brig.-General Cassells (11th Cavalry Brigade) was reinforced this day by an infantry brigade and two batteries R.F.A. from the 18th Division.

The 7th Cavalry Brigade who had been brought back to Fat-Hah on the 26th, also joined General Cassells before dark after a very fine march.

Our halt was therefore curtailed half an hour. "C" Company joined up before we marched, No. 1 Platoon "A" Company, and one section No. 258 M.G.C. were left at Balalij as garrison, in accordance with orders.

The Regiment marched on at 13.30 hours, and almost caught up the 1/10th G.R. After passing through a gap in the hills, we advanced towards the fight in progress in artillery formation across the plain; but Coningham's Column did not come into action, for the 34th Infantry Brigade Column (General Wauchope) had driven back the enemy, though our march across the plain probably helped to accelerate their withdrawal.

We arrived at the junction of the river and desert roads at 17.00 hours. After a short halt, Coningham's Column ceased to exist, the 45th were attached to the 51st Infantry Brigade, and we marched over to a bivouac near their Headquarters. Our rations had not yet come up, but the 14th Sikhs did not let our men starve and shared their rations.

Before going to sleep (all ranks were tired after forty-eight hours' marching, much of it being in single file), we received orders that the advance would be resumed at 06.00 hours (29th).

"A" Company left Ain Dibbs at 11.30 hours with the rations, having cooked them during the halt, and left No. 4 Platoon there as garrison in obedience to orders. They reached Balalij at 15.30 hours, and the cross roads about 20.00 hours, but did not find the Battalion that night so bivouacked on their own.

Thus, the whole 17th Division (less 52nd Infantry Brigade) was concentrated in the vicinity of the cross roads this night with the intention of advancing on Shergat and effecting a junction with General Cassells at Hawaish at 06.00 hours on the morrow.

About 01.15 hours we were rudely disturbed with a Brigade march order issued at 01.05 hours. *October 29th.*

"General Cassells is still holding his own astride Turkish communications about six miles north of Shergat.

"51st Infantry Brigade and No. 2 I.M. Artillery Brigade will march as below. 34th Infantry Brigade and remainder of artillery marches 03.00 hours.

Advanced Guard. — Commanding Lieut.-Colonel F. E. Coningham, 1/10th Gurkha Rifles.

"*Main Body* will pass starting point, marked by Brigade Red Lamp on Mosul Road, west of Brigade bivouac, as follows:

Brigade Headquarters	..	02.25 hours
1st H.L.I.	..	02.25 ,,
45th Sikhs	..	02.32 ,,
No. 257 M.G.C. ..	..	02.39 ,,
No. 2 I.Artillery Brigade	..	02.43 ,,
14th Sikhs	..	02.55 ,,

"14th Sikhs will join main body as it passes through outpost line.

"Halts of ten minutes; from ten minutes before each clock hour to clock hour.

"Pace of march will not exceed one mile per hour.

Reports to Head of main body.

ACKNOWLEDGE."

In accordance with these orders, we slipped into our places, and advanced along the Mosul Road. Enemy Very lights were going up frequently on either side of us, but we reached Shergat (five miles) at daybreak, and advanced still along the road until 07.00 hours without opposition, when the 1/10th G.R. and 1st H.L.I. moved forward along the plateau with a squadron of the 32nd Lancers on their left flank, and the 14th Sikhs in support. The 45th, in reserve, *The Battle of Shergat.*

moved along the road under the plateau, until they reached the point Map No. 8/C.S.11.B.99/70 at 08.00 hours and halted.

Divisional Headquarters came up and established their Headquarters near by, and the artillery a position in the nullah in front of us. After many false alarms the Battalion were allowed to take off their equipment, and send mules to and fro for water about 10.30 hours.

See Plan of Battle of Shergat. Map No. 9.

"A" Company (less two platoons left at Ain Dibbs and Balalij) arrived and joined the Battalion with the rations at 11.00 hours, and the men fairly got down to it for they were ravenous.

The distance marched by the 45th Sikhs since the 26th was:
H.Q., "B" and "C" Companies 66 miles in 63 hours.
"D" Company .. .. 72 miles in 75 hours.
"A" Company .. .. 53 miles in 48 hours.

This was over a bad country, often in single file especially in the hilly part. Only three men fell out all told, and the men were wonderfully fit and cheery.

During this period of waiting the Turkish artillery were very busy and shelled us so that we had to move position twice, but we only had one Sepoy hit. They also turned their attention to the 34th Infantry Brigade coming up, the heavy artillery, Divisional Headquarters and mules going to and returning from water, in fact to anything that moved.

17th Divisional Intention.

About noon an aeroplane dropped a message on Divisional Headquarters giving a very clear description of the enemy dispositions and our own. The H.L.I. and 10th G.R. had been held up and had reached the line shewn in the plan of the battle of Shergat.

It was resolved to attack 800 yards of the enemy's left with one battalion, supported by two more, and thus to break through his line, and join hands with Cassells Force at Hawaish.

The Battalion selected to attack, was the 45th, who were now of a fighting strength of about 530 rifles.

Reconnaissance by 51st Brigade and 45th.

At 13.00 hours Lieut.-Colonel D. A. D. McVean, Major R. H. Anderson, and Captain A. L. Butcher, rode on about a mile to make a reconnaissance with the Brigadier and Brigade Major.

SKETCH MAP OF SHARQAT.

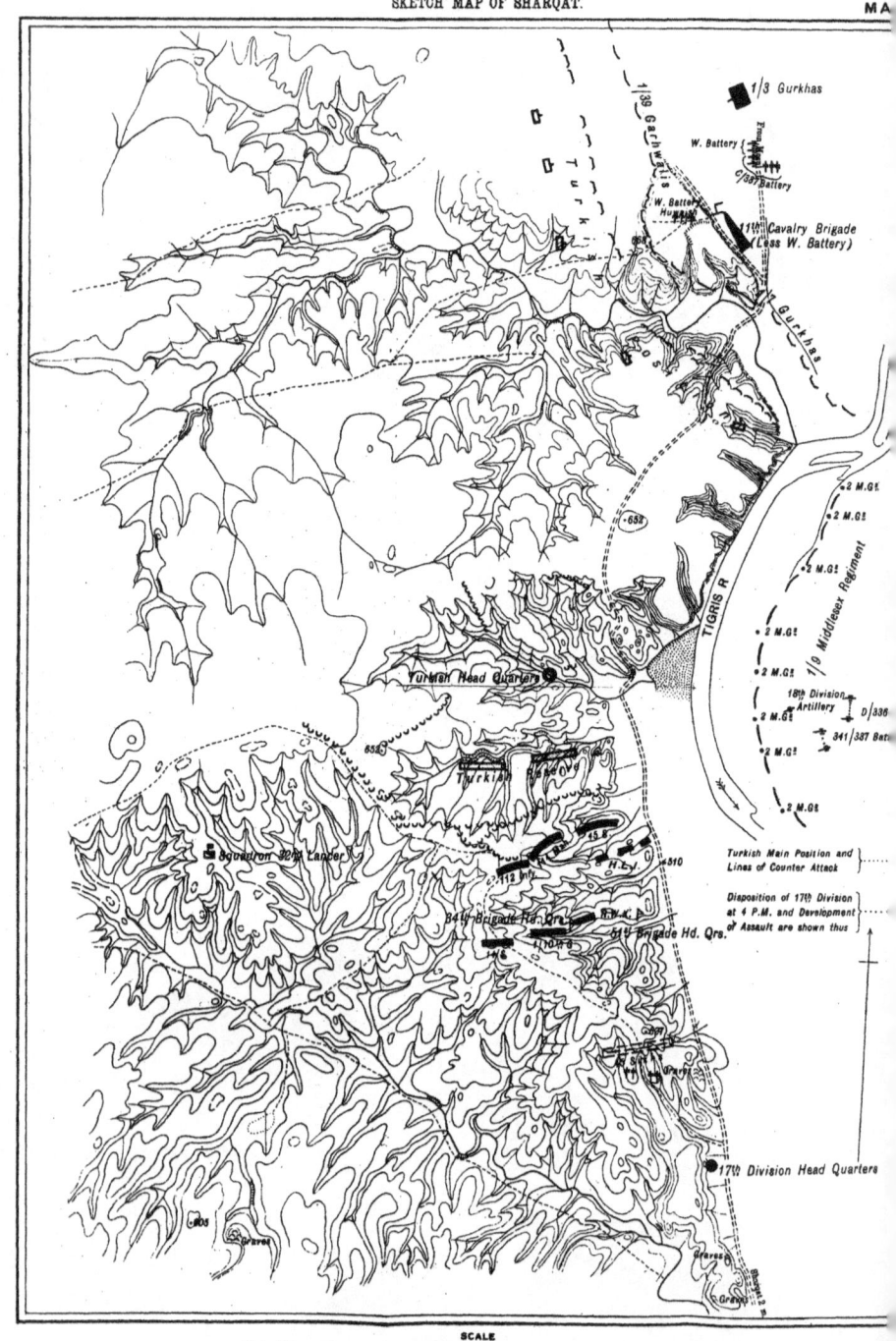

The horses were left, and the party proceeding up a nullah made their reconnaissance under a very unpleasant shell-fire, for the enemy artillery were searching all nullahs. Frontages, etc., were settled and the attack order was written under the shelter of a friendly cliff. It was as follows :—

"To H.L.I., 14th Sikhs, 45th Sikhs, 1/10th Gurkhas. *51st Infantry*
"Aeroplane reports enemy holding the line CZ.92.D.8/2 to *Brigade Order*
CZ.91, Central AAA *No. B.M.*
0101, Map
"2. 51st Brigade will assault left flank of position on a *No. 8.*
front of 800 yards right on cliff above road AAA Pressure to be maintained on remainder of present 51st Brigade front AAA

"3. Field guns and howitzers will bombard front of assault at full rate from zero hour (to be notified later) till assaulting infantry are within 100 yards of position and will then lift 300 yards for three minutes AAA Signal for lift Very lights and by F.O.O.'s AAA Fire will then be controlled by F.O.O.'s and Battery Commanders AAA

"Heavy Artillery 17th and 18th Divisions counterbattery work and harassing fire AAA Mountain Artillery bombard remainder of front AAA 34th Brigade will follow in close support of assaulting troops to confirm success and join hands with Cassells at Hawaish AAA 45th Sikhs will carry out the assault passing through H.L.I. AAA 1/10th Gurkhas will maintain pressure on rest of front AAA Acknowledge.

Five one brigade.
2.38 p.m."

Having completed the reconnaissance the party got back to the Regiment at 15.30 hours, zero hour having been fixed in the meantime for 16.00 hours. The Adjutant had the Battalion under cover in artillery formation, and the orders were hastily explained to all ranks. "D" and "C" Companies ("D" right) in the front line, and "A" (less two platoons) and "B" in the second.

At zero hour the Regiment advanced in four waves, the right of "D" Company directing, followed by the Headquarters' party, and our own artillery barrage commenced. As we topped a rise in front of us, platoons assumed square formation. The Regiment moved with the utmost steadiness through a heavy enemy shell fire of all descriptions, and

arrived at the line of the 1st H.L.I. about 16.45 hours.
Owing to the broken ground and dust and smoke created by the enemy shell fire, " B " Company and the Headquarters' party under Lieut. Henson bore too much to the left.

By good fortune and an extended formation, we sustained very few casualties from the enemy gun fire. On nearing the H.L.I. line we passed through heavy machine gun fire, but passed through this without great damage also.

After having passed through the H.L.I. position to the ridge beyond, a very heavy counterattack was launched by the enemy, the signal for which was a succession of Very lights. This caused our guns which had slacked off considerably to cease fire; and the full force of the enemy counterattack struck the flank of " C " Company and " B " Company who had got rather far out to the left. This drove in " B " Company and part of " C " Company, and for a time things looked ugly.

A few strong tactical positions were seized by " C " Company and " D " Company, Captain A. L. Butcher and Subadar Labh Singh in particular putting up a very gallant resistance at close quarters.

About this time the 114th Mahrattas came up, and in their turn caught the Turkish counter-attack in flank, aided by our fire, which was thrown back about sunset, when a line was held, 45th Sikhs on the right, " A," " D," " C " Companies and " B " Company reorganized and brought up, connecting up with the 114th Mahrattas and with the 112th Infantry on their left.

October 30th.   At one time this counter-attack had got right round our flank as far as the line of the 14th Sikhs.

Very heavy rifle fire and machine gun fire went on most of the night, and on our front the Turks had patrols out, throwing bombs at intervals, but they never looked like making another attack.

At 04.00 hours, the Regiment was ordered into reserve a mile in rear, and the 1st H.L.I. took over our line. There was still a good deal of firing going on, and, as we marched back, we found numbers of our own and other wounded lying and crawling about.

At 06.30 hours we heard the British " Cease fire " blown

several times on the bugle, and at first thought it was a Turkish ruse. But shortly after we saw white flags being put up, which increased in numbers, and then, to our amazement, after the heavy fight of the night before, we heard that the whole Turkish force and its Commander had surrendered to our army.

This was confirmed a few hours later by the whole army headed by its Commander and staff, marching past us unarmed towards Shergat.

Most of the Regiment slept very soundly in the quiet that ensued till 16.00 hours, when we received orders to march to and bivouac on the river at Map No. 8/C.S.12.A.6/1, which we found to be a very dirty spot; but were far too tired to mind anything.

Our casualties in this fight were severe. Lieut. Henson who lost touch with the Battalion put up a fight on his own till he was dangerously wounded, and his party were absorbed in the line taken up by the 112th Infantry. Captain Butcher was wounded in the arm, whilst two of our best Indian Officers, Subadar Mehar Singh, I.D.S.M., and Jemadar Sadhu Singh were both killed in action. Subadar Kehar Singh was desperately wounded and carried off with difficulty. Many brave deeds were done, some of which appear in the Appendix on Honours. But the action was fought just before dusk and much of the initiative lay with platoon and section commanders.

Our casualties were thirty-six killed in action and 144 wounded, and in spite of a temporary retirement in one part of the line in face of an overwhelming and sudden counterattack, the men, who had marched splendidly for three days, did magnificently.

In the evening we got the following message from the Army Commander, addressed to all formations, 1st Corps and attached troops :—

" Order of the Day AAA The following message has been received from the G.O.C. in Chief begins to General Cobbe. My very warmest congratulations to you and all troops under your command at having brought off a great coup which opens the road to Mosul AAA The fighting of the Turks seems to have been unexpectedly stubborn and of course the ground made the task of the troops a most difficult one AAA The feat of the Eleventh Cavalry Brigade has been a most notable feature of the operations AAA General Marshall AAA Ends AAA

"The Corps Commander wishes to inform all ranks of his great admiration for their endurance under fatigue, and their gallantry and dash in action under conditions of ground entirely favourable to the enemy, who has fought most stubbornly."

Our Divisional Commander also issued the following special order of the day.

"For the last ten days the Division, and attached troops, have been strenuously marching over difficult roads and carrying on despite shortage of rations, water and sleep.

"They have fought two rear guard actions and two pitched battles, the last on the 29th instant, against a superior force which they defeated and which, with the co-operation of the Cavalry further north and Infantry and guns across the river, they have forced into complete surrender, resulting in the capture of every man, gun and animal.

"The Troops have given the finest possible exhibition of soldierly fortitude and gallantry in action, and have fully maintained the best traditions of the British and Indian armies.

"I am proud to command such a fine force, and thank it for the superhuman efforts it made to bring the operations to so successful an issue."

October 31st. In the morning the Regiment got the following message from the G.O.C. the 52nd Infantry Brigade at Fat-Hah :—

"Congratulations on your fine performance deeply regret casualties. General Andrew."

At 11.00 hours the Regiment marched down to the river near Shergat under orders of the Division, as guard over the Turkish prisoners-of-war camp. We took over our duties at 13.00 hours from the 14th Sikhs. There were some 9,000 prisoners in this camp, and its state of filth and dirt was indescribable.

The 14th Sikhs remained in bivouac quite close to us.

Major B. W. Shuttleworth was appointed Commandant, prisoners-of-war camp, until such time as the prisoners were evacuated down country to Baghdad.

We remained on duty at the prisoners-of-war camp. About *November 1st.*
noon we heard that an Armistice with Turkey had been
declared, and that all hostilities were to cease.

We were informed by the 51st Infantry Brigade that the
captures on the 30th October included :—
- 430 Officers.
- Over 8,000 other ranks.
- 30 guns.
- 80 machine guns.
- 1,850 animals.

also large quantities of rifle and gun ammunition.

These captures were added to by the Cavalry Brigades,
and it became known to us that a force of the 18th Division
was on its way to occupy Mosul.

We remained on duty over the prisoners-of-war camp. *November*
As we were on half rations, and had been since October *2nd.*
26th, we carried out combined bombing operations for fish
in conjunction with the 14th Sikhs. The results were
extremely good.

Under orders from Corps, Lieut. R. V. Fox proceeded by
Ford van to Ain Dibbs to search for some mysterious war
material. He had about ten minutes' notice, and his kit
consisted of what he stood up in. He was afterwards made
Administrative Commandant of that place, which was very
malarious. So he spent a hard month there.

On duty over the prisoners-of-war camp. *November*
Orders came in for the Regiment to march down to Fat- *3rd.*
Hah in two wings, each escorting Turkish prisoners on the
4th and 5th instant.

Major-General G. A. Leslie, C.B., C.M.G., inspected the *November*
Regiment on parade at 07.15 hours, and made the following *4th.*
speech to the British and Indian Officers, which was afterwards given out to the men :—

"After very hard marching with very little food, sleep,
or water, you were called upon for the hardest task of all,
the assault on the enemy's position, for which you were
specially selected. I have since been over the ground, and
seen how difficult it was. The Regiment advanced most
gallantly under heavy shell fire, and although you went
back in some places in the face of the enemy counter-attack

(which I consider that any troops in the world might have done) yet you went forward again, and took the enemy's first position. I want you to remember that you have fully maintained your high reputation, and that your behaviour in the recent operations has increased that reputation."

Immediately after the parade, the left wing under Major R. H. Anderson (strength : six I.O.'s, 220 I.O.R.'s) took over seventy officers, 830 other ranks and 153 animals from the prisoners-of-war camp, and marched for Qalat al Bint, nineteen miles.

The prisoners all belonged to the 13th Regiment, the march was a waterless one, and the prisoners-of-war felt it very much.

November 5th. Left wing under Major R. H. Anderson with prisoners-of-war reached Qalat Jabbar and halted for the night.

On the way the left wing passed the Turkish position at Mushaq, and the Turkish officers as well as ourselves were much interested in going over the ground.

Headquarters and right wing, Lieut.-Colonel D. A. D. McVean, D.S.O., with Captains Curtis and Ramsbotham, and Lieut. Pybus, marched to Qalat Al Bint with about 1,100 prisoners-of-war, halting for the night.

November 6th. The left wing reached Fat-Hah in the early afternoon, and handed over their prisoners-of-war to the cage and special guard.

The right wing arrived at Qalat Jabbur.

November 7th. Our dump at Fat-Hah under 2/Lieut. F. W. Kelly, and Subadar Major Sundar Singh had risen to 182 I.O.R.'s.

At 07.30 hours 2/Lieut. Kelly with two platoons, made up from the dump, marched for railhead (near Abu Rajash) with the prisoners-of-war brought in by the left wing. Having handed them over they returned to K.11.D. (four miles south of Jift) where the 52nd Infantry Brigade were to concentrate.

Headquarters and the right wing under Lieut.-Colonel D. A. D. McVean, D.S.O., arrived at Fat-Hah at noon with eighty officers and 1,100 other ranks (approx.) Turkish prisoners-of-war.

At 14.45 hours, under Brigade arrangements, the left wing under Major R. H. Anderson marched for K.11.D. sixteen

HISTORY OF THE 45TH RATTRAY'S SIKHS 137

miles. They were given twelve carts with tired mules who had already done the journey once that day. Owing to the vile road, darkness and heavy rain which came on after dark, they came to a standstill, and had to bivouac 1,000 yards south of Shuramiyah Khan.

Left wing under Major R. H. Anderson arrived at the new bivouac at K.11.D. at 08.45 hours, after spending a bad night without any shelter. *November 8th.*

The Headquarters and right wing arrived at K.11.D. at 18.00 hours, having left Fat-Hah at 11.30 hours with fresh transport.

Thus the whole Regiment was together again. They had picked up their kits at Fat-Hah, and were on full rations again, having been on half rations and without kits for eleven days.

Lieut. G. L. Watson rejoined from duty at Baghdad.

The Regiment had its first day's rest since October 26th. During the day Captain A. L. Butcher joined fit from a field ambulance. He was evacuated after the battle on the 29th. *November 9th.*

In the evening we received orders that we in common with the remainder of the Division were to be employed on construction work on the extension of the railway towards Shergat.

300 rifles proceeded in two shifts for work on the embankment of the new railway one mile north of Jift. *November 10th.*

Ten N.C.O.'s and Sepoys marched to railhead for despatch to the depot as drill instructors.

300 rifles worked on the railway. *November 11th.*

There was rain most of the day, but before evening when it rained heavily we got our tents to the great joy of all ranks, as we had been tentless since October 20th.

At 23.00 hours we received the welcome news of an armistice with Germany and on all fronts. We saw visions of returning to India, leave and all kinds of nice things. Little did all ranks realize that we should be in the country for nearly another two-and-a-half years.

The usual working party of 300 rifles worked on the railway. *November 12th.*

The day was rainy and there was an issue of rum, the first for eight months.

13th.	In honour of the Armistice there was no railway work.
14th.	400 rifles worked on the railway.
15th.	300 rifles worked on the railway.
16th.	Eighty rifles completed a six-day task on the railway.

The 14th Sikhs arrived from Shergat, and camped next to us.

Our men had saved up two days' rations, and fed them right royally on arrival.

Lieut. G. L. Watson left the Regiment on appointment to a prisoner-of-war Labour Corps.

17th. There was a holiday from railway work.

Lieut. G. D. Pybus, 14th Sikhs, attached, rejoined his own unit under orders from 1st Corps.

18th. A new five-days' task on a very deep cutting was allotted to the Regiment, and 350 rifles worked daily on it, completing it on the 22nd. At the conclusion of work, we were informed that there would be no more railway work, which gave great satisfaction to all ranks.

23rd. Orders received from the 52nd Infantry Brigade that we should march to Tekrit to-morrow, but at 07.00 hours on the 24th the move was cancelled on account of lack of transport.

25th. The Regiment marched at 10.15 hours from K.11.D. to Abu-Rajash, a short march of eight miles.

26th. The Regiment marched to Tekrit, and went into our old camp at Jibn Wadi. This was on a very nice site, on high cliffs overlooking the river.

During the afternoon Lieut.-Colonel F. S. Keen, D.S.O., G.S.O.I., paid a visit and informed us that the following immediate rewards had been given to the Regiment for the recent operations :—

M.C.—Captain A. L. Butcher, Captain B. W. Key, Subadar Labh Singh.

I.O.M., 2nd Class.—Jemadar Harnam Singh, No. 4489 Havildar Tara Singh, No. 886 L./Nk. Ujagar Singh, No. 1855 Sepoy Harnam Singh.

The remainder of the month was spent in settling in, completing deficiencies of kits, etc.

December The whole month of December was spent in Camp Jibn Wadi (Tekrit). There was a lot of rain, and it was bitterly cold with several degrees of frost for many days.

HISTORY OF THE 45TH RATTRAY'S SIKHS

On the 1st Lieut. R. V. Fox, and No. 12 Platoon rejoined the Regiment from Ain Dibbs.

The Corps Commander held a parade of the whole 17th Division on the 10th. Before this we had frequent practice parades.

The actual day was a very fine and impressive spectacle.

The Division was drawn up in mass, and whilst the Corps Commander was carrying out his inspection, the R.A.F. were flying about overhead, doing many crazy feats. After this immediate rewards were distributed. The Regiment's share was :—

M.C.—Captain A. L. Butcher, Subadar Labh Singh.

I.O.M., 2nd Class.—Jemadar Harnam Singh, No. 4489 Havildar Tara Singh, No. 886 L./Nk. Ujagar Singh, No. 1855 Sepoy Harnam Singh.

I.D.S.M.—No. 4675 Havildar Wazir Singh, No. 52 Havildar Prem Singh, No. 77 Havildar Bagga Singh, No. 4828 Havildar Rur Singh, No. 1109 L./Nk. Nahar Singh, No. 813 Sepoy Narain Singh, No. 1861 Sepoy Gurditt Singh, No. 268 Sepoy Basant Singh, No. 614 Nk. Indar Singh.

After this, there was a march past of all arms, in which the drums and fifes of the Hants played us past. We were altogether under arms for six hours.

There was great activity in the games line, and a Divisional Inter-Company Hockey Tournament started. " D " Company won in the Regiment, and defeated a company of the 113th Infantry on the 29th by two goals to nil.

Lieut.-Colonel D. A. D. McVean joined the 17th Division shooting camp for Christmas.

In the 17th Division races on the 31st, Lieut.-Colonel D. A. D. McVean's " Ossian " came in first in the Arab race.

The following Officers joined the Regiment during the month :—

Capt. J. B. Mudge, R.A.M.C. (2nd).
Lieut. L. G. Mathews, I.A.T.C. (20th).
Lieut. C. A. Phillips, I.A.T.C. (26th).

CHAPTER VI

JANUARY 1ST, 1919—OCTOBER 31ST, 1919.

THE Regiment commenced the year 1919 at Tekrit (Jibn Wadi Camp), and the following Officers were present :—
Lieut.-Colonel D. A. D. McVean, D.S.O.
Major B. W. Shuttleworth, B Company.
Major R. H. Anderson, " D " Company.
Captain A. C. Curtis, M.C., Adjutant.
  „   R. B. Ramsbotham, I.A.R.O., " A " Company.
  „   A. L. Butcher, " C " Company.
Lieut. R. V. Fox.
  „   C. A. Phillips, I.A. (on probation).
  „ · R. W. Kelly, I.A.R.O., Quartermaster.
  „   L. G. Mathews, I.A. (on probation).
2/Lieut. R. N. Moore, I.A.R.O.
Capt. J. B. Mudge, R.A.M.C.
The strength of the Regiment this day was : British Officers, 11 ; Indian Officers, 16. Indian Other Ranks, 744.

January. On the 1st we held very successful combined sports with the 14th Sikhs. We won most of the events, including the tug-of-war, and a great forgathering of British and Indian Officers took place on the conclusion of the sports.

On the 3rd, " D " Company played " C " Company of the 113th Infantry in the Divisional Hockey Tournament. "D" Company won by 2—1 after a close game.

Major B. W. Shuttleworth left the Regiment to join the British Mission at Vladivostok, to the great regret of all ranks.

The Regiment was ordered to move to Samarra left bank on the 4th. Lieut. L. G. Mathews proceeded by route march to that place with the 1st line transport and Officers' chargers, halting for the night at Tel Mahijir.

On the 5th camp was struck, and having entrained, the Regiment left Tekrit at 17.00 hours, arriving at Samarra at 19.30 hours. They bivouacked for the night by the line.

Major R. H. Anderson, 2/Lieut. R. N. Moore and "D" Company hockey team stayed at Tekrit for the next hockey match on the 7th with the 14th Sikhs.

On the 6th, with the aid of the first line transport, 22 carts and the Decauville Railway, the Regiment got settled down in the new camp on the L.B. near Samarra Town.

The site was a delightful one, and was recently 18th Divisional Headquarters. Good huts were obtained for the Mess, Officers' quarters and Gurdwara.

On the 7th, "D" Company played "A" Company, 80th Infantry, in the Divisional Hockey Tournament. After a very exciting game in which two of our goals were disallowed for sticks, the match ended in a draw of one goal all.

The result of the Tournament now depended on if "A" Company, 80th Infantry, beat "C" Company, 113th Infantry on the 9th. In which case we had to replay this match.

Work was commenced on dismantling the defences on the Samarra position left bank. This area was full of interesting old ruins, such as the tomb of the Emperor Julian. We were therefore much on the look-out for old and valuable relics, which, however, did not come our way.

On the 9th, the G.O.C. Brigade visited us and informed us that (i) a certain battalion on the right bank wound 500 yards of barbed wire on an empty barbed wire drum and (ii) that this battalion had actually rolled up 21 miles of wire on the 7th.

On the 10th, spurred on by the above news, the Regiment rolled up and packed on drums, thirty-six miles of barbed wire.

Lieut. G. W. Benton rejoined the Regiment from temporary duty as A.D.C. to the G.O.C. 17th Division.

On the 11th and 12th there was very heavy rain and wind, which cancelled all work for the day.

Late on the 13th, we heard that the 113th Infantry had beaten "A" Company, 80th Infantry. Therefore "D" Company, 45th Sikhs, were the winners of the Divisional Hockey Tournament cup. Much rejoicing in consequence.

142 HISTORY OF THE 45TH RATTRAY'S SIKHS

On the 18th, fifty-two miles of wire were disposed of.

Lieut.-Colonel F. S. Keen, D.S.O., G.S.O.I., came to stay with the Regiment, and brought the unwelcome news that the Regiment was to be part of the post-bellum Army of Mesopotamia. The news was most unexpected as we had been told privately that we were for India very shortly. A draft of 200 men was reported to be coming out to us.

On the 15th, fifty-two miles of barbed wire was rolled up and sent to Ordnance.

On the 16th and 17th, thirty-eight and forty-five miles of wire respectively were rolled up, and work carried out on digging up pipe lines.

On the 18th, very heavy rain and wind stopped all work, and our huts leaked very badly.

On the 19th, we received official intimation that the following Indian Officers and Other Ranks had died as prisoners-of-war in Turkey :—

Subadar Thaman Singh (previously reported), No. 510 Naick Bhagat Singh, No. 1131 Sepoy Kaku Singh, No. 4182 Havdr. Wariam Singh, No. 1200 Sepoy Gurnam Singh, No. 805/B L./Naick Radha Singh, No. 1227 Sepoy Udham Singh, No. 1070/B Sepoy Sant Singh, No. 1400 Sepoy Ram Singh, also a private letter was received from No. 4207 Naick Surjan Singh that the following men had arrived in Karachi, on repatriation to Indian prisoners-of-war after the Armistice, including himself :—

No. 1339/B Hav. Kishan Singh, No. 4850/15 Naick Budh Singh, No. 331 Naick Jagat Singh, No. 413 Sepoy Anokh Singh, No. 528 Sepoy Udham Singh, No. 639 Sepoy Chainchal Singh, No. 688 Sepoy Kehar Singh, No. 1546 Sepoy Sundar Singh, No. 872 Sepoy Lal Singh, No. 900 Sepoy Budh Singh, No. 1163 Sepoy Gobind Singh, No. 1672 Sepoy Gajjan Singh, No. 1216/B Sepoy Jagat Singh, No. 1033/B Sepoy Arjan Singh, No. 505/B Sepoy Amar Singh, No. 1747 Sepoy Indar Singh.

All these men had been captured in the attack of February 1st, 1917, and had almost all been wounded.

On the 20th, eight miles of wire were rolled up, work on the pipe line proceeded, and the work of dismantling dug-outs commenced.

HISTORY OF THE 45TH RATTRAY'S SIKHS 143

On the 21st, "A" Company commenced a course of musketry. Miles of wire were rolled up, the pipe line finished and the work on the dug-outs progressed well.

The work on the wire was now finished, and in nine days the Regiment had collected, rolled up and sent in 266 miles of barbed wire.

On the 25th, under orders from 3rd Echelon General Headquarters, twenty-eight reservists marched out of camp *en route* for India, for discharge and pension. They were as fine a body of men, both in physique and length of service, as any regiment could wish to see, and it was with the greatest regret we saw them march away for good.

Five had re-transferred to the Colours just before, and these twenty-eight were the last of ninety-two who came out to Mesopotamia with the Regiment.

On the 26th, a rumour reached us that the Brigade was to move shortly. We were practising hard for Divisional and Army Sports, and had just completed hockey grounds and running tracks. Late at night we received definite orders that the 52nd Infantry Brigade were to move at once to Baghdad to construct protective bunds for the new Cantonment.

On the 28th, all baggage was moved to the station. Major Anderson and nineteen Indian Other Ranks, the running team for the 17th Division five-mile cross country race, entrained for Tekrit.

On the 29th, the Regiment entrained for Baghdad, arriving there early in the morning, and arrived at the new camp at Es Sulaikh at 12 noon. The whole Brigade camp was pitched in a very constricted site in palm groves on rather sodden cultivated soil.

Captain J. A. Finlay rejoined the Regiment from duty with the Nabha Imperial Service Infantry, who had proceeded to India.

On this date the Divisional cross country race took place at Tekrit. Our team did the course in thirty-two minutes, but were only third. The winning team did it in twenty-eight minutes.

February. The 1st saw the Commemoration Service in the Gurdwara for those who fell on February 1st, 1917. The day was windy and rainy. Regimental sports were held on the 2nd, and were most successful.

The following week was characterized by much rain and cold, and all work and play was out of the question owing to the slippery state of the ground.

On the 10th, the 52nd Infantry Brigade started work on the new " Bund " out in the desert for the protection of the new Cantonment. It was a stupendous affair sixty-three feet broad at the base, ten feet broad at the top, and fourteen feet high. Baskets were provided, and the men settled down to their daily eight-hour task with very good humour. The nature of the work was so colossal, that with only three Battalions working, it was felt that it would take a year at least to complete.

On the 14th and 15th, the Divisional Sports were held at Tekrit. The Regiment won the 100 yards, quarter-mile, half-mile, one mile, relay and obstacle races, also the long jump and the putting the weight, and came out easy winners by thirty-eight points to the next Regiment's eighteen.

On the 15th, the Regiment were employed on their usual daily task on the " Bund," when they were recalled from work at 11.00 hours. The river Tigris was rising very fast, and the " Bund " was reported breached twelve miles north. At 16.00 hours a message was received from the Musketry School, near by, asking for assistance, as the "Bund" opposite them was breached. The Regiment after a full task on their own work, turned out in five minutes, and were at work within ten minutes of the message being received, working until 19.15 hours, at which hour they were relieved by another regiment.

Great anxiety prevailed at General Headquarters about the floods, and at 20.00 hours the Brigade received orders to move at once to Hunaidi. Lorries and carts arrived at midnight, and the loading proceeded easily as there was a bright moon. The night was bitterly cold, so no one got a wink of sleep. The Regiment marched off at 05.30 hours on the 16th, leaving Nos. 15 and 16 Platoons for duty at the Musketry School, reaching a camping ground near Hunaidi railway station at 09.00 hours. After a weary wait for transport, another move was made to a camp on the river bank one mile up stream of Hunaidi railway station. A billet for the mess with electric light was also secured. During the next few days the river fell considerably, and all danger of our old camp being flooded out disappeared.

On the 20th, a Force Order of the day was received, which awarded a Bar to his D.S.O. to Lieut.-Colonel D. A. D. McVean in the following terms :—

"For conspicuous gallantry and devotion to duty. He led his Regiment into action after a series of most trying and arduous marches over difficult country, covering over sixty miles in seventy hours, and in the end through a heavy hostile barrage. He displayed courage, determination and leadership of a high order."

Thus it came to pass that the Regiment, as well as Colonel McVean himself, received official recognition of their splendid marching and stout fight at the Battle of Shergat, and the operations preceding it.

On the 23rd, Lieut. R. W. Kelly, I.A.R.O., left the Regiment for England on demobilization.

On the 24th, the Regiment marched back to the old camping ground at Es Sulaikh and settled in.

The remainder of the month was spent in the usual work on the "Bund," making a good hockey ground for ourselves on the Baghdad Sporting Club ground just outside our camp, and training for the Baghdad Sports. It was rumoured that the 52nd Infantry Brigade was to spend the summer in the desert near Es Sulaikh, and we did many fatigues on brick making, digging trenches for pipe lines and work of a similar nature.

On the 2nd, "A" Company, Capt. R. B. Ramsbotham, and *March.* No. 15 Platoon under Subadar Attar Singh, proceeded by rail to Hillah (for Kifl) and Mahmudiyah respectively, where they were to look after Turkish prisoners-of-war at work. "A" Company proceeded to Kifl by road on the 3rd, twenty-three miles.

The river was again rising rapidly and "B" and "C" Companies were out continuously patrolling the "Bund" on a front of six miles for six days.

On the 11th the Baghdad Sports for the Championship of Mesopotamia were held, and the Regiment won five events out of seven, *i.e.*, the 100 yards, quarter-mile, half-mile,

K

Relay Race and Jemadar Sundar Singh (Jat) won the 120 yards Race for old soldiers in a canter. We lost both jumps and were second in the mile—altogether a very successful day.

On the 13th and 15th were held the Baghdad Races. On the first day Lieut.-Colonel McVean entered his old pony "Ossian" for the Arab Race. But he was pulled at the start, and had no chance whatever of showing his form.

It was now given out that only two battalions of the Brigade would work on the "Bund" in the week; the other was to be struck off duty for training.

On the 17th Captain R. B. Ramsbotham and Lieut. G. W. Benton left the Regiment for India and demobilization to the great regret of all ranks of the Regiment.

On the 19th a more sensible view of the size of the "Bund" we were working on was taken. The profile was altered to thirty-six feet at the base, four feet at the top, eight feet high, and slopes of 1 : 1. Had this been done in the first instance, the Brigade would have completed two miles, whereas the result was 320 yards from February 9th!

Shortly afterwards the site of the new Cantonment was altered to the south of Baghdad, so all our labour was in vain.

On the 26th rumours of trouble in the direction of Diwaniyah on the lower Euphrates reached us, and the 94th were held in readiness at thirty minutes' notice, with the remainder of the Brigade ready to follow shortly afterwards.

On the 28th the 113th were warned for the "War," and the 45th were detailed for Brigade fatigues and duties and work on the "Bund," also on a new Range Stop Butt of colossal dimensions.

On the 30th we heard that the entire 52nd Infantry Brigade was shortly to move to Hillah, which caused great joy as it would get us out of work on the "Bund."

April. On the 1st we got our orders as follows :—

200 men to entrain and leave Baghdad West with ninety 1st line mules and chargers at 12 noon on the 2nd, and Headquarters and the remainder of the Regiment at midnight April 2nd/3rd.

These orders were carried into effect, and the Regiment

(Headquarters, "B," "C" and "D" Companies less No. 15 Platoon), arrived at Hillah on a beautifully cool morning at 5.30 a.m. on the 3rd, detrained and marched into camp one mile north of the town under palm trees, close to the Hillah branch of the Euphrates, and in altogether quite pleasant surroundings.

On arrival also we received news that the threatened "War" further south was off, as all differences were settled, and so the whole 52nd Infantry Brigade was concentrated, with Brigade Headquarters in a billet in the town.

During our first week there was much rain and wind, and the weather remained surprisingly cool for the time of year. Several palm trees blew down with narrow escapes to various occupants of tents, so all that looked dangerous were cut down.

Many small escorts to convoys by road and river were supplied during the month. Lieut. G. M. Worden, I.A. (T.C.) joined for duty on the 16th, and on the 18th Lieut. L. G. Mathews, I.A. (T.C.), proceeded to join the 1/5th Buffs.

On the 19th by the orders of General Headquarters the men of the 8th Rajputs attached to us marched out of camp to rejoin their own unit, and the Regiment became all Sikh again.

They marched out at a strength of one Indian Officer, and eighty-six Indian Other Ranks, and their departure left us rather short of strength temporarily.

Since our arrival in this camp, flies had been increasing till there were, literally speaking, myriads of them, and life for all ranks became a positive burden. Energetic steps were at once taken to combat this nuisance, but it took a good many weary weeks to stamp it out.

On the 22nd we got E.P. tents, and pitched a very nice and regular camp for the summer. Cook houses and company messes were made, and roofed over with reeds from the river.

On the 26th, owing to a flood of the River Euphrates and heavy inundations over the country, Captain Butcher took out a company by train early in the morning to Mile Six on the Hillah-Kifl railway (Decauville) which was expected to be breached at this point. The breach occurred on the night of the 26th/27th, and our men were completely flooded out in their bivouac. They salved nearly all their kit by diving for it, and being able to effect little, returned to Hillah by train in the afternoon.

On the 29th the Indian mail brought us the news of the serious riots and unrest in the Punjab, with the proclamation of Martial Law. The Regiment remained very unmoved and cheery through it all, and were posted up in all news as it arrived. Owing to this they would not send home money orders for some time, and the outbreak of the Afghan War prevented drafts from being sent to us, and, of course, all leave to India was stopped.

Incidentally, Captain B. W. Key took a draft of 200 men from the depot to join the 15th Sikhs at Dakka.

Owing to continual rain showers and thunderstorms the weather kept wonderfully cool for the time of year.

May. Twelve Indian Other Ranks rejoined us from the 14th Sikhs at the end of April, and on May 1st our strength was British Officers, 10; Indian Officers, 17; Indian Other Ranks, 769.

On the 14th "A" Company arrived from escort duty with Turkish Prisoner-of-war Labour Corps, having been relieved by the 113th Infantry. No. 15 Platoon and the 1st line transport of "A" Company still, however, remained out in the "Blue."

On the 17th our men received letters from their homes after a lapse of a month. The news from the Punjab was much more reassuring.

On the 20th the Regiment provided 500 rifles for the Brigade Moveable Column, which then marched through the city as a show of force.

We were inspected by Major-General G. A. Leslie, C.B., C.M.G., the G.O.C. 17th Division, on the 23rd.

On the night of the 26th shortly after midnight our camp was entered by Arab thieves, who got into the Gurdwara tent (the remainder of the camp was well protected). They got away with the Granth Sahib and two or three boxes. The Granthi and his orderly gave the alarm, but the thieves got away from camp. A search party, however, was at once organized by Subadar Labh Singh, and went out. Attracted by the noise of hammering they came on a party of four

Arabs dividing the spoil not 200 yards from camp, and at once gave chase. No. 1965 Sepoy Ram Singh who was leading, closed with the nearest Arab, and pluckily collared him low. The man plunged his dagger into his back, and this plucky young Sepoy died in a few seconds. Two other men who were close behind, secured the murderer, and he was brought into camp in a very summary fashion and lodged in the quarter guard. The remaining three Arabs unfortunately got away in the darkness, but the actual murderer gave away their names to the Political Officer, to whom he was handed over.

On the 28th the first leave party of the year left for India. Strength—3 Indian Officers, 64 Indian Other Ranks and 10 followers. The period of leave was increased to two months.

The month ended with a Moveable Column Exercise, which entailed staying out at night. The hot weather had set in in earnest.

On the 31st Lieut.-Colonel D. A. D. McVean, D.S.O., proceeded to the U.K. on four months' leave, the command of the Regiment devolving on Major R. H. Anderson.

This day also saw the whole Regiment together again, for No. 15 Platoon got in from escort duty with prisoners-of-war by motor mahela, and rejoined the Regiment.

During June, sports, both land and aquatic were held, also wrestling on Sunday mornings. Training in all its branches was carried out, a range was made, and "B" Company carried out a course of Musketry, which consisted of a preliminary course and the old Part III. The results of the whole Regiment are given at the beginning of October.

June.

On the 12th the Battalion was inspected by the Army Commander, Major-General Sir. G. F. MacMunn, K.C.B., K.C.S.I., D.S.O. He inspected the Regiment on parade and was very complimentary on the men's steadiness and the arms drill. He also inspected the lines, and praised the cook houses and the Company mess houses we had built.

Owing to an outbreak of plague amongst the Arabs the whole Regiment were inoculated for plague between the 16th and 28th.

150 HISTORY OF THE 45TH RATTRAY'S SIKHS

July.

On the 29th we got the news by wire that Peace had been signed with Germany.

The month was very hot, and was spent in all branches of training including musketry. The men kept very fit with frequent sports, hockey and wrestling, and were always very cheery.

On the 7th the murderer of No. 1965 Sepoy Ram Singh was publicly hung in the Square in Hillah town in the early morning. We had to send his Company, " A ", to witness his execution.

On the 27th, Arrah Day was celebrated in the Gurdwara, and on the 28th, sports on a large scale were held to which the whole garrison were invited. The Gymnastic Squad, a feature of the Regiment for many years, was revived during the summer, and gave an excellent display.

On the 29th Captain J. A. Finlay left by order to join the 126th Baluchistan Infantry who were proceeding to Kurdistan, and Lieut. R. N. Moore was posted to the 113th Infantry, who were under orders for the same destination.

August.

On the 1st the 113th Infantry left by train for Baghdad *en route* for Kurdistan.

On the 2nd " D " Company—Captain A. L. Butcher with Lieut. R. V. Fox—marched at 17.30 hours for Tuarij, to support the Political Officer, Kerbela, in rounding up six bad and disloyal characters on the 4th.

They reached Tuarij after a very hot march on the early morning of the 3rd, and rested for the day in two " caravanserais."

At 17.00 hours they moved quietly off to the prearranged " Position of Assembly " one-and-a-half miles north of Tuarij and bivouacked for the night.

At 04.30 hours on the 4th Captain Butcher with fifty rifles, two Lewis guns and a stock of bombs, left in Ford vans for the Turkish hospital half-a-mile south of Kerbela to await and take over six political prisoners from the Assistant Political Officer, Kerbela, and if necessary to assist this Officer in their arrest. The rendezvous was fixed for 06.00 hours. Four of the prisoners gave themselves up easily, but two gave trouble and things looked doubtful for some time. However, at 10.30 hours, the arrest of all being effected, they were handed over to our detachment, who at once proceeded to Hillah in the Ford vans, arriving at 15.00 hours. The day was the hottest and dustiest of the year. The prisoners were lodged in our quarter guard, and left under our escort for Baghdad by the night train.

Lieut. R. V. Fox and the remainder of "D" Company made a night march, and arrived at Hillah on the early morning of the 5th.

The remainder of the month passed quite uneventfully in the usual training and games. The weather was very hot, but the health and the cheeriness of the men remained excellent.

On the 13th, the Band and Drums under Bandmaster H. *September.* Rodgers, arrived—strength: forty-nine Indian Other Ranks. The Band was remarkably good, and the Drums gave their first public performance of playing "Retreat" on the 17th.

For months past the men had been buying muzzle-loading single-barrel guns from Arabs for shikar purposes. On the 15th, a follower was shooting doves, when the gun burst and blew off part of his hand. The hasty disposal of these guns quickly followed this accident.

The first leave party to India arrived in driblets between the 24th and the end of the month.

On the 30th, very sudden orders arrived for the Regiment to proceed at once to Baghdad to relieve the 1/6th Gurkhas, who were guarding Prisoners-of-war Labour Corps.

At noon on the 1st, the sudden order was received that the *October.* Regiment would entrain at 08.00 hours on the 2nd. We handed in our tents to Ordnance, and got our kits down to the station by 17.00 hours. The men fed in the dismantled camp, and the Regiment marched to the station at 20.00 hours and bivouacked there.

"D" Company completed their musketry in the afternoon and the results of the whole Regiment during the summer were so good that they are given here.

Company	Marksmen	1st Class	2nd Class	3rd Class	Total
"B"	12	100	44	2	158
"A"	25	130	49	1	205
"C"	17	64	34	—	115
"D"	35	110	23	—	168
Grand Total	89	404	150	3	646

On the 2nd, we loaded up and entrained and left Hillah at 09.30 hours, arriving at Baghdad South at 12.30 hours, where we were met by the General Officer Commanding 17th Division and staff, when it was learnt that the Regiment was to be split up into three detachments for the guarding of prisoners-of-war, so the companies were distributed as follows :—

Headquarters and " C " Company   Hinaidi L.B.
" A " Company   ..   ..   Hinaidi Grove.
" B " and " D " Companies   ..   Daurah.

The day was very hot and close, and by dint of very hard work on the part of the men, owing to shortage of transport, the Regiment got loaded and embarked at 17.30 hours in three steamers, arriving at their destinations and taking over from the 1/6th Gurkhas before midnight in all cases.

We were looking after some nine labour battalions of prisoners-of-war (about 10,000 men) and duties for the men in all camps were very severe.

Capt. J. B. Mudge, R.A.M.C., left us for demobilization on the 4th, and Capt. J. B. D. Galbraith, R.A.M.C., replaced him on the 7th.

On the 10th we received orders to send one company to Mahmudiyah at short notice to guard prisoners-of-war working on a canal, which imposed a further strain on our duties. On the evening of this day the second leave party of the year proceeded to India—strength : one Indian Officer, nine Indian

Other Ranks and four followers, and on the 11th our first draft for months joined from India—three Indian Officers, one Havildar (from leave), 114 Indian Other Ranks. They were badly needed owing to the severe duties.

On the 13th, " C " Company, Capt. A. L. Butcher, left for Mahmudiyah by the midnight train, and took over a labour corps working in the Desert some miles out the next day.

On the 19th, a sentry of " A " Company shot a Turkish prisoner-of-war, who jumped the barbed wire of his enclosure. This news got round, and our men had very little trouble for the future.

On the 21st, Capt. J. A. Finlay rejoined the Regiment from duty with the 126th Baluchistan Infantry in Kurdistan, and on the 27th, Lieut. F. T. Birdwood, 36th Sikhs, joined on attachment to the Regiment.

On the 31st, another leave party of fifty-five Other Ranks left on leave to India under Jemadar Bishan Singh II.

CHAPTER VII

NOVEMBER 1ST, 1919—DECEMBER 31ST, 1919
INCLUDING OPERATIONS IN KURDISTAN.

November. ON November 5th, the General Officer Commanding the 17th Division came into our camp, and gave us the information that the Regiment was to proceed north very shortly to take part in an expedition into Kurdistan, where trouble had recurred in spite of various expeditions during the summer.

The necessary warm clothing was drawn from Ordnance, the relief of all our detachments was effected, and warm clothing issued by the 9th.

On the 10th, the Band and Drums marched us down to a steamer and barges at Hunaidi. They then proceeded to 17th Division Headquarters, where they stayed during the absence of the regiment. We embarked, disembarked at the advanced base, and having entrained, left Baghdad by rail in the evening for Shergat. The Officers with the Regiment were :—

Brevet Lieut.-Colonel R. H. Anderson, Commanding.
Captain A. C. Curtis, M.C., Adjutant.
Lieut. C. A. Phillips, Quartermaster.
Capt. F. T. Birdwood, 36th Sikhs, " A " Company.
Capt. J. A. Finlay, " B " Company.
Capt. A. L. Butcher, " C " Company.
Lieut. R. V. Fox, " D " Company.
Lieut. H. St. O. Will, Transport Officer.
Capt. J. B. D. Galbraith, R.A.M.C., Medical Officer.

On the 11th, we found ourselves passing Jift, Shuramiyah and all the country we had marched and fought over in October, 1918, and all ranks had plenty to interest them. We arrived at Shergat before dark, detrained and bivouacked near the railway station. Our transport for the march to Mosul was drawn overnight.

Marching late we arrived at Hadraniyah (eight miles) on the 12th. The short march gave the young soldiers of the last draft the chance of settling down, as the days were still hot.

On the 13th, we reached Qaiyarah (thirteen miles). Here were situated some old German naphtha works, partially destroyed by the Turks in 1918, and at this time being worked by us. The whole atmosphere was tainted with sulphuretted hydrogen, and highly polished buttons tarnished in a very short time.

On the 14th, we reached Hadra (thirteen miles), and on the 15th Hammam Ali (eighteen miles). This place contained a number of hot sulphur springs.

On the 16th, we entered Mosul (17 miles), a very picturesque city, at noon. The men marched in with a fine swing, and greeted the General Officer Commanding 18th Division, who came to meet the Regiment, with round after round of "fatehs."

The men were billetted in the Turkish barracks, and the mess and Officers in a house near by which had electric light.

On the 17th and 18th, we halted in Mosul. The first day was spent in preparations, and the men took serge into wear. This had been carried on the march up. It was also decided by the Column Commander that only one Lewis gun per platoon was to be taken on. A small escort for a regimental dump was therefore left in Mosul.

On the 18th, the Army Commander, Major-General Sir G. F. MacMunn, K.C.B., K.C.S.I. D.S.O., inspected the Regiment in the Barrack Square at noon, and was very complimentary on their appearance.

The Force had been moving towards Aqra in Echelons, and on the 19th, Headquarters and the left wing marched at 07.00 hours to the starting point near the ruins of Nineveh, and picked up the following units to join Stapleton's Column at the advanced base near Aqra.

    26th Jacob's Mountain Battery.
    No. 13 Wireless Section.
    One Section No. 238 Machine Gun Company.
    Headquarters Stapleton's Column.

After a long trying march of eighteen miles with no water *en route*, the Echelon bivouacked one mile short of Bir Hallan. On the 20th, Headquarters and left wing and Echelon arrived at Badaresh (sixteen miles).

The right wing under Capt. F. T. Birdwood escorted one section 4.5 howitzers and an ordnance dump to Bir Hallan.

On the 21st, the Headquarters and left wing and Echelon arrived at the Advanced Base, Jujar (15 miles), and very soon got settled in.

The right wing and attached Echelon made Badaresh, and marched into Jujar on the 22nd. The advanced base was situated at this place on a pleasant open plateau about ten miles from Aqra. Rain had fallen and the weather was cold and clear.

Lieut.-Col. F. H. Stapleton, C.M.G., Oxfordshire and Buckinghamshire Light Infantry, arrived from Mosul by car the same day, and Stapleton's Column was formed.

Composition of Force.

Column Headquarters and Signal Section.
One Troop 11th Lancers.
Two Sections No. 6 Company 1st Sappers and Miners.
26th Jacob's Mountain Battery.
1/3rd Gurkha Rifles.
1/10th Gurkha Rifles.
45th Rattray's Sikhs.
One Section No. 258 Machine Gun Company.
No. 13 Wireless Section.
Supply Section and Column.
Two Sections 38th Combined Field Ambulance.

Line of Communication Troops.

Two Squadrons 11th Lancers (less one Troop).
One Section C/336th Brigade, Royal Field Artillery (eighteen pounders).
One Section D/336th Brigade, Royal Field Artillery (4.5 howitzers).
One Company 1/39th Garwhal Rifles.
Detachment Light Armoured Motor Battery.
Detachment No. 119 Casualty Clearing Station.

COUNTRY ROUND AKRA.

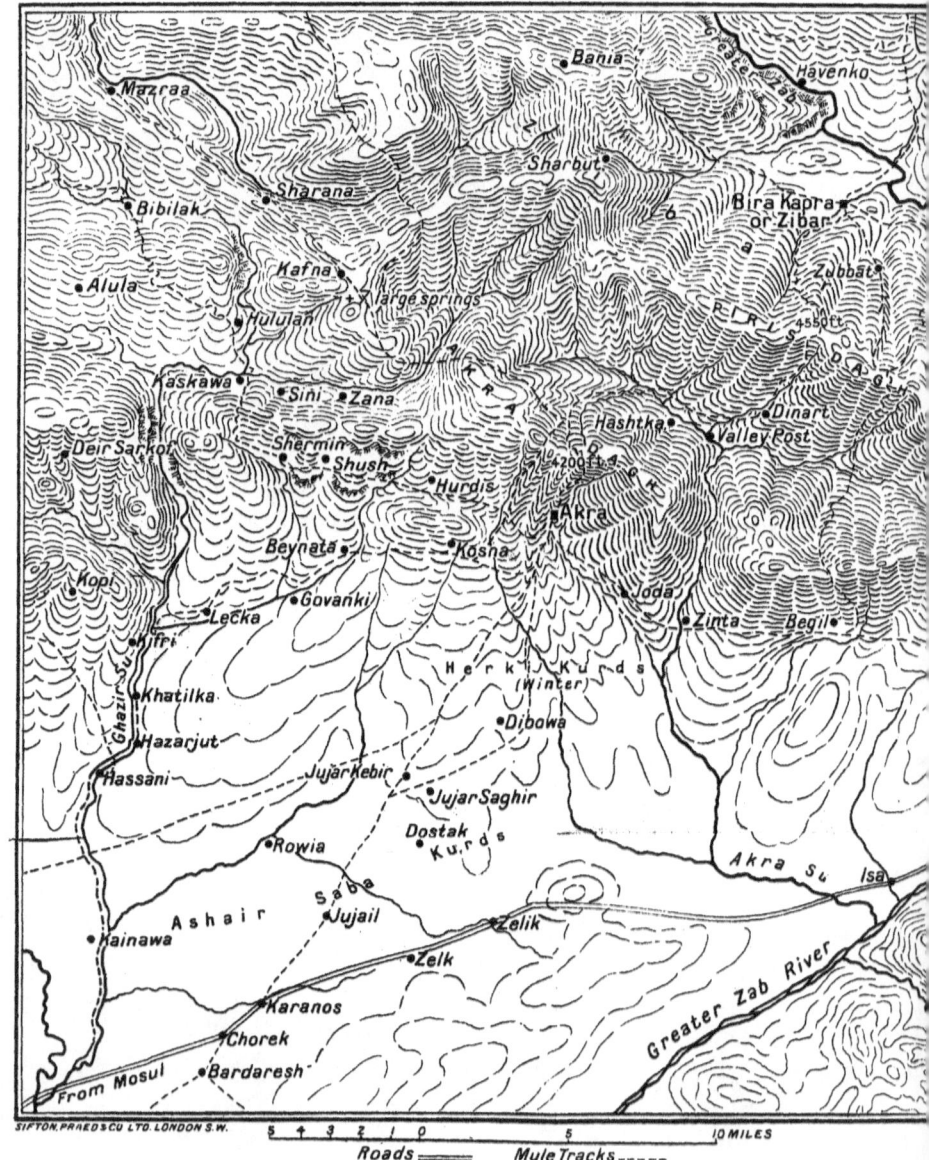

HISTORY OF THE 45TH RATTRAY'S SIKHS 157

Stapleton's Column was formed to carry out punitive operations against the Kurdish tribes implicated in the murders of Mr. Bill, I.C.S., and Capt. Scott, Political Officers, at the end of October, and also against those who had joined in the subsequent rising in the Aqra district.

The area concerned was the mountainous country N.E. of Aqra, the largest village of which was Bira Kapra, and also some of the villages across the Greater Zab north of this place. *Map No. 10.*

On the 23rd, the whole force halted at Jujar, final preparations were made, and the transport was organized from draught into pack. The Regiment learnt on this day that it was to be employed on forward line of communication work, with one Company near Aqra, one on the summit of the Aqra Dagh, where the track passed over, and Headquarters and two Companies in the valley between the Aqra and Piris Daghs.

This news was received with great regret by all ranks, but was slightly softened by the additional news that the 45th would carry out the attack on the Dagh on the 25th.

Dagh was the local name for a range of mountains.

The Column marched from Jujar to a camp about one mile south of Aqra. "A" Company did left flank guard and "B" Company rear guard to the column, which accomplished the march without incident. Aqra was a most picturesque town consisting of stone houses built in tiers up the hillside with gardens interspersed here and there, and with the Dagh standing grim and formidable-looking behind it. *November 24th.* *See Panorama sketch of Aqra.*

The Column Commander held a conference of Commanding Officers before sunset on a small hill which gave an extensive view, and the details of the attack were discussed and settled.

COLUMN ORDERS.

Column orders entrusted the conduct of the attack to the 45th who were to develop the attack from the line of North East Edge of Aqra town at 08.30 hours. *November 25th. The Attack on the Dagh.*

The 1/10th Gurkha Rifles were to be at a point near by at 08.00 hours in readiness to support the attack if necessary.

The artillery were to support the attack as follows:—

158 HISTORY OF THE 45TH RATTRAY'S SIKHS

One section eighteen pounders one section 4.5 howitzers and 26th Mountain Battery from positions S.E. of Aqra.

Registering on the summit of the Pass and its vicinity, was to commence at 07.30 hours, and a bombardment at 08.15 hours.

Two sections Sappers and Miners were to follow the 45th closely, and to improve the track as much as possible for pack transport. [This track turned out to be more of a rocky staircase, with, in many places, overhanging boulders, and proved to be a very tough proposition for such a small body of Sappers.]

Two aeroplanes, based on Mosul, were to co-operate if the weather proved favourable.

THE 45TH ATTACK.

See Panorama.

In dull cloudy weather the Regiment (less " D " Company) paraded at 07.00 hours, with all kits ready to be loaded up by baggage guards. "D" Company—Lieut. R. V. Fox—who were detailed to hold the defensive post on the advanced line of communication one mile south of Aqra town, moved out, less camp guards, at 06.00 hours with orders to occupy a very precipitous and isolated hill that covered our right flank, and from which fire at about 1,000 yards range could be brought to bear on the summit of the Pass itself.

After a very stiff climb, in which men had to help each other up in many places, " D " Company accomplished their task in fine style, and were in full possession of this hill by 08.45 hours.

The remainder of the Regiment marched at 07.30 hours, with " C " Company and one Sub-Section Machine Gun Company as Advanced Guard. The Advanced Guard occupied and held Yellow Hill and Point 3100 in succession, when Headquarters and " A " and " B " Companies pushed through the town of Aqra, and went straight up the Dagh to their objectives, " A " Company on the right, covered by the fire of the Artillery.

These two companies scaled this steep mountain side with such magnificent dash and speed, that they were in full occupation of the Dagh by 09.30 hours (two hours after leaving bivouac), when " C " Company joined them, and " D " Company returned to Aqra.

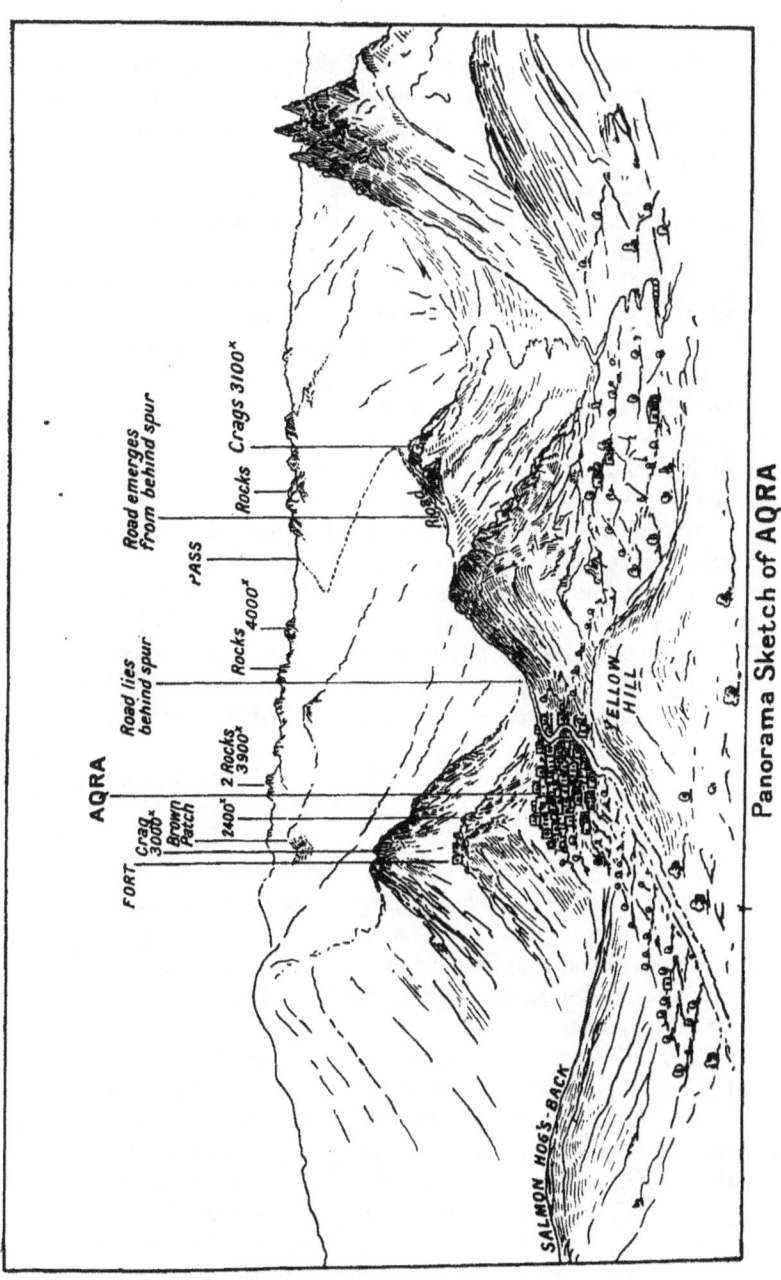

Panorama Sketch of AQRA

There was no opposition, and if there were any Kurds on the Dagh at the commencement of the attack, they did not appreciate the accurate fire of the guns, and made good their retreat.

The Regiment's quick occupation of the Pass was highly commended by the Column Commander as he passed through later in the day.

It began to rain during the attack, and continued in bursts all day, so there was no co-operation by aeroplanes.

Directly the Regiment's message, that the Dagh was occupied, was received by Column Headquarters, the 1/10th Gurkha Rifles marched up by the track, and at about 11.00 hours passed through us down towards the deserted village of Hashtka, the next bivouac, followed by the remainder of the Force and the transport.

The track was so bad, and the Sappers were able to make so little impression on it in so short a time that by 17.00 hours no second line transport whatever had got through. Under column orders this transport was therefore parked above Aqra town under the escort of their baggage guards and the rear guard. The 45th were ordered to occupy the Dagh for the night, and until all the transport had got through the next day.

It was raining and sleeting all night, and the cold on the exposed Pass was intense, in spite of great coats and waterproof capes.

The stream of second line transport commenced to move at 07.00 hours, and the last mule got over at 16.00 hours.

November 26th.

"C" Company—Captain A. L. Butcher—took up their defensive post on the summit of the Pass during the day, and spare sections assisted them to build up their perimeter and pitch their tents.

At 17.00 hours Headquarters, "A" and "B" Companies left the Dagh, and arrived in bivouac at Hashtka at dusk, where they found the Column in a perimeter camp in very wooded country. So far no opposition had been met with, though during the night a bomb had exploded in a Gurkha picquet, killing and wounding eight or nine men.

November 27th.

The Regiment (less two companies) marched at 07.00 hours as advanced guard and picqueting troops to the Column;

the weather was very misty. When they reached the vicinity of Valley Post they left the Column, and were hard at work all day building a perimeter camp. The camp was in ideal scenery, but was commanded on the western side by some thickly wooded hills at 800 yards. Unlimited firewood was obtainable from the oak forests, and clear mountain streams provided excellent water.

The remainder of the Column marched on with a fresh advanced guard, and bivouacked south of the Piris Dagh taking and occupying the Piris Dagh the same day. The only opposition they met with were five or six shots fired at long range.

Our day was spent in improving the defences of our perimeter, and at the end of the day our perimeter was very secure. *November 28th.*

Stapleton's Column had laid down a ground line from Aqra, for which we were responsible up to the foot of the Piris Dagh and back to Aqra. This was continually being cut, generally at dusk, and it entailed sending out a couple of men very often and at all times.

Our three posts were picqueting daily, and in Valley Post we were responsible to half way with "C" Company on the Dagh, and to the foot of the Piris Dagh in the other direction. At night we seldom had less than 800 mules within the perimeter.

The Column occupied Bira Kapra, leaving a permanent picquet of one company on the Piris Dagh.

For the next six days the Column burnt all villages implicated in the murders of the Political Officers, including Birsan and others, which entailed the crossing of the Greater Zab on rafts. The R.A.F. assisted with a good deal of bombing, but the enemy had evacuated the area of operations, and so probably suffered only material damage. *November 29th. December 4th.*

The G.O.C. 18th Division rode up to see the country, and stayed with us for two nights on his way up and down.

On the 4th a small party was sent out to a village five miles north of our post with the Armenian Interpreter. They found only old men, women and children in the village, but brought in three rifles and some twenty-five snider rounds. On the evening of the 4th we got orders to go out and meet the Column returning on the 5th.

December 5th.

So "A" Company—Captain F. T. Birdwood—went out to the Piris Dagh for the last time, and did rear guard to the Column coming in, reaching camp at dusk. There was no following up by the enemy.

"B" Company—Captain J. A. Finlay—marched at noon for Jujar, where they were to take over from the Company 1/39th Garwhal Rifles, who were to garrison Aqra during the winter.

December 6th.

The Column marched at 06.30 hours for Aqra leaving one section 26th Jacob's Mountain Battery, Headquarters and "A" Company 45th Sikhs, and two companies 1/10th Gurkha Rifles as rear guard under Brevet Lieut.-Colonel R. H. Anderson.

The enemy made no attempt whatever to follow up, and the rear guard reached the summit of the Aqra Dagh about 13.00 hours.

The Gurkhas and section Mountain Battery moved on into Aqra, and Headquarters and "A" and "C" Companies remained in observation for another hour, when they marched into the old camp south of Aqra. There was severe rain and a good deal of mist before we left the Pass.

December 7th.

The Column marched into the Advanced Base at Jujar, and ceased to exist on arrival at that place. The following orders of the day were issued to the Column :—

Order of the Day

"Stapleton's Column has completed its task, but before the troops have dispersed I want to say that with such good troops it was too easy, the regret being that we had such curs for enemies.

"None the less, however, are my thanks for, and appreciation of the way in which all ranks tackled the difficult country and conditions in spite of spells of bad weather and privations."

(*sd.*) F. H. STAPLETON, Lieut.-Colonel,
Commanding Stapleton's Column.

Order of the Day No. 2.

"The following telegram has been received from the G.O.C. 18th Division :—

' On return your Column to Advance Base I wish to congratulate you and the fine troops under your command on the complete success of the operations. Although the enemy did not stand, you have traversed his country and punished his leaders. The transport arrangements over very difficult country were excellent.' "

So ended our doings with Stapleton's Column, and we had entered a magnificent mountain and forest country very different from the plains of Lower Mesopotamia. The men were very cheery and ever so fit for they had been marching daily for a month.

The 8th was spent in Jujar, and on the 9th the Regiment marched with that fine Mountain Battery, the 26th, for Mosul, arriving on the 12th.

On the 13th we left Mosul, the 2nd Battalion 5th Fusiliers kindly sending their Band to march us out. Proceeding by the same stages as on the way up, and always marching in friendly rivalry with the 26th Mountain Battery, we arrived at Shargat on the 17th, where the Regiment entrained for Baghdad the same night, arriving there on the afternoon of the 18th.

On the 19th we embarked on a river steamer and disembarked at Hunaidi, when the Band and Drums marched us into the same camp as we had left on November 10th.

We got comfortably into camp before the rains broke and spent a pleasant enough Christmas. A good deal of hockey was played, and we entered for some sports got up by the Young Men's Christian Association, which were much interfered with by rain.

We learnt that the 52nd Infantry Brigade, which we had rejoined, was to proceed early in the New Year to the Kirkuk area, and there was much speculation as to whether the Regiment would see India in 1920.

On Christmas Eve the following telegram was received from Colonel Stapleton : " The Chief has directed me to convey his thanks to you for the fine efforts of the Regiment on the recent operations."

The Band got a good many engagements during Christmas week, including two at the High Commissioner's.

CHAPTER VIII

JANUARY 1ST, 1920—JUNE 30TH, 1920

January. THE Regiment commenced the New Year with a strength of nine British Officers, fifteen Indian Officers, and 746 Indian Other Ranks.

On the 2nd Nos. 5 and 6 Platoons left by rail for Baqubah to take over guards on the huge Armenian refugees' camp at that place.

On the 3rd Captain J. B. D. Galbraith, R.A.M.C., left for England on demobilization.

Map No. 11. On the 4th Captain J. A. Finlay left for Qaraghan by rail with Nos. 7, 8, and 14 Platoons. It was known now that our destination would shortly be somewhere in the Kirkuk area.

On the 6th the finals of the Young Men's Christian Association Sports took place. They had been postponed from Christmas week owing to continual rain.

We won most of the events, the chief of which were the relay race, the one mile and the tug-of-war, and came out first for the Championship Cup with twenty-eight points to the next regiment's twenty.

We also won the cup given for the tug-of-war.

There was much rain during the month, and it was extremely cold, but we got a good deal of hockey against various teams, including two very good games against the Officers of Baghdad.

2/Lieut. A. Paterson joined the Regiment from the depot on the 16th.

On the 21st we got definite orders that our destination was to be Kingerbah (railhead) with detachments on the road to Kirkuk.

On the 24th Lieut.-Colonel D. A. D. McVean, D.S.O.,

rejoined from leave in the United Kingdom, and resumed command vice Brevet Lieut.-Colonel R. H. Anderson.

On the 25th Nos. 7 and 8 Platoons under Lieut. G. M. Worden, rejoined the Regiment from duty at Baqubah, and on the 26th we received a very welcome draft of 180 Indian Other Ranks from the depot.

On the 1st a service was held in the Gurdwara in memory of all ranks who fell in the attack on the River Hai on this day in 1917. *February.*

On the 2nd, Headquarters, the Band and Drums and "A" Company, also half of the 1st and 2nd line transport left by rail for the new destination, Kingerbah, and arrived there on the 3rd in bitterly cold weather.

"B," "C," and "D" Companies (less three platoons) and the remainder of the transport under Captain A. L. Butcher, entrained at Baghdad South Railway Station on the evening of the 3rd, and left for Kingerbah.

Brevet Lieut.-Colonel R. H. Anderson left by rail for Kut the same evening, also Captain F. T. Birdwood. The former to proceed on five months' leave to the United Kingdom, and the latter to rejoin the 36th Sikhs in India.

Owing to worn-out engines, and frequent breakdowns, the parties who left Baghdad on the 3rd did not arrive at Kingerbah until after dark on the 4th. The Regiment first entered the rest camp, to stay there until the 94th Infantry left for Kirkuk.

The camp at Kingerbah was very scattered, and contained besides the 94th (less detachments) and ourselves, one company Sappers and Miners, a Mechanical Transport Company, a Labour Corps, hospital and large supply and ordnance dumps.

On this date No. 6 Platoon took over Sallahiyah Post from the 94th Infantry. This post guarded an important bridge.

Nos. 7 and 8 Platoons remained at Qaraghan, and No. 14 was situated at Mirjana. These three platoons under Captain J. A. Finlay, had come on in advance of the Regiment to Qaraghan on January 4th.

The Persian mountains, covered with snow, were plainly visible from our camp, and a little snow actually fell in camp on the 5th.

The country we were now in was very bare and stony, and a line of bare and stony hills to the north reminded those who had served there of the Waziristan Frontier.

On the 5th Nos. 1 and 2 Platoons proceeded to Tuz under the command of Lieut. H. St. C. O. Will. Strength: two Indian Officers, 111 Indian Other Ranks.

On the 6th No. 13 Platoon proceeded to Tazah under Lieut. G. M. Worden. Strength: forty Indian Other Ranks.

On the 9th a hockey ground and running track was cleared of stones, and much hockey, running, and tug-of-war practice for the forthcoming Baghdad Sports took place for the next month.

On the 12th and 13th snow fell in camp for two hours on each day, and a bitter cold wind made it intensely cold.

On the 14th Nos. 3 and 4 Platoons marched to take over Tauk Post from the 94th Infantry. Strength: one Indian Officer, 101 Indian Other Ranks.

At Tuz No. 2134 Sepoy Sharm Singh was accidentally killed by a rifle by another Sepoy in " A " Company.

A summary general court martial subsequently awarded this man a nominal punishment.

We also moved this day into the camp recently vacated by the 94th Infantry, who had moved up to Kirkuk. Several days were spent in clearing it up, dressing tents, etc.

On the 18th the first leave party of the year, ninety-one Indian Other Ranks, left for India full of good cheer.

The Officers got one or two good shoots in the neighbourhood during the month. On the 22nd a party of guns with the G.O.C. 17th Division, got 47 birds, mostly duck and teal.

On the 24th Lieut. C. A. Phillips, Lieut. H. St. C. O. Will, and the hockey team left for Kirkuk to play off the Brigade ties, and Captain A. C. Curtis and the running teams left for Baghdad by train for the eliminating tests which were to take place on the 26th, weather permitting. Very heavy rain on the 25th postponed the first hockey match against the 113th Infantry until the 27th, and the running heats till the 29th.

The camp was, as usual, transformed into a sea of mud.

On the 27th our team defeated the 113th Infantry team by five goals to two, having things all their own way in the second half.

HISTORY OF THE 45TH RATTRAY'S SIKHS 167

On the 29th they defeated the 94th Infantry by six goals to two, and thus qualified to play at Baghdad for the remainder of the tournament.

The strength and distribution of the Regiment on the 1st *March* was as follows :—

	B.O.'s	I.O.'s	I.O.R.'s	
Kingerbah	..	5	9	451	
Qaraghan (and Mirjana)	..	1	2	88	Nos. 7, 8, 14 Platoons.
Sallahiyah ..	..	–	1	34	No. 6 Platoon.
Tuz	..	2	1	107	Nos. 1 and 2 Platoons.
Tauk	..	1	2	103	Nos. 3 and 4 Platoons.
Tazah	..	1	–	42	No. 13 Platoon.
With 9th Labour Corps	..	–	–	11	
On Command	..	–	–	8	
Total	..	10	15	844	

The heats at Baghdad were run off on the 1st, and our men won every heat in the 100 yards, quarter-mile, half-mile, one mile, long jump, and relay race (eight in the team).

On the 2nd our tug-of-war team beat the 49th Mountain Battery team easily. They were passing through *en route* to Kirkuk.

The hockey team left for Baghdad by train in heavy rain on the 4th, and played the 2/9th Delhi Regiment, and won very easily by thirteen goals to one.

The Athletic Sports in connection with the "Baghdad Commemoration Week" took place on the 13th with the following results :—

100 *Yards*.	1. Jemadar Harnam Singh, I.O.M.
	2. No. 770 Sepoy Jaswant Singh.
	3. 114th Mahrattas.
440 *Yards*.	1. No. 770 Sepoy Jaswant Singh.
	2. Jemadar Harnam Singh, I.O.M.
	3. No. 2143 Sepoy Sucha Singh.
Half-Mile.	1. No. 1042 Naick Indar Singh.
	2. No. 1357 Sepoy Wariam Singh.
	3. No. 2009 Sepoy Buta Singh.

One Mile.   1. No. 3324 Sepoy Wariam Singh.
                2. No. 1179 Sepoy Kishan Singh.
                3. No. 2090 Sepoy Lal Singh.
Long Jump.   1. No. 770 Sepoy Jaswant Singh.
                2. No. 2740 Sepoy Arjan Singh.
                3. Guides Cavalry.
Relay Race.   1. 45th Sikhs.

Thus, with the exception of the high jump, we practically swept the board.

On the 14th we played our second round in the hockey tournament, against the 31st Signal Company, and won by two goals to one after a close game. We thus entered the semi-finals.

This game took place on the 15th against the 13th Rajputs. The Regiment were the better side, and dominated the game throughout. We finally won by five goals to love.

The finals were played on the 17th instant against the 122nd Rajputana Infantry, the winners of the tournament in 1918 and 1919. Extracts from the *Baghdad Times* described the game in the following terms:—

"The 122nd won the toss, and immediately started pressing. The Sikhs did not seem to settle down to their usual game, and lost both opportunities and ground through excitement and injudicious hitting. Lieut. Will played the best game we have seen him play, stopping several dangerous attacks on the part of the 122nd forwards. After some twenty minutes play, the 122nd scored a beautiful goal—the Sikhs were still not playing their best. Havildar Bagga Singh did several good runs, but the inside forwards could never get past O'Leary and Levingstone. Half-time came with the 122nd leading one goal to nil.

The second half provided some very fast even hockey. Both goals had one or two narrow escapes. The 122nd missed what should have been a certainty by giving sticks. Halfway through the second half a penalty bully was given close to the Sikhs' goal line, and O'Leary scored without difficulty. After this, for the first time, the Sikhs really got going. Their forwards played with great dash and were unlucky not to score. Jemadar Sundar Singh did a fine run, but had the misfortune to kick the ball just outside the circle. Another movement was spoiled by Sher Singh being offside. In spite of this, the defence was taxed to its utmost, and forced to concede several corners. Final score :—

    122nd Rajputana Infantry .. 2 goals.
    45th Rattray's Sikhs .. .. Nil.

The 122nd played better together as a team, and their combination at times was of a very high standard. The Sikhs were the faster team but lacked cohesion; there was too much individual effort, and too much indiscriminate hard hitting."

The 45th team was : *Goal*, Lieut. R. V. Fox ; *Backs*, Lieut. H. St.-C. O. Will and No. 249 Naick Jiwan Singh ; *Half-Backs*, Lieut. C. A. Phillips, No. 4908 Naick Bhagat Singh and No. 424 Sepoy Mahain Singh ; *Forwards*, No. 77 Havildar Bagga Singh, No. 520 Naick Lal Singh, Jemadars Surain Singh and Sundar Singh, and No. 143 Lance Naick Sher Singh.

Altogether the Regiment did well in the " Commemoration Week," winning the sports almost outright and being the " runners up " at hockey.

The remainder of the month passed uneventfully. A range was made at Kingerbah. On the 31st two sections of No. 14 Platoon proceeded to Tazah, to relieve a platoon of the 94th who were still there.

April. With the advent of April the weather became warmer, and the dust nuisance commenced. Musketry was carried out during the month, and as much training as possible.

On the 5th our detachment at Sallahiyah was relieved by Arab levies, and on the 10th Captain J. A. Finlay arrived from Qaraghan with Nos. 7, 8, and 14 Platoons.

On the 13th one Indian Officer and two sections of No. 14 Platoon proceeded to Tazah, which brought the garrison of that place to a strength of two platoons.

On the 18th the Commander-in-Chief, Lieut.-General Sir Aylmer Haldane, K.C.B., K.C.M.G., D.S.O., spent a day in Kingerbah, and met and conversed with the Indian Officers.

There were several bad thunderstorms during the month, and on the 19th a very wild one with much hail and rain. The lightning was terrific and killed four mules of the Sapper and Miner Company, camped about 100 yards from our camp.

On the 23rd Major-General G. A. Leslie and staff stayed on their way through to Kirkuk, and the Army Commander passed through on his way to Baghdad.

May.   From the 1st the name Kingerbah was changed to Kingarban. The Commanding Officer proceeded to Baghdad to raise the question of more leave for the men. The Regiment had now been on service over four years.

On the 5th a wire was received from Basra announcing the arrival there of Subadar Nidhan Singh and 101 Indian Other Ranks. This was a great surprise, as no word of their coming had been received from the depot.

This very welcome draft joined the Regiment on May 10th, having left the depot at Multan on April 21st.

During the middle of the month a succession of the wildest dust storms, which played much havoc with tents, and also with the gardens recently planted, was encountered.

On the 19th a new general routine order was published regarding leave for the Indian Ranks. The limitation of 10 per cent. of establishment was removed, and the new rule laid down that 600 effective rifles per battalion were to be kept up. This order caused great rejoicing.

By the end of the month the men had built a very fine Gurdwara with a thatched roof of reeds.

June.   On the 3rd the Regiment paraded and fired a *Feu-de-joie* in honour of His Majesty the King's birthday. This was the first time after a lapse of seven years owing to the Great War.

On the 6th another, and as it turned out owing to subsequent events the last, leave party left by train for Baghdad and India. Subadar-Major Sundar Singh, I.O.M., Sardar Bahadur Subadar Labh Singh, M.C., and 168 Indian Other Ranks went with it. Also two Indian Other Ranks for pension, and two Indian Other Ranks for discharge.

On the 15th the General Officer Commanding the 52nd Infantry Brigade arrived to discuss internal security measures, and on the 16th the Commanding Officer proceeded by car with him to inspect our detachments at Tuz, Tauk and Tazah, returning to Kingarban on the 18th.

On this date a telegram was received that the 45th Sikhs were to concentrate at Kingarban as soon as possible.

This wire was followed by another on the morning of the 19th that two companies were to be ready to proceed to Baghdad at eighteen hours' warning. About 17.00 hours yet another wire was received giving orders that two companies would leave for Baghdad at once, and that the remainder of the Regiment would follow as soon as truckage was available.

"B" and "C" Companies were warned to proceed.

The Tazah detachment marched to Tauk to-day. The Regiment was to be relieved by the 94th Infantry from Kirkuk.

On the 20th "B" and "C" Companies left by train for Baghdad at 20.00 hours under Captain A. L. Butcher, M.C.

We learnt that the Regiment was being sent to Baghdad because the situation there had been and was somewhat critical. The local Arabs, thinking that the British ought to clear out of Mesopotamia, had organized meetings, etc., and there was considerable unrest prevalent in the city. A proclamation was distributed to-day telling them that we did not mean to leave Mesopotamia at this juncture.

Headquarters, "A" and "B" Companies (less two platoons "A" Company left in Kingarban as a temporary measure) left in two trains on the evening of the 21st and arrived at Baghdad South about noon. The heat was very great after Baqubah, and one goat out of the men's herd of 300 and all but two of the mess fowls died of heat.

We took over a camp at Hinaidi from the 99th Infantry just opposite our old camp of the previous winter, and this regiment left for Hillah the same evening.

On the 23rd some goats strayed from the improvised pen: three men were sent after them, and the Arabs fired some rounds at them, to which our men replied. No damage was done and the goats were recovered. Firing in Baghdad showed that events were not normal.

On the 30th, Subader Pertab Singh, Jemadar Sadhu Singh and seventy-one Indian Other Ranks rejoined the Regiment from leave.

On July 2nd General Leslie and staff came into camp in the evening, and watched the Drums playing "Retreat."

From him we got the information about events down the Euphrates, which in a short time were going to test the Regiment very severely, but the Regiment was more than fully equal to this test, as coming events will show.

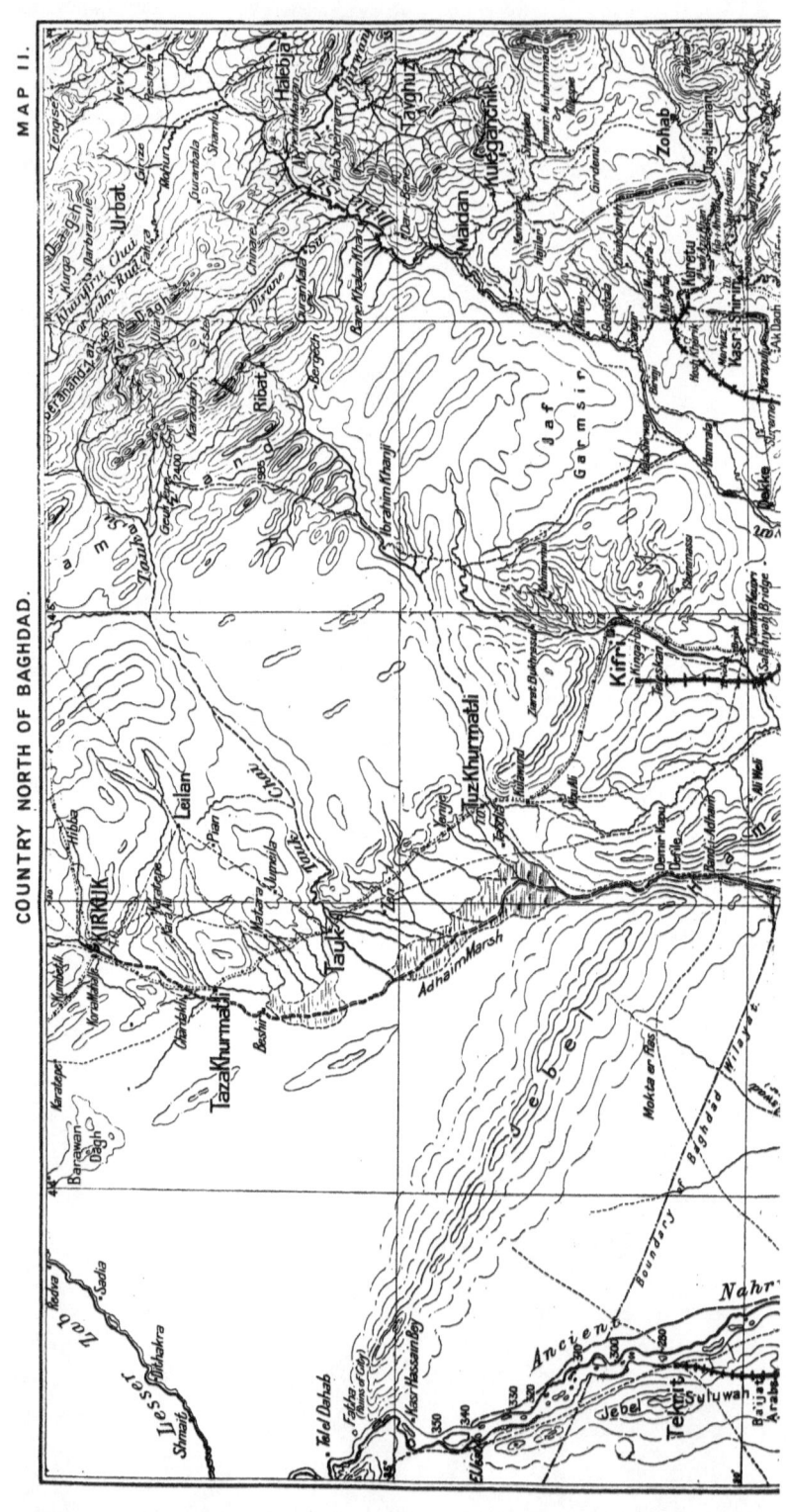

MAP II.

COUNTRY NORTH OF BAGHDAD.

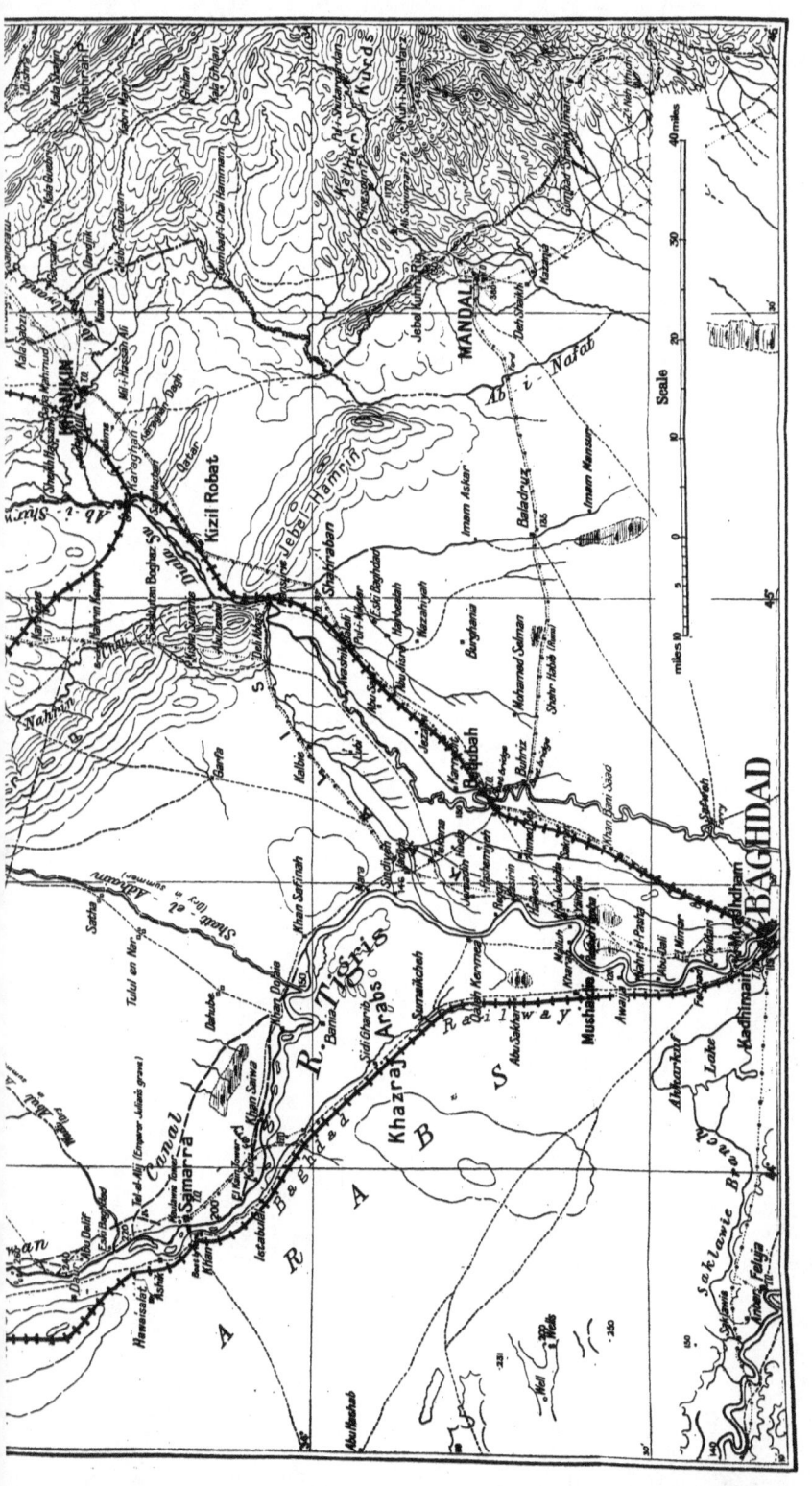

CHAPTER IX

THE ARAB INSURRECTION, JULY 2ND—SEPTEMBER 30TH, 1920

July 2nd. NEWS reached us that the Arabs were showing increasing signs of unrest in Baghdad, and we were all buoyed up with the hope that we should be sent to clear the Bazaar.

Later, information was received that the Arabs had broken out into open rebellion, cut the Baghdad-Basra railway line in two places in the vicinity of Samawah, and had attempted to destroy two railway bridges at that place, where they had been repulsed with loss by the detachment of the 114th Mahrattas stationed there.

We were informed that should the troops on the spot not be able to cope with the Arabs, we should be sent down to help to restore order and open up the railway.

July 3rd. The next morning saw the commencement of the Regiment's participation in the Arab insurrection.

Whilst on a manœuvre parade, and some three miles distant from camp a mounted orderly appeared from 17th Division Headquarters ordering Headquarters and two companies to proceed at once to Hillah.

The Regiment returned to camp Headquarters, "A" and "B" Companies packed kits, and entrained at Baghdad West railway station *en route* for Hillah at about 14.30 hours.

On arrival at Hillah about 20.00 hours the train was met by the General Officer Commanding 34th Infantry Brigade who explained to Lieut.-Colonel McVean that the situation was most obscure, the outstanding known facts being that the garrison of Rumaitha was closely invested, and was short of food and water, and that it was of the utmost importance to relieve it at once. Also that the railway line had been cut in several places between Diwaniyah and Rumaitha by the insurgents.

One company of the 99th Infantry had got through from Diwaniyah that day, but that the railway line was now cut.

Finally, that five platoons of the 99th Infantry and one section 45th Mountain Battery under the command of Major Townsend, R.A., had been ordered to establish a post as far ahead as possible between Diwaniyah and Rumaitha.

July 4th. After a rest for food and water the train moved on and arrived at Diwaniyah at 04.15 hours on July 4th, to find that the column under Major Townsend had not yet left that place.

Colonel McVean interviewed the Political Officer (Major Daly), but obtained little information of value from him, except that a small train-load of coolies attempting to repair the breach in the railway line ahead had been caught by the insurgents the previous day. The train was derailed, and most of the escort and all the coolies had been scuppered.

Major Daly emphasized the necessity of pushing on at once, and by showing a bold front, to attempt to stay the tribesmen.

Colonel McVean decided to move on that evening with the following force :—

One section 45th Mountain Battery.

Headquarters and two companies 45th Rattray's Sikhs.

Headquarters and five platoons 99th Infantry (Captain O. Masters).

This column proceeded by train at dusk, and arrived at Imam Hamzah, where a halt was called for the night.

A party of about 200 Arabs, mounted and on foot, were observed in the village and fired on by the mountain guns. The railway station was found to be looted and gutted, and several mutilated and naked corpses of railway coolies were lying about, the place having witnessed an engagement the previous day.

July 5th. The following day the Column proceeded slowly to the scene of the derailment, a construction train under Lieut. Clarke (Railways) having arrived during the night from Diwaniyah with repairing materials.

At this point the Hillah branch of the River Euphrates ran within some 400 yards of the railway line, so good water was obtainable and was most acceptable.

Here a halt was called, and the railway coolies commenced work making a diversion round the wrecked train, whilst a burying party was told off to bury the dead, who had been killed two days previously. All the corpses were mutilated.

Many Arabs congregated in the vicinity, but kept at a respectful distance, though they indulged in long range sniping.

Work ceased at dusk, and the Column went into a perimeter camp for the night.

During the night the Column was reinforced by one squadron 37th Lancers under Lieut. Finch.

In the meantime, the left wing, "C" Company (Captain A. L. Butcher) and "D" Company (Lieut. H. St.-C. O. Will) which had been left in Hinaidi camp, received orders from the 17th Division on the afternoon of July 4th to proceed at once to join Colonel McVean.

They entrained on the evening of that day, and proceeded to Hillah, where they were able to get no information whatever as to the movements of Colonel McVean's Column. The left wing, however, was ordered to proceed as soon as the men had fed, to join Colonel McVean wherever he should be found down the line.

The left wing left Hillah by train on the night of July 5th and proceeded to Diwaniyah. On arrival at that place Major Townsend, who had been left as Base Commandant there, informed Captain Butcher that as far as he knew Colonel McVean should be in Rumaitha by that time, but that he was not in communication with him, as the Arabs had cut all telegraph wires. He ordered the left wing to proceed at once to join Colonel McVean, which orders the two companies carried out, leaving Diwaniyah at 04.00 hours by train, to arrive at the derailment and report its arrival to Colonel McVean at 08.00 hours on the 6th.

McVean's Column, for such was its official designation from *July 6th.* now onwards, was now made up as follows :—

1 section 45th Mountain Battery.
1 squadron 37th Lancers.
45th Rattray's Sikhs.
Headquarters and five platoons 99th Infantry.
30 sabres of the Arab Levies.
Railway coolies (about fifty).

This Column marched at 10.00 hours taking with it one

train—the train in which the left wing arrived having been sent back to Diwaniyah—with the intention of marching straight through to Rumaitha.

"B" Company (Captain J. A. Finley) was acting as advanced guard and was heavily fired on from the left flank, but pushed on resolutely. The squadron 37th Lancers who were operating on the right flank were also heavily engaged, and had several horses hit and lost two Hotchkiss guns.

See Map 12. The advance continued till dusk, when a point E.Y.59.D. was reached, where water was plentiful.

Here bivouacs were erected, and the Column went into a perimeter camp for the night. Many hundreds of Arab horse and foot were observed on all flanks. The Arabs sniped continuously, but kept at a respectful distance.

The fire of the mountain guns inspired awe, if they actually did not do much damage.

Sniping died down at dusk, and we slept undisturbed that night. There was much singing, drumming and noise from all sides during the night which was kept up until the early hours of the morning, and which we interpreted to mean the gathering of the local tribes.

Our casualties this day were (all of the 45th Sikhs):—
1 Sepoy killed.
13 Non-Commissioned Officers and men wounded.
1 mule driver wounded.

July 7th. The first Battle of Rumaitha. Dawn brought a ration train from Diwaniyah, which was unloaded and sent back to that place. It returned shortly and reported that it had encountered a breach and had had four trucks derailed, which had to be left behind. These trucks were looted and burnt by the insurgents later.

The advance was resumed at 05.30 hours with "A" Company (Lieut. R. V. Fox) acting as advanced guard.

The Column had proceeded about one mile, when very heavy fire was opened on the advanced guard from a "Bund" which crossed the railway immediately across our line of advance.

"B" Company (Capt. J. A. Finlay) was sent up in support of "A," and "C" Company (Captain A. L. Butcher) was sent in on the right of "A." Company.

The assault took place under cover of the fire of the mountain guns, and reached a line some 200 yards from the enemy position. The enemy rifle fire was most intense and many casualties ensued, and it was at once realized that the " Bund " was occupied in great strength.

The last 200 yards of the assault was found to be boggy, which hampered our movements considerably, so that a check occurred, and a fire fight ensued.

The heat was most intense and the men, lying out as they were in the open, suffered considerably from want of water.

It was at this time that a Regimental Bhisti, Dhunni by name (village Lohar Majra, district Ludhiana), performed one of the most gallant actions on record.

He carried his " mashak " from the train, some 800 yards in rear, to the front line repeatedly over the open desert, taking no thought whatsoever for his personal safety, and gave each man lying in the firing line water to drink, though only 200 yards from the enemy, and under a very heavy fire the whole time. Although twice wounded, he carried on until at last a bullet dropped him dead. He laughed and joked with each man as he gave him water ; and his gallantry was most conspicuous.

He was recommended for an I.O.M. by the Regiment ; we heard this was altered to a V.C. by a higher formation, but this did not materialize.

It became very evident that the Column was greatly outnumbered, as many hundreds of Arabs could be seen on all flanks—it afterwards transpired that we were up against 9,000.

Lying in the open was the cause of rapidly increasing numbers of casualties, and the centre of the front line in moving back some 100 yards to the cover of a small irrigation cut, had the effect of bringing out of their position great numbers of Arabs, who charged down upon the front line moving back in extended order.

Colonel McVean at once sent in two platoons of the 99th Infantry (from reserve beside the train) in support.

The sight of these two advancing platoons had the desired effect upon the Arabs, who turned tail and fled back to their position, pursued by fire from the Column, the front line of which had reached the irrigation cut. Many Arabs dropped in the boggy ground in front of their position.

A fierce dust-storm now sprang up blowing from the enemy position into our faces, and of such intensity that it was impossible to see even ten yards ahead, so that firing became desultory, and the action died down to some extent.

At about 13.00 hours Colonel McVean summoned Captain Masters (Officer Commanding detachment 99th Infantry) and company commanders, and decided that a further advance was impossible owing to our heavy casualties—at this period well over 150, and representing about 20 per cent. of the total strength of the Column—and also to the enemy strength greatly exceeding ours. (Enemy strength was estimated at 3,000–5,000.)

Colonel McVean, therefore, very wisely decided to take advantage of the dust-storm, which still raged, break off the action, and slip away back to our former camp of two nights before, there to reorganize and await reinforcements.

Accordingly, dispositions having been made, the Column commenced to retire at 14.00 hours, all the wounded and the few dead that could be collected being put in the train, and had retired about a mile before the Arabs made the discovery. They then followed up closely, but rather half-heartedly, and the Column by fighting a strong rear-guard action reached its former camp at E.Y.49 by 17.00 hours.

Map No. 12. Here we discovered that a nullah running to the river had been blocked, so that drinking water was only obtainable from the river itself.

The Column went into a perimeter camp here and slept unmolested that night, somewhat depressed at having failed to carry out its object, and having had no time to bury its dead. Practically the whole train was used as a hospital for the wounded.

Our casualties this day were:—

Killed in Action.—Jemadar Sant Singh, 19 N.C.O.'s and men.

Died of Wounds.—Acting Subadar Major Nidhan Singh and 9 N.C.O.'s and men.

Wounded.—Lieut. R. V. Fox, Jemadar Bishan Singh I, Jemadar Sundar Singh and 110 Indian Officers and men.

MAP 12.

RIVER-EUPHRATES
HILLAH TO RUMAITHA.

Scale 1 Inch 4 Miles

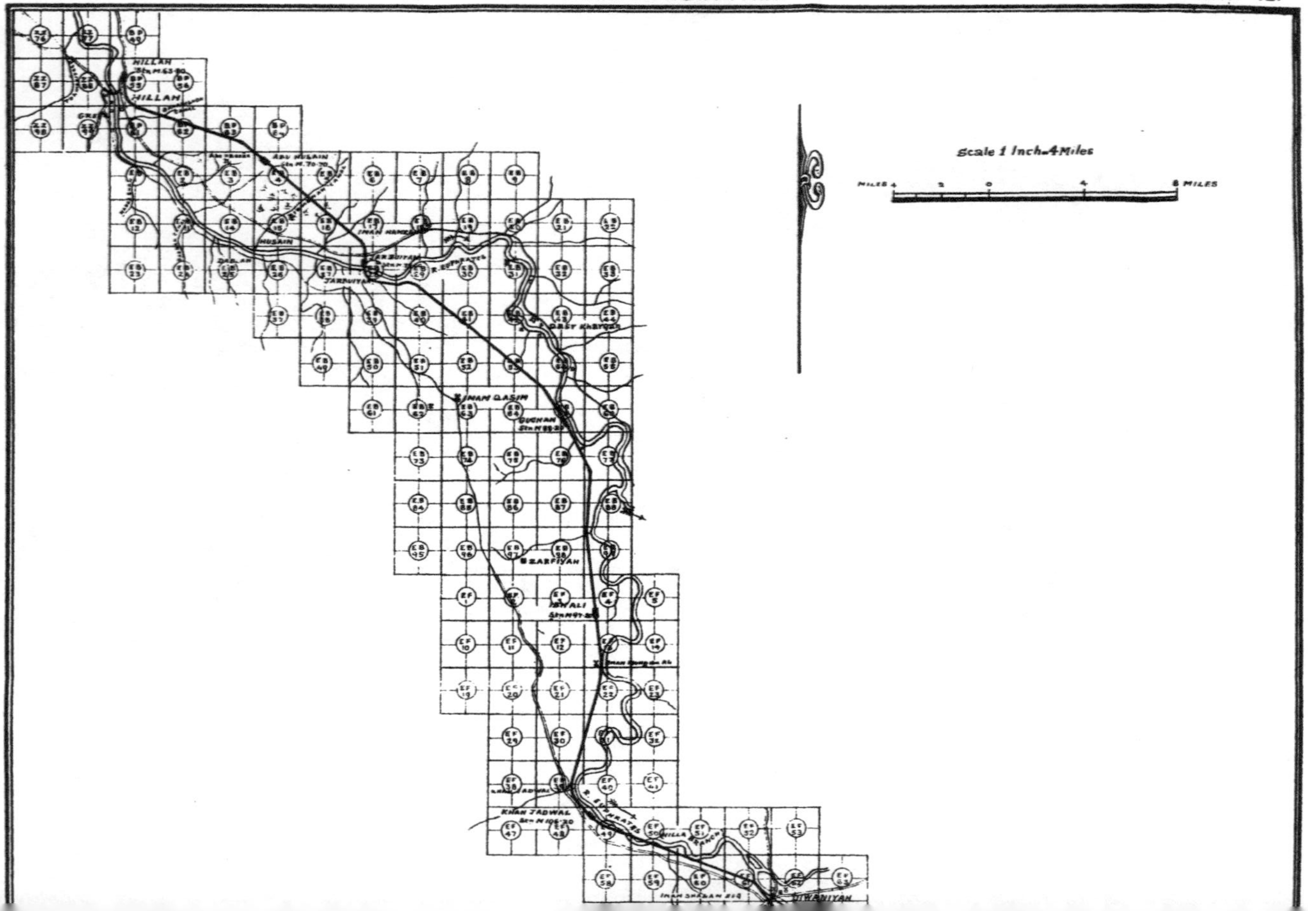

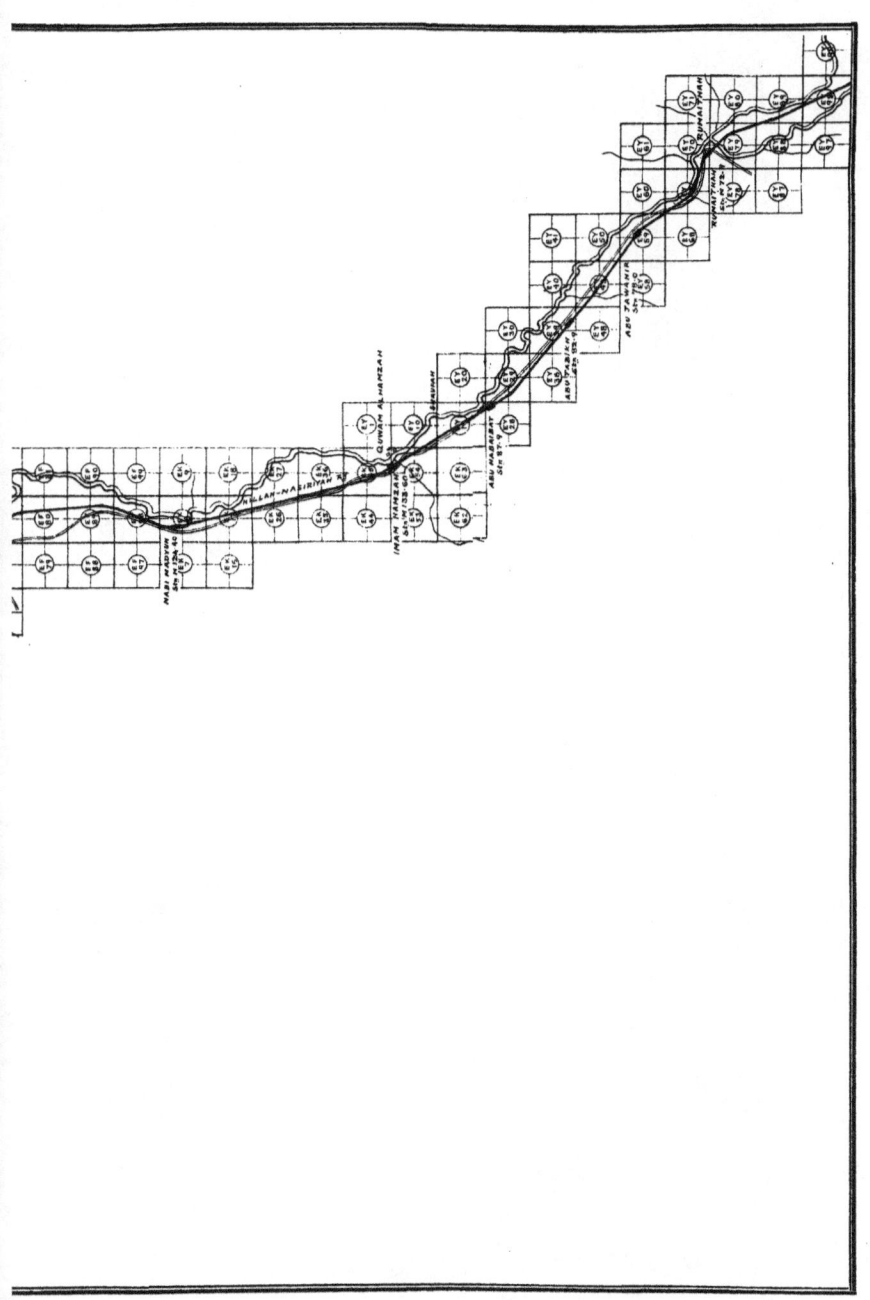

A very great loss to the Regiment this day was the death of acting Subadar Major Nidhan Singh, the beau ideal of an Indian Officer, who succumbed to his wounds, received in the morning, some hours later.

Though grievously wounded in the abdomen himself, he continued to hearten the wounded round him with brave words such as " Oh men, what does it matter about us, if it is well with the Regiment ? " until a few minutes before his death.

The behaviour of all ranks of the Regiment in this action, fought in the intense heat of July, was magnificent. The rewards for gallantry on this occasion are contained in the Honours Appendix.

Captain McCarthy of the 99th Infantry was the only British Officer killed in this action, leading his men with great gallantry.

Our camp being the scene of the lesser derailment on the 6th, some hours were spent in making a clearance of the railway line in the morning, during which time the Arab indulged in a certain amount of sniping. The Column eventually got on the move, and was followed up by the insurgents until the vicinity of E.Y.19.D. was reached. Here a halt was called, to water the horses of the 37th Lancers, and the 1st and 2nd line transport mules. *July 8th.*

These animals had been without water for over twenty-four hours, as on the only occasion on which they could obtain water on the march several were killed or wounded and had to be abandoned.

Here also a relief train met us under **Major Lubbock** (Railways), and after a brief halt the Column proceeded to Imam Hamzah, where it was joined by the 51st Company Sappers and Miners. The Column went into camp profoundly thankful for a rest, to be able to get under canvas and shelter from the fierce rays of the July sun, which had been endured for four days—and greater boon still to be able to bathe in the river. The relief train proceeded to Diwaniyah, taking the wounded.

The Column was reinforced by one section 97th Battery Royal Field Artillery (eighteen pounders). *July 9th.*

The total casualty list of McVean's Column for the past four days was made up and read as follows :—

	Killed and died of wounds				Wounded			
	B.O.'s	I.O.'s	I.O.R.'s	Followers	B·O·s'	I.O.'s	I.O.R.'s	Followers
37th Lancers	–	–	1	–	–	–	4	–
45th Sikhs	–	2	36	1	1	1	106	1
99th Infantry	1	–	5	–	–	2	24	–
Kurdish Levies	–	–	2	–	–	–	1	–
Railway Coolies	–	–	–	–	–	–	–	2
Total	1	2	44	1	1	3	135	3

July 10th. There was no sniping, and the rest was greatly enjoyed, our men were very happy.

Map No. 12. The 87th Punjabis (Lieut.-Colonel B. M. Carroll) passed through us with orders to form a camp at E.Y.19.D. They were recalled the same day, however, to Diwaniyah, to help to protect the railway line to the north of that place, as the Arabs had attempted to destroy it between Hillah and Diwaniyah.

July 12th. The Column marched from Imam Hamzah to E.Y.19.D., and camped there, and on the 13th morning carried out a small demonstration against villages in the vicinity, shelling any Arab concentrations seen. No opposition was met with.

Here the Column remained without incident until the 16th, when it was reinforced by a second section of the 97th Battery Royal Field Artillery, another of the 45th Mountain Battery, and the 116th Mahrattas (Lieut.-Colonel A. H. Bridges, C.I.E., D.S.O.). As Colonel Bridges was senior, the command of the Column passed out of the hands of Lieut.-Colonel D. A. D. McVean, D.S.O.

July 17th. Some excitement was caused by the appearance on the left bank of the river of a small party of Arabs carrying the white flag, which turned out to be the Assistant Political Officer of Rumaitha (Captain Hyatt) and a Railway Engineer (Lieut. Harper). These two Officers had escaped the previous night from Rumaitha under the protection of a friendly

Sheikh, and had run the gauntlet in order to bring information as to the plight of the invested garrison.

They reported that the *moral* of the garrison was good, but food was scarce.

A ration train arrived, and in it came Brigadier-General F. E. Coningham, C.B., C.M.G., D.S.O., and staff. He was the new Column Commander, and the Regiment knew him well.

On the 18th the Column was further reinforced by the 132nd Battery Royal Field Artillery (4.5 howitzers), another squadron of the 37th Lancers and the 2nd Battalion Royal Irish Rifles.

Coningham's Column, as it was now known, marched out before dawn to relieve Rumaitha, composed as under:— *July 19th. The second Battle of Rumaitha.*

2 squadrons 37th Lancers.
132nd Battery Royal Field Artillery (4.5 howitzers).
97th Battery Royal Field Artillery (18 pounders).
45th Mountain Battery.
51st Company Q.V.O. Sappers and Miners.
2nd Battalion Royal Irish Rifles.
45th Rattray's Sikhs.
87th Punjabis.
116th Mahrattas.

The 45th Sikhs, one section 132nd Battery R.F.A., and one squadron 37th Lancers formed the advanced guard troops to the Column.

It was dark when we left camp, and we felt our way till daylight to Abu Tabikh without opposition.

When dawn broke, it disclosed large parties of insurgents on the left bank, which proceeded to snipe the advanced guard, though retreating before our steady advance.

The train which accommodated Column Headquarters, the field ambulance, etc., had to proceed very slowly as several minor breaches in the line were encountered and had to be repaired. In spite of such delays we got to within one-and-a-half miles of the " Bund," our obstacle of the 7th, by 17.00 hours, and from there saw plentiful evidence of its again being occupied in considerable strength.

Brigadier-General Coningham decided to attack at once, using the 45th Sikhs and 116th Mahrattas as front-line troops, with the 87th Punjabis holding on to the left or river flank, with orders to minimise the heavy sniping that was coming from the other side of the river, and to assist the attack by fire.

Both batteries of artillery took up positions in rear, and having registered the " Bund " put down a barrage on it at " zero " hour (17.45 hours), under cover of which the 45th Sikhs and 116th Mahrattas went into the attack, the 45th having, as their front, from the railway inclusive to the river (about 800 yards) and the 116th Mahrattas, rom the railway exclusive eastwards for some 800 yards.

Intense rifle fire was opened by the enemy as soon as the attack commenced, both from the " Bund " and from the other side of the river, which took its toll of the Regiment. The advance, however, continued with great steadiness until a point about 450 yards from the enemy position was reached, where a halt was made preparatory to the assault.

During this halt we suddenly observed that the Battalion on our right was retiring--it afterwards transpired that every British Officer except the Commanding Officer had been hit.

This withdrawal had the effect of bringing in a heavy counter-attack by the Arabs, and as our right flank was left in the air, it became necessary to turn it to meet this new menace. Accordingly two platoons of " B " Company right-formed and lined the railway embankment, thus catching the insurgents in flank and inflicting heavy casualties. The counter-attack which developed on our front was beaten off with considerable loss, and the position was thus restored.

Darkness was then almost upon us, so all positions were consolidated as far as possible for the night. The 87th Punjabis were sent up to replace the 116th Mahrattas, who were sent into reserve.

Just after dark news reached us and was passed round the Regiment that the 1/10th Gurkha Rifles had by marching to the " sound of the guns " joined the Column after a forced march, and were being sent up to guard our left flank, by crossing the river if possible, and destroying concentrations of snipers on the left bank. This information was received by one long "fateh" by the 45th, such was the confidence placed in our comrades of previous fights.

The action now died down, and, but for desultory sniping throughout the night, nothing of moment occurred.

Dawn the following morning broke on an entirely different situation. Our patrols found that the enemy had entirely evacuated the position, and we promptly occupied it. The cavalry were sent forward to clear up the situation and to get into touch with the insurgents. They reported the country clear, so the 99th Infantry were pushed on to within one mile of Rumaitha with the 87th Punjabis in support. The 45th remained at the village of Abu Qifah. *July 20th.*

No serious opposition being encountered, the squadron 37th Lancers entered the town of Rumaitha and relieved the garrison.

Our casualties in this attack were as follows :—

Killed in Action.—2 Non-Commissioned Officers and men.

Wounded.—Lieut. G. M. Worden, Jemadar Adjutant Bishan Singh, and 50 N.C.O.'s and men,

out of a total number of casualties in the Force, of three British Officers and thirty-two Indian Other Ranks killed, and two British Officers and 150 Indian Other Ranks wounded.

The night and the following day were quiet as far as we were concerned. *July 21st.*

A column was organized to enter Rumaitha and bring out its garrison. It left at 05.00 hours, and " B " Company (Captain J. A. Finlay) joined it as it passed our camp. The Column only stayed long enough to evacuate the garrison, and got back at 09.30 hours. We did rear-guard from our camp to the " Bund " with the cavalry.

There was practically no firing by the enemy, but Lieut. Will had his charger killed.

On arrival at the " Bund " we took up the defence of the the camp on its southern face from the railway line to within about 100 yards of the river, where the Royal Irish Rifles came in. There was a good deal of sniping from a village just on the other bank of the river, which resulted in a good many casualties to men and animals going to the river to drink.

We had one man wounded this day.

184 HISTORY OF THE 45TH RATTRAY'S SIKHS

July 22nd.
The retirement on Diwaniyah begins.

Orders were received that night for a general retirement on Diwaniyah to be commenced the following day.

Accordingly, after a fairly quiet night the Column commenced to move off at 05.00 hours. As dawn broke, many thousands of Arabs were seen to be hovering in the vicinity on all flanks, and knowing their propensities in following up a retreating force, we anticipated lots of fun. We got it!

As the 45th held the southern face of the camp, with one squadron 37th Lancers, orders were issued that we should hold on to that position until the train and the main body of the Column had got under way, and then passing through the 87th Punjabis, who were to take up a position behind us, join the main body beside the train, leaving the duties of rear guard to the 87th Punjabis.

All went well at first, though much delay was caused by the artillery waiting to shell the hostile concentrations all round us, and we passed through the 87th Punjabis about 09.00 hours.

A dust-storm had by this time sprung up, which added considerably to the confusion of the next half-hour.

About fifteen minutes later without any warning a seething mass of Arabs suddenly appeared in our midst out of the dust. They broke our ranks here and there, and utter confusion resulted for a few minutes. Hand-to-hand fighting ensued in many places, so keen were the Arabs to seize a rifle if possible. Our men quickly rallied after their surprise, and the rush was completely stopped by our men and order restored, but not before we had lost several killed and wounded though we also took our toll. Some of the Arab dead presented a weird spectacle, being hung round with rifles, bandoliers and haversacks, etc., all captured in their first mad rush out of the dust. The 87th Punjabis lost heavily both in officers and men.

The Column Commander sent back the Royal Irish Rifles, who, together with ourselves, supported the 87th Punjabis as rear guard for the remainder of the march.

We were followed up by snipers, but these kept at a respectful distance.

E.Y.19.D. was reached towards evening, and the Column encamped at that place, very grateful for a rest and a drink of water, as all ranks had gone through the hot dusty day with only one water bottle and a few " chaguls " per platoon.

Our casualties this day were five N.C.O.'s and men killed and fifteen wounded.

After a good sleep the Column pushed on to Imam Hamzah in two portions, the General Officer Commanding and Column Headquarters proceeding with the first, leaving Lieut.-Colonel McVean in command of the 2nd portion. *July 23rd.*

Imam Hamzah was reached without any untoward incident, and the whole Force went into camp.

General Coningham left by train for Diwaniyah, leaving Lieut.-Colonel H. L. Scott, D.S.O., M.C. (1/10th Gurkha Rifles), in command of the first column, Colonel McVean being left as before in charge of the second column. The first column, consisting of one section 45th Mountain Battery, 10th Gurkhas and the transport of the Royal Irish Rifles, marched at 05.00 hours, leaving Lieut.-Colonel McVean's Column at Imam Hamzah with orders not to evacuate the place until all stores, etc., had been dismantled and loaded on to the train which would be sent from Diwaniyah, so as to arrive by 10.00 hours. This train did not turn up till noon, and the task of loading vast quantities of stores fell to the Regiment. Our men having loaded the train, the whole Column marched at 14.15 hours for Nabi Madyun, which was reached at 18.00 hours without incident. We found Scott's Column already in camp, and settled down beside them with a plentiful supply of drinking water. The train containing the stores from Imam Hamzah was sent on into Diwaniyah under escort, where it arrived in some forty minutes in safety. *July 24th.*

After a quiet night the Force again made an early start, Lieut.-Colonel Scott's Column marching at 04.30 hours, and Lieut.-Colonel McVean's Column an hour later. No opposition was met with, so both columns marched straight into Diwaniyah, our column arriving there at 10.00 hours. *July 25th.*

Here we found our Divisional Commander, Major-General G. A. Leslie, C.B., C.M.G., who sent for Lieut.-Colonel McVean and congratulated him on the good work the Regiment had done, which message he wished to be conveyed to all ranks. He left later by air for Baghdad.

The Regiment crossed the river and went into E.P. tents

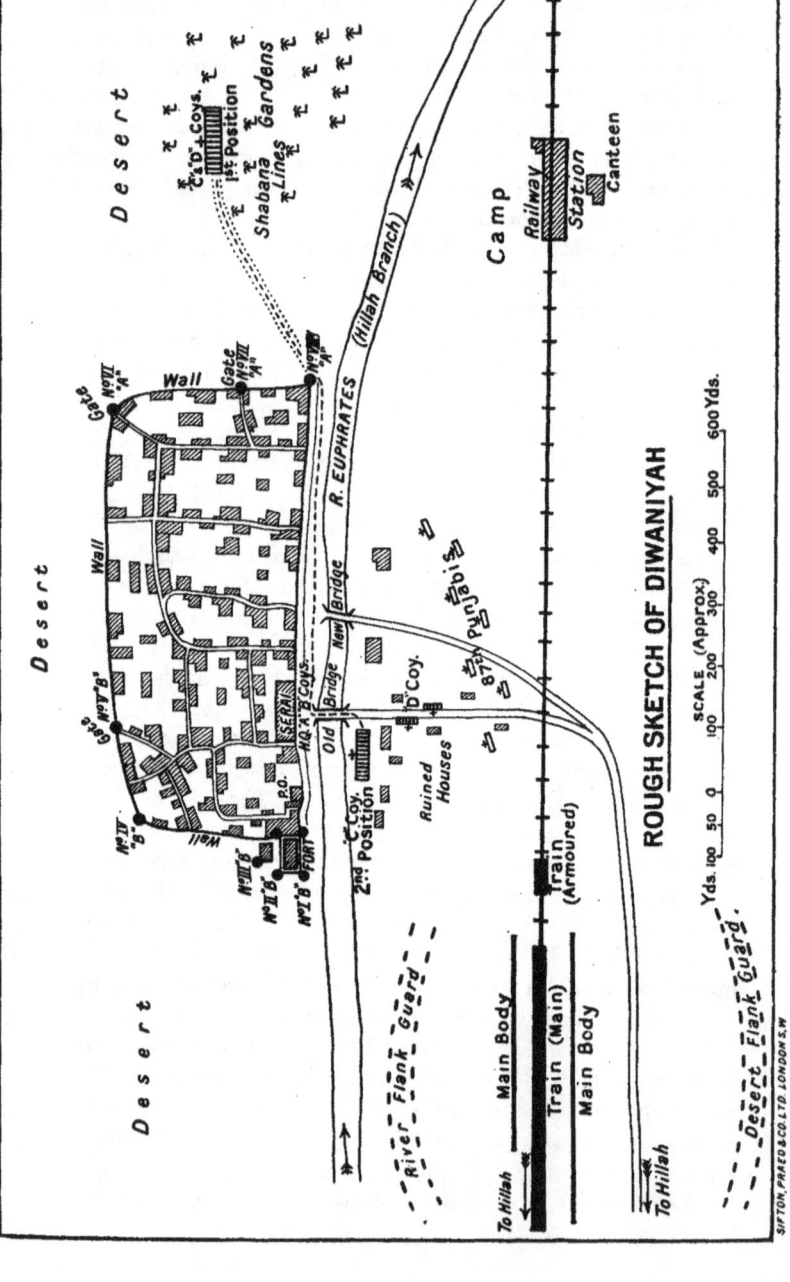

ROUGH SKETCH OF DIWANIYAH

Fig. 3.

in the old lines of the 37th Lancers beside the fort, and prepared for a few days' rest and enjoyment. On the 27th, however, the defensive positions round Diwaniyah were reorganized. The Regiment left the camp and were distributed as follows:— Headquarters and the right wing in the civil " Serai," and the left wing outside the city to the south in the Arab Levy lines. As the loyalty of the Arab levies was strongly suspected, with the exception of the Kurdish levies, they were disarmed by " C " and " D " Companies on arrival in their camp.

On the 29th a conference was held at Column Headquarters, and it was decided to evacuate Diwaniyah and retire on Hillah, as repeated requests for reinforcements from that place were received, and that important town was short of troops and partially invested. All possible rolling stock was to be taken, and the train was to accompany the Column, the line of the railway and river was to be taken by the Column. It was decided to leave all camps, etc., standing, also the railway station, electric light plants, pumping stations, etc. These would naturally fall into the hands of the Arabs, and this decision involved a cost of many thousands of pounds, but was unavoidable. *Decision to evacuate Diwaniyah, and the arrangements made for carrying this decision out. See sketch map of Diwaniyah, Fig. 3.*

The evacuation of the town was of necessity a most difficult undertaking, for whereas the town lay on the left bank of the river, the railway line lay up the right bank, and there were but two bridges over the river, one of which was a very old boat bridge, not capable of taking heavy traffic.

It was, therefore, decided to move the whole Force, with the exception of the 45th Sikhs, over to the right bank before dawn on the 30th (the day fixed for the evacuation). When all was in readiness on the right bank three blasts on a railway engine whistle was to be the signal for the 45th to evacuate the town and cross over to the right bank as quickly as possible, and " leap frog " the 87th Punjabis, who were to take up a position about one mile north of the town at right angles to the railway line to cover our retreat. Having passed through the 87th Punjabis our rôle was to be that of " desert flank guard."

All troops, except the 45th, were evacuated over to the right bank on the night of the 29th, and it fell to the lot of

188 HISTORY OF THE 45TH RATTRAY'S SIKHS

the 45th to provide all picquet duties on the left bank in readiness for the next day.

Orders to the Regiment were issued by Lieut.-Colonel McVean whereby the left wing under Captain A. L. Butcher was to get away from the Arab Levy Camp at 03.00 hours (30th) as quietly as possible, cross the Old Bridge and with " C " Company and one section 17th Division Machine Gun Company to take up a position in the ruined houses opposite the Old Bridge to cover the retirement of Headquarters and " A " and " B " Companies when the time came for the final evacuation. " D " Company (Lieut. H. St.-C. O. Will) were to be sent on to picquet the houses close behind " C " Company's position.

July 30th. The evacuation of Diwaniyah, and the retirement on Hillah begun.

Thus, dawn on this morning broke to find the 45th Sikhs disposed as shown on the sketch map of Diwaniyah, with the 87th Punjabis in position in rear of them.

To judge from the noise issuing from the direction of the railway station, huge preparations were going on round the main train. It transpired afterwards that the large canteen situated beside the station was being loaded on to the train, or rather as much of it as could be taken. Needless to say, the many hundreds of cases of beer were taken, and such delicacies as " Plum and Apple " left to delight the stomachs of the Arabs.

Very patiently did we wait for the signal of the three blasts on the engine whistle, and this came at last at 06.00 hours. Nos. IV and V Picquets held by " B " Company (Captain Finlay) and No. VI Picquet held by " A " Company retired first, followed by Headquarters from the " Serai," then Picquets III and VII, and then finally Nos. I and II (" B " Company) and VIII (" A " Company).

The evacuation was carried out in the most unobstrusive manner possible, but no sooner had we commenced to move than swarms of Arabs rushed in from an easterly direction, and it looked as if we should have to fight for the bridges.

The sight of the loot, however, distracted the attention of the insurgents, and the last picquets got away unmolested. The town was simply a mass of fighting and screaming Arabs, into which " C " Company managed to put several well-directed bursts of fire, having done which it proceeded to evacuate its position, and follow the rest of the Regiment to its allotted place on the south-east flank of the main body as "desert flank guard," the 87th Punjabis in their turn closing in as rear guard.

The trains presented a truly amazing sight. The main portion, some 500 yards in length and pulled by five engines, was surrounded by coolies and refugees, including a local friendly sheikh and his retinue. Following this was a small train of some four armoured coaches, the engine of which was also armoured. On the last two coaches two machine guns were mounted under Major Baker (17th Division Machine Gun Company). This train puffed backwards and forwards firing on any too venturesome hangers-on.

It did great work, and certainly kept the Arabs from coming in too close to the rear guard.

As may be imagined, the first hour of the retirement was somewhat sticky, but improved later and good progress was made.

After some five miles, a large number of Arabs attacked the Column, but were beaten off; the eighteen-pounder guns doing heavy execution. The Force then proceeded without further incident until Khan Jadwal was reached, where picquets' positions were taken up for the night.

Our casualties this day were light—only five N.C.O.'s and men wounded. A moderately quiet night ensued, which was greatly enjoyed by all, assisted no doubt by the issue of some Diwaniyah canteen beer to the Officers' messes. The camp here was a natural stronghold, being guarded on three sides by high bunds, upon which picquets were easily placed.

The Force marched early. We had no protective duties *July 31st.* to perform, so marched in the main body beside the train. Arabs followed up the Column as usual sniping, but they were not very venturesome. They did give some trouble, though, to the 99th Infantry who were doing rear guard.

Progress was extremely slow, as the railway line had been pulled up and taken away every few hundred yards, which necessitated the metals from behind the train being taken up by our coolies, and relaid in front of the train to enable it to proceed at all.

This labour of necessity took a considerable time, and our

average progress was seldom, if ever, more than three hours per mile, a most trying performance.

Added to this the railway coolies were inclined to be "Bolshy," for which one can hardly blame them, as the heat was most intense and water none too plentiful.

The railway did not follow the exact line of the river, indeed it was sometimes as far as two miles distant.

After a weary and dusty day we eventually reached camp late at a point (Map No.12) E.B.99.C., where the river touches the railway. Here we were allotted a very long front on the perimeter, and one platoon "D" Company under Lieut. Will was left in position outside the perimeter in a ruined village to guard the water supply.

August 1st. An early start was again made, and we found ourselves doing advanced guard with one squadron 37th Lancers under Captain Boileau.

The railway line was very badly damaged in this vicinity, so that progress was even slower than on the previous day. No opposition, however, was met with, though we had to contend with a fierce dust-storm, which blew all day and did not add to the enjoyment of the proceedings.

Towards evening, the dust-storm having abated, we saw a construction train working south from Guchan, a small wayside halt about four miles away, and held by our troops as a post.

A halt was called at a place called Raqaniyah, our total progress this day having amounted to three-and-a-quarter miles, over which distance we had expended nearly twelve hours.

August 2nd. Column Headquarters and the train guarded by the 1/10th Gurkhas and a battery of field guns moved off early to effect a junction with the construction train at Guchan, the remainder of the force under Lieut.-Colonel McVean remaining at Raqaniyah until Column Headquarters and both trains should reach Guchan.

The Arabs sniped our watering parties from some cultivation on the left bank of the river, five casualties resulting. We had one sepoy hit, who died almost at once. Colonel McVean ordered the guns to fire a few rounds into this cultivation, which had the desired effect.

At about 14.00 hours the Column got on the move with the 45th doing "desert flank guard" and the 87th rear guard, and reached Guchan without incident about 18.00 hours. Near Guchan we met four eighteen-pounder guns and three platoons 10th Gurkha Rifles, who were left behind to guard some sleepers for which a train was to be sent out. Thinking this escort too small Lieut.-Colonel McVean left the 87th Punjabis to bring them in. Lieut. R. V. Fox and a small party of slightly-wounded men of July 7th rejoined the Regiment at Guchan from hospital in Baghdad.

From Guchan northwards for some eight miles, the railway left the river, which made a big sweep to the north, so that we had to rely for water on the irrigation cuts which crossed the railway, in many cases a snare and a delusion as we had learnt to our cost on previous occasions.

The railway line from here bent north-east and was known to be very badly damaged, so that the progress of the Column would still be very slow. Accordingly early on the morning of the 3rd, the G.O.C. sent a small column, consisting of one *August 3rd.* squadron 37th Lancers, one section Howitzer Battery, 45th Sikhs and 99th Infantry, under Lieut.-Colonel McVean, orward with the construction train as far as possible, to repair the line and reconnoitre for water for the following day.

The line was found to be torn up and the metals and sleepers removed for distances of sometimes 1,000 yards. However the coolies worked well, and a stretch of line some four miles in length was repaired.

Water in plenty was discovered in a cutting which joined the Jarbuiyah canal, a wide and deep canal which took off from the river at Jarbuiyah and ran south, some six-and-a-half miles to our desert flank.

Lieut.-Colonel McVean asked permission of the Column Commander to stay out on the water with his force for the night, but was refused permission, as Arab concentrations were observed from Guchan.

One amusing incident happened this day. A large house stood about 2,500 yards on our right flank, upon the roof of which there suddenly appeared an Arab, who proceeded to divest himself of his "abah" (Arab cloak) and wave it frantically, endeavouring no doubt to signal our approach.

Lieut.-Colonel McVean called up Captain Aitkenhead of the gunners, who, taking the range on this house, put his very first shell slap on to the roof—we did not see that Arab again!

We returned to camp at Guchan at dusk. The Column Commander arranged for two machine guns to be laid up the four miles of newly repaired line, which fired periodical bursts of fire throughout the night, hoping thereby to catch any Arabs who attempted to undo our day's work. It certainly had the desired effect, for the line was untouched next morning, though there was plentiful evidence of interrupted attempts at demolition, including one bloodsoaked "abah," which was lying on the track.

August 4th. The next day the whole Force moved off at 05.00 hours, and good progress was made up to the limit of our repair work of the previous day. From here onwards the progress was terribly slow, but the Arab displayed no hostility, except the usual long range sniping.

We did desert flank guard together with a section of the Machine Gun Company and a section of the Mountain Battery. All houses or villages encountered were burnt to the ground by the rear and flank guards, such procedure being the order of the day from now onwards until Hillah was reached. These houses and villages were of course deserted and their contents removed, but one occasionally came across stray chickens and goats; these were invariably seized and augmented the daily rations.

A camp about five miles south of Jarbuiyah was reached towards evening, the Column having marched about seven miles. Water was a long way off owing to the deviation of the river, so that the watering of men and animals took a long time. "D" Company was out on water picquet, and it was 21.00 hours before they were inside the perimeter.

August 5th. On the following day it was hoped that we should reach the important town of Jarbuiyah, and relieve the invested garrison on the railway bridge, consisting of one company 32nd Sikh Pioneers under Major H. S. Mitchell.

The railway at this place crosses the river from the right to the left bank, as the latter swings west here for a distance of fifteen miles.

The Column again made an early start, but the going was very slow owing to the usual line repairs necessary.

Towards noon the advanced guard (1/10th Gurkha Rifles) and the river flank guard (86th Carnatic Infantry, who had joined the Column at Guchan), came under heavy fire from the date gardens on the left bank of the river.

The 86th therefore established themselves on the river bank, and the 1/10th Gurkha Rifles, having forded the river, in a most determined attack drove the large enemy concentrations back at the point of the bayonet into the village of Musaidiyah, which place they entered and thoroughly enjoyed themselves with bomb and "kukri" before they retired on to the main body.

The Column halted about five-and-a-half miles short of Jarbuiyah for the night, but as the camp was commanded by a high bund on the desert flank about one mile distant, "C" and "D" Companies under Captain A. L. Butcher were sent out there to make a "strong point" and stop out for the night, during which there was some fairly heavy sniping.

Communication having been established with the bridge garrison at Jarbuiyah, it was ascertained that all was well, though Major Mitchell had unfortunately received a severe wound in the thigh, and several men of the garrison were wounded. The enemy had made several attempts to destroy the bridge, which were always frustrated. *August 6th.*

The railway line was badly damaged hereabouts, so the Column remained in its camp of the previous night with the exception of a covering party for repair work, until 15.00 hours when the line was reported fit for traffic into the town of Jarbuiyah itself.

The Column therefore moved at that hour with the 86th Carnatics doing rear guard, the 10th Gurkhas river flank guard, and the 45th desert flank guard.

Just short of the bridge, we took up positions astride the railway, and the whole Force passed through us, leaving the Regiment to do rear guard. We then fell back almost on to the bridge itself.

Here we had to remain all night, as the train now about a mile in length, had encountered a breach on the far side of

Jarbuiyah station, and so could not get on far enough to permit its total length getting over the bridge before nightfall.

It was a truly awful night, for myriads of mosquitos fattened on us in the palm groves, and sleep was impossible.

August 7th. A party of Arabs bumped into "A" Company's picquet line, and got severely dealt with, and it was not before 04.00 hours on the 7th that we were permitted to cross the river and camp down as best we could inside the perimeter. Once inside, the whole Regiment was in the river at once to try and cool their bumpy bodies—a most gratifying performance.

We then received orders that the Column was to continue its retirement at 14.00 hours that same day. It was decided to leave the 86th Carnatics to guard the bridge over the river, as otherwise it would most certainly have been destroyed after our evacuation. Two companies of this regiment were accordingly sent into the bridge head defences, and rationed for a fortnight.

The Regiment's rôle was that of rear guard. We anticipated the usual trouble, as the country here was very enclosed with walled gardens and palm trees. But, strange to relate, not an Arab followed up, and we got clear away into the desert again unmolested.

The railway line was found to be in fairly good repair, so that progress was good, and about four miles were covered by the Column before a halt for the night was called in the region of the Birmanah marshes, some four miles north-east of the river.

Water was very scarce here, of a coffee-coloured stickiness and most unpalatable. By dint of straining it through a handkerchief, however, it became tolerable, and by so doing many of us learnt quite a lot about "Life in our Ponds and Marshes."

A quiet night ensued, though the mosquitos were very busy, and thousands of frogs sang us to sleep.

August 8th. The Regiment was up early (03.00 hours) as our duty this day was that of advanced guard and the starting point was a mile away.

Before we had proceeded very far we ran into a train from Hillah, in which was Major-General Leslie, our Divisional Commander. He called up Lieut.-Colonel McVean and again

HISTORY OF THE 45TH RATTRAY'S SIKHS 195

congratulated him on the splendid manner in which the Regiment had fought throughout.

He also gave some more exact information about the terrible débâcle of the "Manchester Column" on July 24th, only vague rumours of which had reached us, and which had the unfortunate result of bringing all the tribes round Hillah in against us.

We also learnt that the troops of the 51st Infantry Brigade in our Column were to form a column and work north of Hillah, taking punitive measures against hostile concentrations in the vicinity of the Hindiyah barrage and Musaiyib, for the famous barrage had fallen into the hands of the insurgents, thus giving them control of the whole water supply of the Hillah branch of the Euphrates, on which the town of Hillah itself was dependent.

Accordingly all troops of the 51st Infantry Brigade then with Coningham's Column were entrained there and then, and taken back to Hillah. The remainder of Coningham's Column returned to the Birmanah marshes for the night, with the exception of the right wing of the 45th Sikhs under Captain J. A. Finlay, which remained out at this point (E.B.16 Central). *Map No. 12*

The Column, now a small one, marched at 10.00 hours for *August 9th.* Hillah, the right wing under Captain J. A. Finlay acting as advanced guard and the left wing as river flank guard.

No opposition was encountered, and good progress was made, Hillah being reached after a dusty march of about fifteen miles by 17.00 hours.

The Regiment crossed the river, and went into the same camp on the right bank, which it had occupied in 1919 when part of the garrison of Hillah with the 52nd Infantry Brigade.

That night was one of much rejoicing, as we found ourselves next to the 1/10th Gurkhas, so that after a long and refreshing bathe in the river, much *bonhomie* prevailed amongst all ranks of both regiments.

Thus ended a most memorable forty days, which included two big actions and numerous small ones, as well as the unique feat of retiring with a train a mile long for 100 miles in the intense heat of the July sun, with the line damaged so much that the Arab was astonished beyond measure how it

196 HISTORY OF THE 45TH RATTRAY'S SIKHS

was all achieved. But the Regiment had plenty before it yet.

August 10th. The fighting round Hillah. We were not left long in this camp, as on the 10th we were ordered to take over the northern defences of Hillah on the left bank; and accordingly moved over into a new camp beside the railway station, where we found ourselves alongside the 132nd Howitzer Battery.

Into this camp was brought our dump, and all ranks were very grateful to get at some extra kit, all of which had been left under a small guard in Hillah on our downward journey of July 3rd.

Our drums beat "Retreat" every evening in front of Divisional Headquarters situated in the old Turkish barracks. Crowds of Arabs always watched them, and then made their way home as "Curfew" was at sunset.

We remained in this camp four days cleaning up, and trying to replace losses in stores and animals due to enemy action. It was found that our total losses in Lewis gun mules and first line mules amounted to twelve mules killed and thirteen wounded.

The tribes between Hillah and Baghdad, having up to the present "sat on the fence," now began to give trouble, egged on no doubt by the news of the "Manchester Column."

They cut the lines, both railway and telegraph, in many places so that we were cut off from Baghdad, and communication perforce had to be maintained by wireless, and the mails carried by aeroplane.

To counteract this continual cutting of the railway lines, the General Officer Commanding-in-Chief adopted the plan, utilized with such success in the South African campaign, of building block houses along the railway lines.

This plan again proved most effective, though the garrisons required presented a problem which was only solved by arming some 2,500 volunteers from labour corps existing in the country. These stout fellows gave the lie to the doubtful trust placed on them in some quarters, and shewed themselves eminently suited to the task allotted them.

August 14th. After four days peace and quiet, we got orders to take over the garrisons of Hillah town, or that portion of it which lay on the left bank of the river.

"C" Company (Captain A. L. Butcher) accordingly took over the various picquet positions from the previous occupants (a company of the Royal Irish Rifles), and found themselves on the roofs of Arab houses on the southern outskirts of the town. The Regiment was also allotted two strong platoon picquets on the southern defences (left bank), so it was decided to move camp to a new position in some date palms further south. This move was completed on the 14th.

The following day news was received that the Arabs were collecting south of the town on both banks of the river, though the majority were reported to be on the right bank, and that an attack on the town was inevitable.

That night, however, nothing unusual happened, though the southern defences were very much on the *qui vive*.

August 16th. We were given to understand that we were to be attacked that night by 8,000 Arabs, who had collected in the palm groves south of the town, and who had been reinforced by the tribes from Diwaniyah and that vicinity. The attack, however, did not mature that night and although Divisional Headquarters persisted in their song of "To-night's the Night," nothing was heard of the 8,000 on the following nights (17th, 18th) either.

August 18th. Major-General Leslie decided to blockhouse a high canal bund which took off from the river about one-and-a-half miles south of Hillah on the left bank.

The General Officer Commanding personally went out to this bund—known as the Banashshah canal—on the morning of the 18th at an early hour, and "B" Company (Captain J. A. Finlay) preceded him in order to put out picquets, whilst he selected sites for the proposed blockhouses.

During their advance through the palm groves, "B" Company encountered many Arabs, many of whom were perched up in palm trees, who were summarily dealt with.

The General Officer Commanding having made his reconnaissance, "B" Company returned to camp about 13.00 hours without further incident.

August 19th. In retaliation for our encounter on the previous day and its results, the enemy about 01.45 hours opened a rapid fire on the blockhouse picquet line, concentrating on one of our platoon picquets, known as Pioneer Post, but retired hurt under the answering fire of the garrison (" A " Company). Collecting again, they came in on " C " Company's front and tried to force an entrance into the town. They were driven back with rifle fire and bombs, and eventually retired at 04.00 hours. Their numbers were estimated at several hundreds.

When dawn broke, the small village of Grata, which is almost a suburb of Hillah, was searched by " B " and " C " Companies, whilst the 32nd Pioneers were engaged in clearing the ground up to the Banashshah canal, which was picquetted by " A " Company (Lieut. R. V. Fox). Our search proved fruitless except for a few harmless individuals, who were handed over to the Political Officers for interrogation.

The work of clearing the ground continued on the following day, " D " Company providing the covering force on the Banashshah canal.

August 21st. Saturday the 21st provided some real excitement. It was " B " Company's turn to act as covering party to the clearance work, and they were in position on the Banashshah Canal by 06.30 hours.

At about 10.00 hours heavy sniping started, which increased in volume to such an extent that Lieut.-Colonel McVean in consultation with General Leslie, who was out with his staff, asked for artillery support, and also requested the General to leave as the fire was so hot.

He sent up two platoons of " A " Company under Lieut. Fox to reinforce " B " Company (Captain Finlay) on the Banashshah Canal, and finally as the situation did not improve, the whole of " D " Company (Lieut. Will).

This force together with one squadron 37th Lancers under Captain Boileau, was put under the command of Captain A. C. Curtis, the Adjutant, as Lieut.-Colonel McVean, as Officer Commanding Left Bank, was required at Left Bank Headquarters beside the railway station.

Before the arrival of the reinforcements, " B " Company had been charged by masses of Arabs, who had come to within forty yards on four occasions. They held their ground stoutly, and inflicted heavy casualties with bombs and rifle fire, though they suffered considerably themselves. The position held was situated amongst thick palm groves, under cover of which the Arab was enabled to come in close with impunity.

By 14.00 hours a regular battle was going on, so having reinforced " B " Company with the other two platoons of " A " Company, Captain Curtis decided to drive the Arabs off the Banashshah Canal, where a footing had been obtained by the insurgents on " B " Company's left flank, by attacking with " D " Company, and at the same time to send the squadron 37th Lancers under Captain Boileau well out on to the left, or desert, flank, to take up positions to enfilade the enemy positions.

" D " Company under Lieut. Will therefore pushed in a strong attack, which drove the Arab off the bund, and sent him running, thus giving Captain Boileau magnificent targets for his Hotchkiss guns, of which he took full advantage.

It was estimated that the enemy was many thousands strong, so that the long-promised attack of the 8,000 had at last materialized, though the enemy had crossed from the right to the left bank of the river.

The struggle continued and the enemy made several more assaults on " B " and " A " Companies, thereby getting severely hammered, until about 17.00 hours when Lieut.-Colonel McVean ordered a retirement back to camp.

Captain Curtis was now faced with a most hazardous undertaking, for though " D " Company's retirement would have been comparatively easy, as they were in more or less open country, the two platoons of " A " Company and " B " Company would, for some 1,000 yards, be fighting in a most enclosed terrain, and would no doubt be followed up most closely, and at the same time be powerless to prevent the Arab from coming to close quarters owing to the thick woods and undergrowth.

" D " Company was therefore withdrawn from the Banashshah Canal, and took up a position on to which " A " and " B " Companies could fall back, and leapfrog so as to gain the protection of " C " Company's picquet positions on the outskirts of the town.

Following the withdrawal of " D " Company, " A " and " B " Companies accordingly commenced to withdraw about 15.30 hours, and by taking up a series of positions worked their way back. As had been expected they were very closely pressed by the Arab, who, jumping from tree to tree, kept up a constant fire at a few yards' range.

The movement was splendidly executed, and the enemy kept back by rifle fire and bombs until "D" Company's covering position was reached, when these companies closed and withdrew to camp.

The enemy was not all at inclined to take on "D" Company, and gradually withdrew, leaving this Company unmolested, when the time came for its eventual withdrawal behind the permanent picquet positions of "C" Company.

We suffered fairly heavy casualties considering the numbers of the Regiment engaged, though only one man was killed. Twenty-two was the number of our wounded, a good ten per cent. of the numbers engaged.

We heard next day that the Arabs had suffered severely, having had five killed and 150 wounded, so we had good reason to be pleased with ourselves.

The Politicals reported that the Arabs' strength was from 6,000 to 8,000, their intention having been to attack Hillah that night, but their plans were frustrated by us.

The 22nd and 23rd were peaceful, except that a small party of Arabs fired on Pioneer Post, which was held by us, without any damage being done on the latter day.

They resumed again on the early morning of the 24th in greater strength, and attacked our defences in a half-hearted manner. The artillery put down a barrage in front of our positions, which had the effect of producing an absolute pandemonium amongst the Arabs, who shouted and screamed, and kept up an ill-directed fire for about three hours before they retired.

Apparently the guns caused some damage, as a platoon of "A" Company searched the ground in front of Pioneer Post after daylight, and found much blood, besides many cartridge cases of all calibres, from a .303 to an awful thing of about .500—a most unpleasant missile to stop and known as the "Whizz-Bang."

August 25th. Formed part of a column to relieve Jarbuiyah.

We received orders this day that a column under Brigadier-General Coningham, of which we were to form part, were to proceed to Jarbuiyah to extricate the 86th Carnatics from their guard over the bridge there, and bring them back to Hillah.

The Column was to march at dawn the next day; meanwhile it was to concentrate on the left bank, behind the Banashshah Canal.

Accordingly at 15.00 hours we took up positions on the Banashshah Canal in order to cover the concentrations of the force in our rear.

No train was to accompany the Column on this expedition, and all rations, etc., were to be carried on 2nd line mule transport.

The concentration took a considerable time owing to a ration train leaving the rails whilst bringing rations up to the Column ration dump. This necessitated units sending back their army transport carts to collect the rations, so that it was midnight before all was ready for the start at dawn.

The composition of the Column was as follows :—
37th Lancers.
132nd Battery Royal Field Artillery (4.5 howitzers).
97th Battery Royal Field Artillery (18 pounders).
No. 12 Company Q.V.O. Sappers and Miners.
32nd Sikh Pioneers.
1/10th Gurkha Rifles.
45th Rattray's Sikhs.
99th Infantry.
116th Mahrattas.
A field ambulance.

As we formed the infantry of the advanced guard, we *August 26th.* were early astir and in position before dawn broke, and the whole column moved off when it became sufficiently light to see.

After proceeding some four miles, and when approaching a high canal bank, known as the Hassan Canal, a weird spectacle met our gaze. The Hassan Canal cut the road, our line of advance, at right angles, and flowed into the Euphrates about one-and-a-half miles away on our right flank to the westward. At this point masses of Arabs were observed standing on the canal bank, gesticulating wildly, and gathered round large white, green and red standards, obviously the Headquarters of Sheikhs.

A second large concentration directly barred our advance, and a third was away on the left bank.

Heavy sniping was opened on the advanced guard cavalry (37th Lancers) from all flanks, and especially from some sand hills away on the left flank. The Lancers reported their inability to advance, as they were greatly outnumbered, to the advanced guard commander, Lieut.-Colonel McVean.

The guns were accordingly ordered to take up positions from which to shell the bund, and opened fire on the mass waving their banners.

The first shrapnel shell was a beautiful burst. The banners were hauled down, and every Arab was off that part of the Bund in about one second.

Some H.E. followed in rapid succession, and it was hoped that much damage was done.

The General Officer Commanding had by this time come up to the advanced guard, and agreed with Lieut.-Colonel McVean that an infantry attack on the Arabs barring our path was necessary.

Accordingly "C" and "D" Companies 45th Sikhs under Captain A. L. Butcher, were ordered to attack the Bund to the left of the railway, whilst two squadrons 37th Lancers were to co-operate on the left flank.

The left wing made a determined walking attack on the Bund, and succeeded in pushing the enemy off it without a single casualty, though the enemy opened heavy fire on it. The Arabs, however, did not wait too long and bolted before we were in actual possession of the Bund, so that though "C" and "D" Companies pursued them with fire, no great losses were inflicted on them.

The attack was supported by the artillery, who made very good shooting.

The Arab having fled in the direction of the river, we took no further notice of him, but pushed on, and reached the Birmanah marshes towards evening, where a halt was called for the night.

"C" and "D" Companies occupied two small villages ahead, with "A" and "B" Companies in support on a

canal "Bund" about 500 yards in rear of them, from which *August 27th.*
the animals were watered. An uneventful night ensued.

An early start was made, and our duty was again that of advanced guard.

Progress was slow, as the Arabs had flooded the road, which hampered the movements of guns and transport enormously. The railway line was badly torn up in this vicinity, though happily this did not impede our movements on this occasion, as we had no train with us.

We pushed on slowly, however, and reached Jarbuiyah by noon, to be greeted with much joy by the 86th Carnatics, who had had no communication with the outside world since they were left behind on August 8th. They appeared very snug, however, their trenches being deep and well dug down.

They told us that the Arabs had on two occasions attempted to burn down the railway bridge by floating down stream bellums (native boats) full of burning pitch. But on neither occasion had the attempt proved successful.

The Column camped in the gardens surrounding Jarbuiyah, and all enjoyed a delightful bathe in the river that evening, and slept unmolested, except for mosquitos, that night.

A village called Imam Hamzah lay some three miles northeast of Jarbuiyah, which was known to harbour many hundreds of insurgents, and to be the home of a sheikh of the Dargara tribe who had fought against us.

It was therefore decided that, prior to the return of the Column to Hillah, this village should be "strafed," and the houses of well-known inhabitants burnt to the ground.

Accordingly in the early morning the dispositions for the *August 28th.*
attack, discussed overnight at a conference, were taken up.

The 99th Infantry and the 116th Mahrattas were to be the assaulting troops, with the 1/10th Gurkhas in support. The Regiment (less one company) was in reserve. This company ("D" under Lieut. Will) acted as escort to a section of machine guns which was pushed forward to a flank to help on the attack.

The remainder of the Regiment sat up on a bund, and had a perfect view of the whole show.

The guns having taken up a position, put down quite an

effective barrage, under cover of which the 99th and 116th advanced to the attack.

Imam Hamzah appeared to be stiff with Arabs, who opened fire at a very long range on the advancing lines of infantry. They did not wait for long, however, but fled through the town leaving everything behind them, including women and children.

The 1/10th Gurkhas thereupon pushed through the town in pursuit, and passing right through took up positions on the far side to cover the work of the demolition parties, which consisted of the 61st Company Sappers and Miners and the 32nd Sikh Pioneers.

The houses told off for destruction were quickly in flames, whereupon the order was given to retire, and the whole column returned unmolested; the men of the Sappers and Miners and Pioneers well content, having managed to pick up a fair amount of poultry in the course of the work.

The little Gurkhas also managed to pick up a few hens and goats on their way through, and were all anxious to be allowed half an hour to themselves in the town, a boon which our men craved too.

The Force returned to camp, and heard that the watering places for animals had been sniped, causing some casualties amongst the muleteers. The 86th Carnatics who had been left behind to guard the camp, were therefore sent to burn two villages upstream from the camp, which they did successfully. They killed several Arabs, but escaped casualties themselves.

The total losses for the day in combatants were extraordinarily light, amounting to two only. One British Officer of the 116th Mahrattas was most unluckily hit in the attack on Imam Hamzah and died later, and one sepoy of the 99th Infantry was slightly wounded.

This paucity of casualties was due to the fact that the insurgents fled long before our troops got to close range.

The Column having accomplished its object at Jarbuiyah, it was decided to return to Hillah if possible the following day. The orders for the retirement were issued, which detailed the Regiment for the duties of rear guard.

August 29th. The Column marched at 06.00 hours, and it was decided to stick to the main road, and not to the line of the railway. It was 09.45 hours before the Regiment as rear guard got on the move, and whilst waiting in position, we witnessed an amusing incident.

An aeroplane was flying overhead, and suddenly became very interested in an Arab Levy picquet, which was fairly close to us. Having thought about it for a long time, the aeroplane eventually decided that the unfortunate picquet was hostile, so dropped a couple of "Eggs," which, however missed the picquet by a good 100 yards. We all laughed heartily though it might have had its tragic side, had the 'plane taken a better aim.

We got going at last, and splendid progress was made, though occasional halts were necessary, as the 10th Gurkhas were working up the river bank burning and destroying everything they encountered.

On one occasion they spotted a bellum load of Arabs crossing over to the other bank, and actually succeeded in dropping a bomb into the boat, which scattered those left to tell the tale into the water.

Not a shot was fired at the Column the whole day. The Arabs ran like rabbits on our approach, and got away on to the right bank of the river.

The Column got on so well that the General Officer Commanding decided to go straight on into Hillah, which was eventually reached by 18.30 hours after a long march of well over twenty miles.

We were all glad to reach camp, and to have a quiet night without any defensive duties to perform. But we were told upon arrival that our sojourn in Hillah was to be of a very short duration, as we were to leave almost at once for Baghdad *en route* for Baqubah, there to join the 15th Sikhs, and to form part of another column which was to carry out punitive measures in the vicinity of that place.

Map No. 11.

We were all, however, delighted to hear that we should again be under the command of Brig.-General Coningham, for we looked upon him as a friend, besides being a leader in whom we had implicit faith. It would have been hard, too, to find a better, or more popular Brigade-Major than General

Coningham's (Brevet-Major F. V. B. Witts, D.S.O., M.C., R.E.), in whom, we knew, we also had a friend.

The next day was spent in preparations for the move, and loading our heavy kits and army transport carts on to the train, so as to be ready the following day, which was the one appointed for the move.

The 1/10th Gurkhas were to accompany us for which we were very thankful.

The objects of this expedition were first to secure the safe passage of the women and children who had been isolated at Karind in Persia, and also to rescue a Mrs. Buchanan, who had fallen into the hands of the Arabs in the town of Shahraban, where she had been living with her husband, an Officer of the Irrigation Department. Captain Buchanan, together with the Political Officer of that town and several others, had been killed by the insurgents after a most heroic defence in an isolated bungalow on August 15th.

As may be realized, considerable anxiety was felt as to Mrs. Buchanan's fate in the hands of these unscrupulous blackguards, and preparations for her speedy release were therefore hurried on as much as possible.

August 31st. The move to Baqubah, etc.

We left Hillah at 09.45 hours in one long train with the 1/10th Gurkhas. After a long and uneventful journey we arrived at Baghdad West station at 18.45 hours the same day. The line was blockhoused throughout its length, and some of the blockhouses nearer Baghdad reported attacks by Arabs in the early morning, which had been beaten off. We saw no signs of any enemy.

Map No. 13 (Shahraban area).

Upon arrival at the West station, we were met by a staff officer from General Headquarters, who intimated that we were to march at 02.30 hours the following morning to the East station, there to entrain for Baqubah. As time was very limited, we bivouacked beside the station for the night, and snatched what sleep we could, before being up and away across Baghdad at the time appointed.

Having entrained again by 06.00 hours, we left on the thirty-five mile journey to Baqubah, and were thoroughly pleased to arrive there at 16.00 hours.

Baqubah was a place of considerable importance, as the railway from Baghdad to Quraitu (whence a motor road ran

BAQUBAH - SHAHRABAN.

MAP I

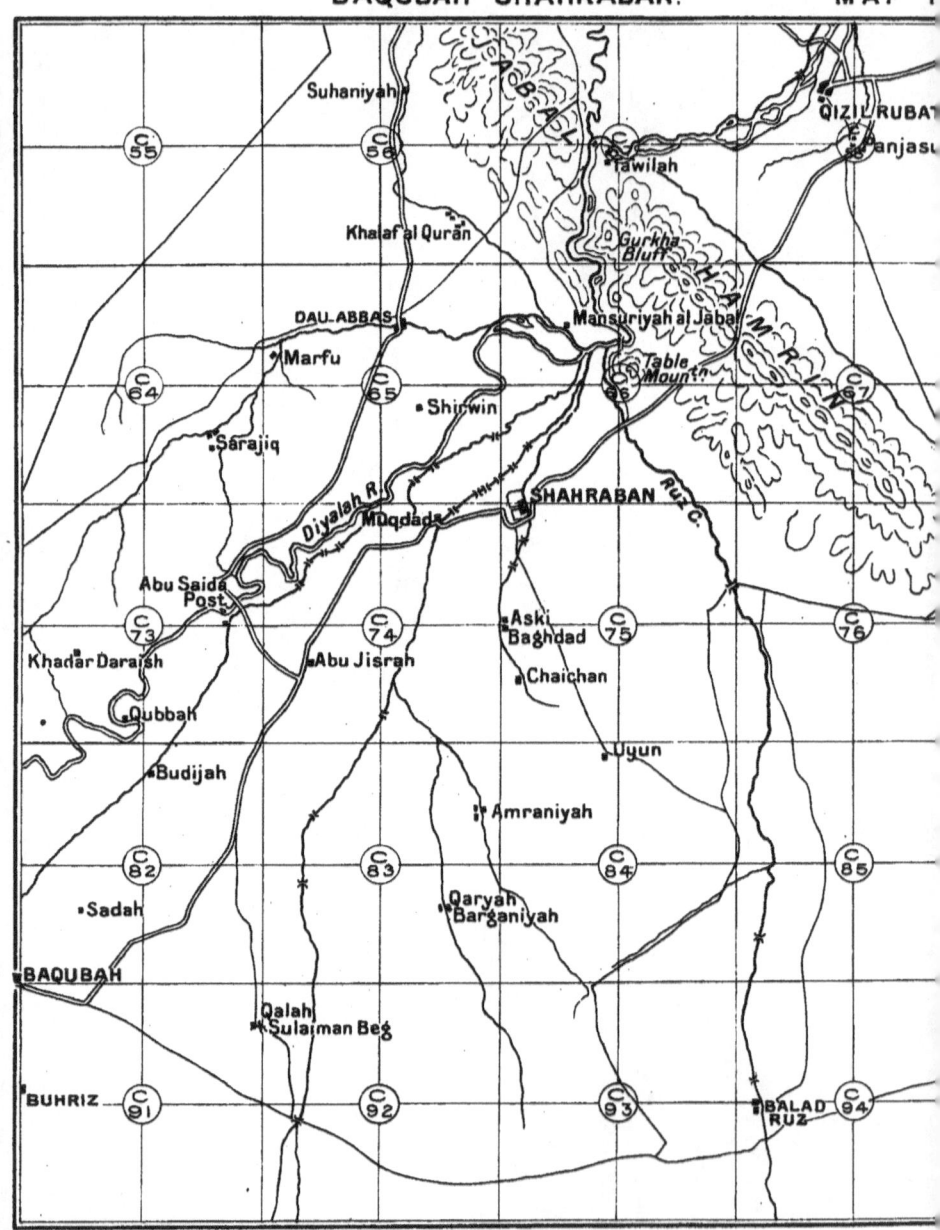

Scale : 6 miles to 1 inch.

to Karind and beyond) crosses the Diyala river, a big tributary Map No. 13
of the River Tigris, by a fine bridge. It was also the site of
the famous refugee camp, for Armenians, Assyrians and
such-like folk.

This camp had, however, been dismantled on the outbreak
of the rebellion with the idea of repatriation of its occupants.

Upon arrival at Baqubah we met the 15th Sikhs (Colonel
H. S. E. Franklin, C.M.G., D.S.O.) who had but recently
arrived in the country from India. They had succeeded in
driving the Arabs out of Baqubah, which place had been
captured and held by the insurgents for some time.

The 15th Sikhs were in occupation of the town itself, the
whole of which lay on the left bank of the Diyala river. We
camped on the right bank, beside the wireless station, but
that did not prevent parties of men of the 15th from coming
over to see their friends and relations in our ranks, and a very
happy evening was spent.

The next few days passed uneventfully, except that we
took over the duties of bridge guard, and the concentration
of the new Column went on apace. General Coningham
arrived on the 4th.

It did not take the men long to discover the presence of
fresh fruit and vegetables, which were found to be growing
on the left bank some distance away. Parties under Indian
Officers were sent out and returned daily with goodly supplies,
which however lessened as days passed, as our hunting grounds
did not remain secret long.

The troop concentration was completed by the evening
of September 4th. Orders were therefore issued that the
whole Force was to concentrate on the left bank on the 5th.
The Regiment was to move first, and take up positions behind
which the remainder could collect.

We therefore moved off at 08.00 hours, and crossing by September
the railway bridge passed through the town and took up 5th.
picquet positions on the far side of it.

Serious misgivings were entertained as to the behaviour
of the mules when crossing the bridge, which was a good
100 feet above the river bed. These animals, however,
negotiated the passage without mishap, though some of
them needed a lot of coaxing.

The whole Force had crossed by dark, and went into a perimeter camp for the night, with the intention of moving off the following morning *en route* for Shahraban.

The Column was composed as follows :—
    32nd Lancers (less two squadrons).
    35th Scinde Horse (less two squadrons).
    97th Battery Royal Field Artillery.
    132nd Battery Royal Field Artillery.
    No. 9 Company Q.V.O. Sappers and Miners.
    12th Pioneers (less two companies).
    1/10th Gurkha Rifles.
    15th Sikhs.
    45th Sikhs.
    99th Infantry.
    Field Ambulance.

Aeroplanes had, for the past day or two, flown over our intended line of advance and dropped leaflets for the Arabs, informing them that no party would be fired on except under provocation.

This course was adopted as there were still many tribes in this vicinity who had not come in against us, and it was thought that perhaps the policy of leaving such tribes alone would prevent them from joining in against us. Further, it was known that Mrs. Buchanan was still alive, but considerable doubt was entertained as to her remaining so if the drastic measures practised on the Euphrates were adopted in this vicinity.

A train was to accompany the Column, as the line was reported as undamaged by aerial reconnaissance.

September 6th. The Column moved off at 06.30 hours, with the Cavalry and "A" and "B" Companies doing advanced guard. The line was found to be damaged in places but not very seriously. Repair work was well and quickly carried out, so that fair progress was made.

As we had again to rely for water on the irrigation canals shown on our maps, we expected the supply to be limited. However, a good and plentiful supply was encountered at noon, from which we replenished.

Towards evening the village of Abu Hawa was reached, where the Column camped for the night. At this place watering facilities were very poor, and at some distance from the camp.

A few snipers collected and fired on our watering parties. They wounded one mule, but did no further damage, and we passed a quiet night.

We were off by 07.00 hours, considerable delay having been caused by the animals being forced to march some one-and-a-half miles to water. "C" and "D" Companies formed the Infantry of the advanced guard. *September 7th.*

The telegraph line was found to be badly damaged which necessitated repairs, and progress was as a result slow. No opposition was encountered, and the village of Abu Jisrah, which was reached at 16.00 hours, was selected as a camping ground, as there was a plentiful supply of water there.

The 15th Sikhs supplied the Infantry of the advanced guard, and the Cavalry formed a huge screen in front of them. *September 8th.*

We now began to traverse much more interesting country, cultivation being very plentiful, and water much more easily come by.

Towards midday, the advanced guard was opposed by almost 400 Arabs, who fired from some thick cultivation bordering on the railway line. They made off, however, when fired on by machine and Hotchkiss guns, except for one daring spirit, who hiding in the undergrowth, waited until a British Officer of the 32nd Lancers was almost on top of him. He then jumped up, and firing at point-blank range, knocked this Officer out of the saddle with a bullet in the shoulder, and with a second shot killed his orderly. He then ran for his life, and, unfortunately, escaped.

We camped that night at the village of Muqdad, where plenty of water was easily obtainable from the Marut Canal which ran through it. The ground hereabouts was very marshy, and pig and snipe abounded. Though several efforts were made to bag a pig, they proved unsuccessful. From this camp we were almost in sight of Shahraban.

The Column advanced at an early hour. The Regiment were detailed as advanced guard, with orders to enter the town, covered by the 1/10th Gurkhas outside it, and to the south, and by the Cavalry who were to work round to the *September 9th. Entry into Shahraban.*

o

north. The 15th Sikhs and the Artillery remained in reserve, whilst the 99th provided the escort to the train.

We advanced up to the walls of the town without opposition, and entered it by the south gate, there to be met by salaaming dignitaries, who professed great friendship for the British, and imparted the information that the hostile tribes had only just left the town by the northern gate, having battened on the inhabitants for a long time.

Major Bourdillon, the Political Officer of Baqubah, who accompanied the Column and acted as interpreter, asked about Mrs. Buchanan, and received the reply that she was well cared for in a petty sheikh's house in the town. He thereupon searched her out, and found her little the worse for her terrible experiences, though truly thankful for her release. She was put into a Ford car, and sent back to Column Headquarters beside the train in the vicinity of Muqdad.

With her was one British Other Rank and one Indian servant, the sole survivors of the party who had made such a gallant stand in the "Kushla" (or Headquarters of the Arab levies) on August 14th. This was situated just outside the south gate, upon the roof of which the Regiment put up a picquet position upon arrival.

The "Kushla" was gutted and looted, having been the scene of a most despairing effort on the part of its defenders. They only numbered about twenty, mostly Arab levies, and lacked food and water.

They were closely invested for several days, but finally in making a sortie to obtain water were butchered, the insurgents not even sparing their co-religionists, the Arab levies.

It was said that they died most gamely, accounting for more than their own numbers, before being wiped out themselves. No trace could be found of their bodies, though Captain Buchanan was buried about 200 yards away, as he was murdered before the siege commenced whilst walking in the town accompanied by his wife.

He was shot at point-blank range, and then stabbed to death by an Arab, who then proceeded to drag Mrs. Buchanan away by the hair, only being prevented from doing so by the intervention of a friendly Sheikh, who took charge of her, until finally rescued by us.

The murderer was caught by us, as very luckily he had not fled the town upon our entry, and was caught as he was about to leave some few hours after our occupation. He was tried by Military Court and condemned to death that same evening, Mrs. Buchanan having come into Shahraban in order to identify the man. He was shot the next evening by a firing party of "B" Company, under the Adjutant, Captain Curtis.

After our entry we held the town by picquets on the roofs of the houses, and our Mess was established in the Buchanan's bungalow.

We were joined that evening by Captain G. B. Fyldes and a draft from the depot at Multan. He took over the command of "A" Company.

The Political Officer was busy all day on the 10th collecting rifles from the townsmen, who yielded up about 175 modern weapons.

The hostile tribes had used Shahraban as a dump, and had left many tents behind them, which alone were valued at from 60,000—70,000 Rs. These were confiscated, together with any other articles of value, and subsequently taken back to Baghdad by train.

We were allotted the task of burning the houses of five notables, who had taken a prominent part in the rebellion. From these houses a good many chickens and eggs were obtained.

We were only in Shahraban two days on this occasion, but they were happily spent, and the men ate their fill of the most beautiful grapes, which the inhabitants were ordered to bring in.

September 11th. We were given orders overnight to evacuate Shahraban this morning, and return to Muqdad where we were to remain with one squadron 35th Scinde Horse, one section Sappers and Miners, one section 132nd Battery Royal Field Artillery and two platoons 12th Pioneers.

Before moving, 150 carts were sent from Column Headquarters, and all Arab tents, etc., were removed to the station, where the remainder of the Column was encamped, loaded on trucks and sent to Baghdad. The remainder of the Force, except our small column, began to retire at 07.00 hours for Abu Jisrah. We followed them at 09.30 hours.

Both Columns retired without a shot being fired at them, and we established ourselves at Muqdad, whilst the remainder went on to Abu Jisrah. After the departure of the Columns from Shahraban, the tribesmen poured into the town and proceeded to loot it.

During the afternoon the Political Officer of Deli Abbas, Captain Lloyd, who had been a prisoner in the hands of the Arabs for nearly a month, rode into camp with a party of Arabs, and a sheikh of that vicinity. He appeared well, and reported that he had received kindly treatment at the hands of the Arabs.

He had left his fellow-prisoner, one Strachan of the Irrigation Department, in Deli Abbas.

He told Major Bourdillon, who was with our Column, that the Arabs were thinking of throwing up the sponge. They were doubtful, however, as to what treatment they would receive at our hands, and were really waiting for a lead by the big sheikh, Beni Tamin, whose example they would follow.

September 12th.

Work was commenced on blockhouse construction along the railway line, "C" and "D" Companies with the squadron 35th Scinde Horse acted as covering party to the 12th Pioneers, who were working towards Abu Jisrah.

Several sheikhs appeared in camp and surrendered unconditionally; some went on to see the General.

They were well armed, and the hilts and scabbards of the swords and knives that many of them carried were beautifully engraved. They were well treated and provided with food and water.

It was now evident that the back of the insurrection was broken hereabouts, so arrangements were made whereby the line should be opened up between ourselves and Quraitu, and from thence the motor road should be kept open to Karind, at which place most of the wives of the British portion of the Mesopotamian garrison were living at the time.

A column under Lieut.-Colonel Greer 1st Battalion Royal Irish Fusiliers was working down the road from Karind to Table Mountain, and wireless communication had been established between it and our Column.

It (Greer Column) reported its position in the vicinity of Table Mountain, though it had not reached that place.

One squadron and the right wing of our small Column was covering working parties making blockhouses towards Shahraban, when orders came in that both Columns were to concentrate at that place. *September 13th.*

The covering troops got back to camp at noon, and followed the Column from Abu Jisrah at 15.30 hours, reaching camp beside the Shahraban railway station, where a quiet night was spent.

The Column, less the 1/10th Gurkhas and 99th Infantry, marched early for Table Mountain. The left wing was detailed as right flank guard and experienced much difficulty from the country, which was intersected by innumerable deep canals, most of them unbridged. *September 14th.*

Table Mountain was reached about 14.00 hours without opposition. The Column camped on the plain below, and the right wing of the 45th was sent to scale the heights, and picquet an eminence known as Cairn Hill.

Table Mountain is a flat-topped hill in the Jebel Hamrin Ridge, which in these parts does not rise to any great height, such as we encountered at Fat-Hah in 1918. The River Diyala flows through the range at this point, and has made a gorge similar in many respects to the Fat-Hah Gorge, but more picturesque.

The railway line follows, more or less, the line of the river, keeping to its left bank, and it was in order to obtain an estimate of the damage done to the line that " A " and " B " Companies picquetted Cairn Hill. Major Witts, the Brigade-Major, carried out the reconnaissance, and found the permanent way undamaged as far as he went.

Table Mountain station was found to be gutted, and the cemetery containing the bodies of those killed in action against the Turks in the Great War was also found to be desecrated. Further, the obelisk erected as a memorial to the 14th Indian Division and situated on the top of the Jebel, was also found to be tampered with, though no serious damage had been done.

The right wing was withdrawn to camp at dusk.

The Diyala River at Table Mountain is a truly beautiful

sight, the water being very deep, and clear as crystal, so that men and animals thoroughly enjoyed themselves during the short time we were there. Moreover it was found to be well stocked with fish, and bombing produced good results.

September 15th. News having been received that Greer Column had reached a point only seven miles distant from us, the Regiment (less " A " Company) went out along the railway line, and picquetted the heights as far as a bridge some four miles away.

Brig.-General Coningham accompanied us, and met Lieut.-Colonel Greer at the bridge, which on examination was found to be badly damaged, one stone pier having been partially blown away with dynamite. Several slabs of dynamite had been looted from the Irrigation Headquarters at Shahraban, and had evidently been put to use.

As the relief of the women and children from Karind was of vital importance, the damage of this bridge necessitated the trans-shipment of all passengers and baggage from one train to another, as repairs would have taken a very long time to execute.

Major-General Leslie arrived in the afternoon, and having received satisfactory reports from Greer Column that the line was undamaged and picquetted as far as Quraitu, the railhead, sent word to General Headquarters, Baghdad, that all was ready for the evacuation of Karind.

We returned to camp at Table Mountain in the evening without incident, though a few Arabs were seen loitering about on the hillsides.

We had known for some days that Brig.-General Coningham was about to leave us, as he had been given command of a newly-formed column for the relief of Samawah, and upon arrival in camp that evening we found that our new Brigadier (Brig.-General G. A. Beatty, C.M.G., D.S.O.) had arrived. He assumed command of the Column forthwith, and it was with very genuine regret that we said goodbye to General Coningham and his staff the following morning upon their departure for Nasiriyah.

September 16th. This same day the 1/10th Gurkhas left camp, and proceeded to the damaged bridge, the heights round which they picquetted, to enable repair work to be carried out. The 15th Sikhs had taken the place of the 10th Gurkhas at Shahraban railway station, which left us at Table Mountain with the guns, and all the local protective duties to perform.

The camp was drawn in and the next three days were happily spent, everyone enjoying the bathing and the feeling of restfulness.

The blockhouse construction work had been proceeding all this time, and the garrisons were found by the 99th Infantry, much to their chagrin, from Table Mountain to Baqubah. We had a lucky escape, having been ordered by General Headquarters to perform the same duties from Baqubah to Baghdad. Our Divisional Commander, however, came to our rescue and got us off.

We received orders on September 18th to construct two blockhouses, one beside the 13th Division monument and the other by the 14th Division monument *i.e.*, one on either side of the river at the entrance to the gorge.

We were busy the next two days on this work but having completed it were ordered to withdraw to Shahraban on the 20th leaving one company to garrison the newly made blockhouses. " A " Company was left.

We left Table Mountain at 08.00 hours, together with two squadrons, three sections of guns and the bridging train, and arrived at Shahraban after an uneventful march. On arrival we went into camp beside the 15th Sikhs at the railway station. Much *bonhomie* prevailed that night, as the 15th Indian Officers had our Indian Officers over to share a case of whisky, to the great content of all. *September 20th.*

Shahraban was depleted of all troops except the 45th Sikhs, one squadron 32nd Lancers and one section of the Howitzer Battery. The remainder all marched off early to Baqubah, from which place a small column was to destroy the village of Deltawah, about twenty miles distant. This place was known to harbour many insurgents, and an attempt was to be made to capture the lot by throwing a cordon of troops round the place before dawn. *September 21st.*

Lieut.-Colonel McVean was given command of the extensive Shahraban area and its numerous blockhouses. A wire was also received that the first train-load of women and children from Karind was to come through Shahraban, *en route* for Baghdad. *September 22nd.*

Many were the precautions taken to safeguard the expected train, whose progress was wired through every fifteen minutes. It was scheduled to reach Table Mountain by 15.00 hours, but was delayed at the "damaged bridge," at which place trans-shipment took a long time, and the train did not reach us until three hours later.

Lewis guns were mounted on carriage roofs manned by British Other Ranks, and the whole train bristled with rifles.

The women and children looked weary, though well and fairly happy, and they must have been thankful to get out of Karind, the delights of which did not compare favourably with the Indian ideas of a hill station.

The Army Commander had by this time decided what terms were to be imposed on the sheikhs who had surrendered in this locality, and it was decided that a "Jirga" should assemble inside the town of Shahraban, at which all sheikhs were ordered to be present in order to hear the terms imposed on them by Government.

September 25th.

This "Jirga" was held at 15.30 hours.

At 13.00 hours the left wing under Captain A. L. Butcher entered the town and picquetted the approaches, and certain houses commanding the "Serai" where the "Jirga" was to be held, against the arrival of Major-General G. A. Leslie.

Major-General Leslie accompanied by Lieut.-Colonel McVean and Major Bourdillon, the Political Officer, entered the "Serai" at 15.30 hours.

The Government terms were read out and translated to the twenty-two assembled sheikhs. Eventually after much discussion they signed their names to the document presented for that purpose. Sheikh Hamid of the Beni Tamin tribe and the "big noise" locally, was present at the "Jirga." It was the first time he had actually shown up, though he had been expected daily.

Negotiations terminated at about 18.00 hours, and the left wing returned to camp.

September 26th.

We were ordered to entrain for Baqubah. The task of loading up the train proved a stiff one, as the only ramp available was small—we had made it ourselves in two days —and also all shunting had to be done by hand.

The seventy trucks were eventually loaded, however, and

we got away by 14.30 hours, and arrived at Baqubah three hours later.

It was rumoured that a well-known outlaw, Abdika by name, was lying up in the small village of Qarnabit on the left bank of the Diyala about four miles from Baqubah.

This outlaw had been the scourge of the whole countryside for two years, since he escaped from jail on the eve of his execution for murder.

He had a small following, in company with whom he terrorized the inhabitants.

It was decided therefore to attempt to catch him by surrounding the village.

After one day's rest in Baqubah, the Regiment with a squadron of the Scinde Horse set out in the early morning with orders to throw a cordon round the village on the left bank of the river, whilst the 15th Sikhs and another squadron were to close the means of egress on the right bank. *September 28th.*

The right bank troops were part of the returning Deltawah Column.

All went splendidly, but when the time came for "B" and "C" Companies to enter the village, it was found that the bird had flown. He was actually seen making good his escape by a squadron, who fired at him but, unfortunately, without effect.

Whilst "C" Company were working their way through the very thick gardens which surrounded Qarnabit they encountered a few Arabs concealed in the undergrowth, and these were dealt with with the bayonet, as it was impossible to fire owing to the surrounding cordon of troops.

The village was thoroughly searched, but apart from a few carpets and sewing machines, nothing of value was found, and the Force returned to camp.

We entrained for Baghdad, and arrived in the afternoon, where we found Lieut.-Colonel Anderson on the platform. He had been recalled from leave with some 500 other Officers on the outbreak of the insurrection. *September 29th.*

The Regiment marched over to the right bank, and camped near the advanced base railway station.

CHAPTER X

THE FINAL STAGES OF THE ARAB INSURRECTION UNTIL THE
ARRIVAL OF THE REGIMENT IN INDIA

OCTOBER 1ST, 1920—MARCH 3RD, 1921

October. AFTER a day's rest, and orders that the Regiment would proceed to Musaiyib had been received, the Regiment on October 1st was inspected by Lieut.-General Sir A. Haldane, K.C.B., K.C.M.G., D.S.O., the Army Commander, at 07.00 hours.

The Regiment was drawn up in three sides of a square and he first of all presented the ribbons of honours won since July. Those absent for any reason are so marked :—

M.C.—Captain J. A. Finlay.

I.O.M., *2nd Class.*—No. 304 Hvr. Tara Singh, " C " Company ; No. 4766 Hvr. Harditt Singh, " C " Company ; No. 2255 Sepoy Ram Singh, " C " Company, invalided wounded, July 7th, 1920 ; No. 254 Hvr. Ganga Singh, " D " Company, invalided wounded, July 7th, 1920 ; No. 733 Sepoy Chanan Singh, " D " Company, died of wounds, July 19th, 1920 ; No. 1712 Sepoy Gurditt Singh, " A " Company, invalided wounded, July 7th, 1920.

I.D.S.M.—No. 161 Hvr. Ishar Singh, " B " Company ; No. 4441 Hvr. Jiwan Singh, " D " Company ; No. 520 Hvr. Lal Singh, " D " Company ; No. 696 Hvr. Maghar Singh, " C " Company ; No. 785 Hvr. Bakhtawar Singh, " B " Company ; No. 817 Naick Tehal Singh, " A " Company ; No. 1075 Naick Hazura Singh, " B " Company ; No. 1124 Sepoy Chattar Singh, " C " Company ; No. 1680 Sepoy Ganga Singh, " C " Company ; No. 1343 Sepoy Seta Singh, " B " Company ; No. 1154 Sepoy Kishan Singh, " A " Company ; No. 1868 Sepoy Kehar Singh, " B " Company ; No. 1212 Sepoy Mehar

Singh, " D " Company ; No. 20 Bhisti Wiru ; No. 770 Naick Jaswant Singh, " B " Company, invalided, wounded, August 21st, 1920 ; No. 2335 Sepoy Bhag Singh, " D " Company, invalided, wounded, July 30th, 1920 ; No. 1097 Sepoy Sewa Singh, killed in action, August 21st, 1920 ; No. 1405 Sepoy Indar Singh, " A " Company, invalided, wounded, July 7th, 1920 ; No. 2284 Sepoy Mukand Singh, " B " Company, invalided, wounded, August 21st, 1920 ; No. 3281 Sepoy Jit Singh, " C " Company, killed in action, July 22nd, 1920.

The Army Commander then made the following speech :—

" Colonel McVean and all ranks of the 45th Sikhs. I have not before had the opportunity of seeing the Regiment on parade, and I am very glad that on the first occasion on which I do so, I should have the pleasure and satisfaction of presenting the ribands of decorations won for gallantry during the recent fighting. I much regret that many of those who have won rewards for bravery are not present to-day through death or wounds.

" Your Regiment has been through the whole of the fighting of the past three months under very trying weather conditions, and on every occasion it has been engaged, has distinguished itself.

" I may tell you now that in the relief of Rumaitha and the withdrawals therefrom and from Diwaniyah I felt considerable anxiety, as the position in which the Force of which you formed part was, with hostile tribes on both flanks and a line of communication that was constantly interrupted, a very dangerous one. The fact, however, that you formed part of the Force made me feel sure that the difficulty and danger would be overcome, and that, come what might, you would live up to the great reputation which you have earned in past wars. You did all I expected of you, and I now thank all ranks for their grand soldier-like behaviour.

" The Sikhs, from time immemorial, have been magnificent fighting men, staunch and loyal, and it is a great satisfaction to me, and I am proud to have the 45th Sikhs in my command, more especially as I knew them in 1898 on the North-West Frontier.

" All troops require a rest from time to time, and although

I can ill spare you, I have decided to send you to take care of the Hindiyah barrage and Musaiyib.

" You will be all the better for a short stay at these places, and all the fitter to rejoin the Brigade when your Brigadier returns from the carrying out of the relief of Samawah.

" I must congratulate you, Colonel McVean, and all of you on your smart soldier-like appearance on parade, and the admirable way in which you have handled your arms. Considering that you have only just returned from operations your turnout is a high tribute to your fine soldier-like spirit and discipline."

After this parade the Regiment marched to the station and entrained for Musaiyib Canal siding, arriving there at 15.20 hours. There a record detrainment was carried out, and the train was empty and handed over to the railway authorities at 16.05 hours.

The mules were just jumped out over rough ramps made of hay bales. We spent a quiet night though the mosquitos were of a very fierce variety.

October 2nd at 06.30 hours " D " Company under Lieut. Fox marched and took over the fifteen blockhouses along the Musaiyib Canal from the 8th Rajputs. The Regiment marched at 07.00 hours, arrived at 10.10 hours and relieved the 8th Rajputs in the posts of the town, and also in a large detached post on the Husaniyah Canal which was taken over by " B " Company (less two platoons) under Captain Finlay. This post was over the regulator which shut off water from Kerbela.

We only held the part of the town on the left bank, as the Arabs held the town on the right bank. They made their presence felt by constant sniping. Our Headquarters were in a Serai on the south side of the town on the river, and in the garden of this were two guns of the 45th Mountain Battery, and a trench mortar.

On the 3rd the 8th Rajputs marched for Hillah at 08.00 hours.

Snipers were busy in the town and also shot at convoys between the town and Husaniyah post.

At midnight a cypher wire was received ordering us to take over the Barrage with 250 rifle strength.

Accordingly at 09.00 hours on the 4th, "A" Company (Captain Fyldes) and "B" Company (less two platoons) under Brevet Lieut.-Colonel R. H. Anderson marched to the Barrage, and took over from the Manchester Regiment.

The relief was effected by 14.00 hours, and the Manchesters marched for Musaiyib, being sniped as they left the barrage. This move left only Headquarters and "C" Company in Musaiyib, and they were all used up in garrisoning the various picquet posts. This state of affairs was relieved on the 6th by the arrival of 115 rifles of the 8th Rajputs, who took over the Musaiyib Canal blockhouses again from "D" Company.

The Barrage was sniped on the night of the 7th. This post was easily defended by seven posts : one on the right bank at the western end of the barrage and six on the left bank. There were also one sixty-pounder, one six-inch howitzer and two eighteen-pounder guns in the post, as well as two trench mortars. By laying with the latter for snipers at night, this nuisance was completely cured after two or three nights. We also made an O.P. round the summit of the Turkish obelisk, as a result of which the six-inch howitzer and sixty pounder did some good shooting when opportunity offered.

The usual sniping continued, and on the 12th one of "D" Company's picquets saw a sniper in a palm tree. A Lewis gun very soon had him out. On the 12th we heard that Tuarij had been occupied by the 53rd Brigade Column; the sound of heavy gun fire reached us this and the previous day from the south. On the 13th four 'planes flying south over the river were heavily fired at by our friends across the river, of course without effect.

The Barrage garrison was doing excellent work catching fish in the lock. At night the gates were opened and closed at dawn. The water was then let out and hundreds of fish were slain with pickhelves.

A fish six-foot long with a girth measurement of thirty-four inches was sent into Musaiyib this day. After the opening of the road to Hillah on the 17th a daily Ford convoy of fish was sent into that place for use of the hospitals.

Samawah was relieved on the 16th, and Kufa on the 17th,

so no beleaguered garrisons existed. We still suffered some sniping in our area, and on the night of the 18th/19th, the Arabs removed 300 yards of telephone wire.

On the 20th the Barrage garrison sent out 100 rifles to co-operate with the 53rd Infantry Brigade who were advancing up from Tuarij in four columns.

We only got one Arab. All four columns bivouacked at the Barrage for the night. A novel sight was some twenty mahelas (Arab boats) with the rations of the Column, as no boat had been seen near the Barrage for months.

General Leslie and staff motored up in the wake of a column and returned the same day. In order to stop the sniping from the right bank, he decided to send a column up the right bank to Musaiyib.

On the 21st a column consisting of two squadrons cavalry, two sections Royal Field Artillery and a battalion from the 53rd Brigade Column moved up the right bank of the river from the barrage. As soon as they passed our post on the Husaniyah Canal, they came under heavy fire. The cavalry worked round the enemy left flank, whilst the infantry pushed on supported by the guns and drove the enemy before them. Four 'planes also dropped bombs during the attack in a very effective manner. The Arabs put up a spirited fight, but were driven upstream, and came under a very effective fire from our Lewis guns on the roof of the Menzil or caravanserai.

As the Column entered the town, we passed over fifty men to the other bank in a boat to co-operate. The town was burnt and the 53rd Column returned to the Barrage, and our fifty men were brought back again.

The six-inch howitzer at the Barrage fired four rounds into the town right bank in the evening at a range of 8,300 yards, and wrecked portions of it.

On the 22nd a portion of the Column returned to Musaiyib by the right bank, their transport marched by the left bank and was sniped *en route* without damage however. Several Arabs were shot, over this affair. This Column came to build blockhouses on the right bank for us to occupy, and the boat bridge was to be put right by the Arabs and Sappers and Miners at the same time.

This work was completed by the 25th when " C " Company

HISTORY OF THE 45TH RATTRAY'S SIKHS 223

took over four blockhouses on the right bank. They were all wired in, and the foreground cleared.

On the 26th " A " Column of the 53rd Brigade returned to the Barrage, less the squadron and one section Royal Field Artillery. " A " and " B " Companies came in from the Barrage and Husaniyah post, having been relieved for two nights by two companies 12th Pioneers.

This was to enable them to take part in a big drive on the 27th towards the Baghdad railway.

On the 27th "D" Column under Lieut.-Colonel McVean consisting of one squadron 5th Cavalry, one section No. 2 Battery Royal Field Artillery and 400 rifles of the 45th under Lieut.-Colonel R. H. Anderson assembled outside Musaiyib at 08.00 hours and commenced their drive towards the line of blockhouses on the Baghdad railway at 08.15 hours.

" D " Column was responsible for clearing the ground between the Musaiyib and Nasiriyah Canals. On our right was a stronger Column of one squadron, one-and-a-half squadron levies, one section Mountain Battery, and a battalion. They were responsible for the Nasiriyah Canal exclusive to the Khan Mahawil Canal inclusive.

It was a very hot day, and the enemy losses were one armed Arab killed, 285 prisoners (by the cavalry), three revolvers, 482 rounds S.A.A., fourteen ponies, and 180 sheep. The Regiment burnt two villages close to Musaiyib as punishment for sniping on their return, and we got into Musaiyib at 17.00 hours. There was no opposition.

On the 28th " A " and " B " Companies returned to the Barrage and Husaniyah Post. The 12th Pioneers proceeded to Tuarij by boat.

On the 29th a telegram was received which surprised us all very much intimating that Major-General G. A. Leslie was proceeding to India and would pass Musaiyib Canal siding at 11.00 hours.

Lieut.-Colonels McVean and Anderson went to meet him.

General Leslie as our Divisional Commander from December, 1917, had been a very staunch friend of the Regiment, and his departure was very keenly regretted by all ranks of the Regiment, and, indeed, throughout the Division.

His farewell order to the Division dated October 29th was as follows :—

"I relinquish to-day the command of the 17th Division, which I have held since December, 1917, when the Division was only two months old.

"A child of war it has been engaged, in whole or part, almost continuously in the occupation of war.

"As I leave it, it is in full enjoyment of triumphs gained despite the worst conditions of climate and hardship.

"To all ranks, past and present, I wish goodbye and give them my heartfelt thanks for their invaluable loyalty and devotion to duty, to which alone are due the laurels won by the 17th Division.

"It has been my greatest pride to command such a Division and I now leave it with the greatest regret."

November. The disarmament of the Arabs commenced, and proceeded well though gradually. A certain amount of sniping of picquets took place early in the month, especially at nights.

As duties at Musaiyib were very heavy owing to the four strong posts on the right bank, two platoons of " B " Company proceeded there from the Barrage, leaving only one company at the latter place for the future.

A draft of twenty-eight Indian Other Ranks joined on the 6th under Subadar Harnam Singh.

As the men were unsettled at no definite prospect of getting back to India, Lieut.-Colonel McVean proceeded to Baghdad on the 7th to find out how matters stood. He returned on the 10th with no definite promise, but that it was hoped to get us away by the end of February and we were high up the list.

On November 9th the nomenclature of the 34th Infantry Brigade, to which we belonged, was altered to the 77th Infantry Brigade.

On the 10th the two heavy guns at the Barrage left for Hillah by road under an escort of two platoons of " D " Company.

There was rain on the 11th, and the nights were turning cold, so the Regiment went into serge on the 12th.

Owing to the more settled conditions large numbers of

Persians passed through our picquet line daily on their way back to Persia.

They had been to Kerbela on pilgrimage, and had been held up for months owing to the disturbances.

On the 13th Brig.-General Dent visited us from Hillah. We learnt that we should move in about a fortnight, and the probable destination of his Column would be Diwaniyah. A dump of surplus rations was to be formed at the Barrage, and this work now proceeded daily.

On the 16th the Barrage garrison went out to a village a mile distant to search it for suspected rifles. The Political Officer accompanied them. No rifles were found, but the outline of the village was altered, and everything capable of burning was burnt. The men spent a thoroughly happy morning.

Two Political Officers motored through from Kerbela on the 17th. They reported the country as quiet. In our district good modern arms were continuing to come in well. The Arabs preferred the Mauser to our rifle, and Mausers predominated.

On November 18th Subadar Labh Singh rejoined with 146 Indian Other Ranks. These men were mostly of the leave party which left Kingarban in June last. This brought the Regiment well up to strength.

The Arabs were now settling down on the Musaiyib canal in large numbers, as the Politicals had granted them permission to do so. Sniping also ceased about this time.

On the 21st a telephone message was received from the Brigade that we were not for the Diwaniyah Column. From enquiries about roads to the north it looked as if Feluja was to be our destination. This was confirmed by the Brigade Major, who paid us a visit the next day. The demolition of blockhouses on the right bank at Musaiyib, and from thence to Musaiyib canal siding was also ordered. This work was completed in the next four days and was a stiff one, as each blockhouse which held seven men took four army transport carts to remove the sandbags and wire. *See Map No. 14.*

Lieut.-Colonel McVean motored over to Hillah on the 27th to discuss arrangements for the new column moving north.

P

226 HISTORY OF THE 45th RATTRAY'S SIKHS

He returned in the evening with the information that the move would commence on December 2nd.

On the 28th some of us had a good shoot on the "jheel" near the Barrage, and got twenty-eight duck and teal. A very large convoy of supplies arrived at the Barrage for the 77th Brigade Column.

On the 29th on a bitterly cold day, with ice on pools for the first time, the Army Commander paid short visits by car to Musaiyib and the Barrage. Whilst at Musaiyib a very sad incident occurred, for Lieut. F. Adams, M.C. (attached), was accidentally killed. He had only been with us two months and was a gallant young officer, who had seen a lot of hard fighting in France.

On the 30th all blockhouses in Musaiyib were demolished, also the defences in Husaniyah Post. The two platoons "C" Company at this place returned to Musaiyib.

December. The 87th Punjabis arrived at the Barrage to relieve us, and all the troops of the new Column passed through on their way to Musaiyib.

A regimental dump of surplus kits was made at the Barrage to proceed eventually to Baghdad. Subadar Wadhawa Singh and eighty Indian Other Ranks, mostly weakly men, were left as a guard with it.

On the 2nd the Regiment encamped outside the Menzil. "D" Company marched in from the Barrage, and a company of the 87th Punjabis took over all duties.

The following day the Regiment joined the 77th Infantry Brigade Column in camp on the left bank north of Musaiyib Town.

See Map No. 14. The composition of the Column was as follows :—

77th Infantry Brigade Headquarters, Commanding Brig.-General B. C. Dent, C.M.G., D.S.O.

5th Cavalry (less two squadrons).

1 section No. 131 Battery Royal Field Artillery.

No. 40 Pack Battery.

32nd Sikh Pioneers (less two companies).

45th Rattray's Sikhs.

108th Infantry.

Two battalions, the 2nd Battalion East Yorkshire Regiment

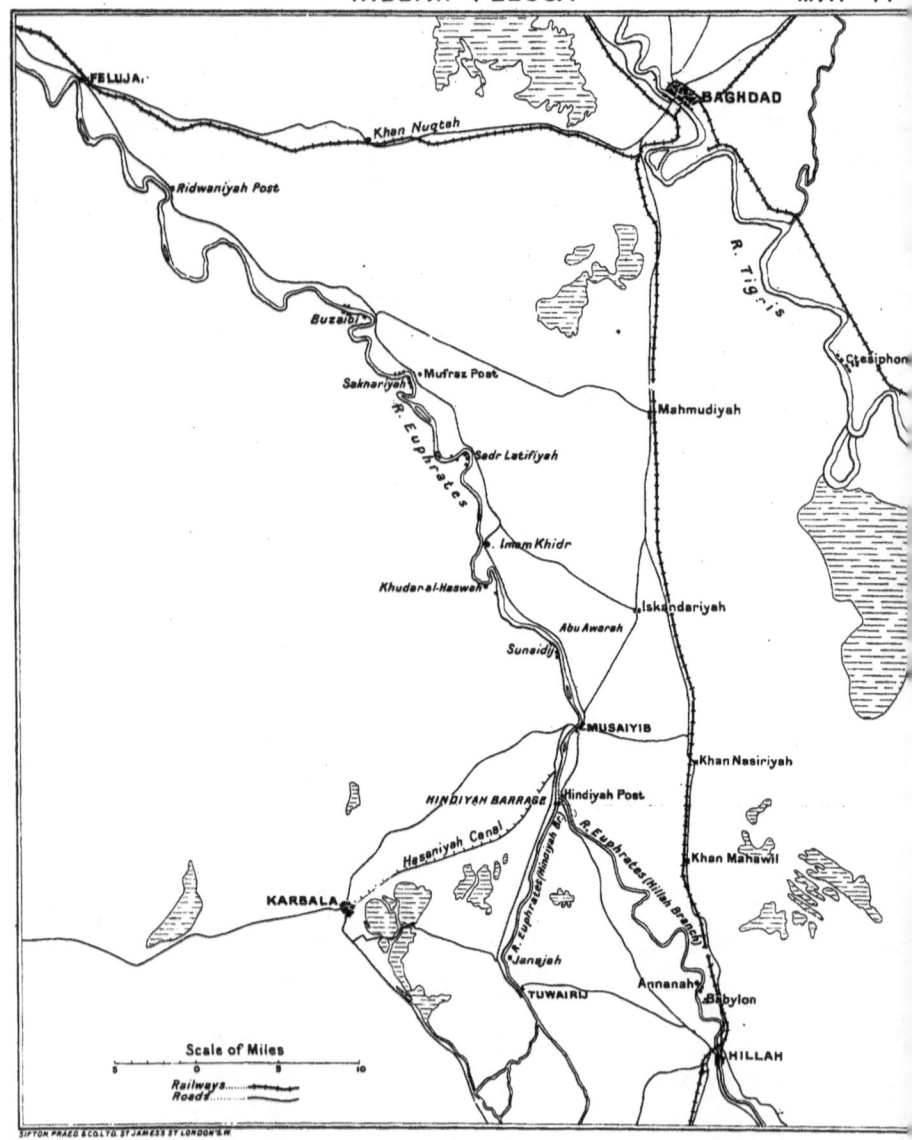

HISTORY OF THE 45TH RATTRAY'S SIKHS 227

and the 1/10th Gurkha Rifles, were starting from Mahmudiyah and were to join us on the 4th day.

The transport was mostly mahelas (Arab boats).

The object of the Column was to sweep a broad tract of country to Feluja and thence to Baghdad, and so to smash any opposition that might be encountered.

The Force marched off in two Columns. Left: one section 131st Battery Royal Field Artillery, and 45th Sikhs under Lieut.-Colonel D. A. D. McVean. Right: remainder of Force under General Officer Commanding Brigade. *See Map No. 14. December 4th.*

This was a short march of six miles and we camped at Y.Y.39 Central.

A Sepoy was put under arrest this day for wearing outside his uniform a sword which he called a "Kirpan." He had returned from leave recently, and the weapon was confiscated. We had heard but little of the Kirpan agitation in those days.

We marched in two columns: we were with the right column this day. No Arabs were seen at all, and we camped after a short march at Imam Khidr. *December 5th.*

There was splendid shooting just north of camp and four guns got thirteen brace of black partridge. A friendly sheikh gave the Regiment a present of thirty sheep.

Another short march of six miles in two columns on a wide front. We marched with the left column on the road. No opposition was met with, and we camped at Sadr Latifiyah. *December 6th.*

The cold seemed to increase daily, and to-day we had very thick ice on standing water.

We marched in the right column and made a wide detour. We burnt two small villages and picked up one .303 rifle with forty rounds. *December 7th.*

After a march of fourteen miles, we arrived in camp at the mouth of the Yusufiyah Canal, and found the Column consisting of the East Yorkshire Regiment and 1/10th Gurkhas already in camp, having arrived from Mahmudiyah.

The Arabs made themselves very scarce and there was therefore no opposition.

The mahela convoy did not get in till midnight, so we were without tents and the night was bitterly cold.

Captain Aston, Political Officer of Musaiyib, who had *December 8th.*

lived with us till now, left us for Musaiyib as we were out of his district.

On account of his cheery personality we were very sorry to lose him, and he had always brought much comfort to the men in the procuring of much milk, charcoal and other comforts from the Arabs.

We marched with the left column along the road, and got into camp at Karushiyah (nine miles) by 14.00 hours. The mahelas were again late, but we got tents up after dark. The night was not so cold, and for the first time for a fortnight it did not freeze.

December 9th.

We marched at 07.00 hours as part of the right column right out in the "Blue." No Arabs seen. The Brigade informed us that the Arab estimate of the Column was 16,000!

We camped north of Ridhwaniyah Post. The day was cloudy and not nearly so cold and rain looked imminent.

December 10th.

We marched straight into Feluja about six miles. The new Divisional Commander flew over by 'plane from Baghdad, but we did not see him.

We got heavy rain about sunset, but managed to get our tents up just in time.

The following day we halted at Feluja. Two guns accompanied the General out shooting, and brought back twenty-one-and-a-half brace of black partridge.

December 12th.

The Column marched straight across the desert on a broad front to Khan Nuqta, twenty miles. "C" Company did rear guard.

We camped close to the Khan where Colonel Leachman, the famous Political Officer, was foully murdered in August. Not an Arab was to be seen. Tents and blankets were to have come by train, but there was some bungle and we got none. There was a very heavy dew at night, which turned to frost, and a heavy mist in the early morning.

The following day we marched at 07.30 hours in a dense mist towards Baghdad (twenty miles) which was reached at 15.00 hours. The Brigade went into camp at the Khirr Depot, a dusty and dirty spot. Our tents and blankets arrived by train before nightfall.

On arrival we were warned to march to Hillah on the 15th,

but this was cancelled the next day to the joy of all, as India looked closer in sight.

We stayed in camp at the Khirr Depot until the 18th, when we marched over to our old camp at Hinaidi headed from the bridge of boats onwards by the Band and Drums.

We made the camp ship-shape, got the running track going, and practised for the forthcoming sports. The Gymnastic Squad also got going.

On the 20th the 15th Sikhs arrived from Hillah, and encamped at Jalani, one-and-a-half miles from us. A great *entente* between all ranks prevailed. On December 23rd we dined their Officers in our mess.

On the 24th our Drums marched the 15th Sikhs to Baghdad East station, whence they entrained and left for Kingarban at 02.00 hours on Christmas morning. They first dined us at the Officers' Club, Baghdad. " Some " night was spent, and their Officers went straight off to the train after dinner.

It was known now that the Regiment would proceed down the Shatt-El-Gharraf (River Hai) with a column in January, and return to India afterwards if all went well.

There were torrents of rain on the 26th, 27th and 29th and many of our tents were completely flooded out.

On the 30th an order of the day was received gazetting Captain A. E. Curtis a bar to his M.C.

On the 31st Brig.-General B. C. Dent and his Brigade Major, Brevet Lieut.-Colonel Hastings dined with us and we drank in the New Year with excellent rum punch.

The beginning of the New Year found the Regiment with *1920.* a strength of thirteen British Officers, eighteen Indian Officers, *January.* and 955 Indian Other Ranks.

There was much rain and wind for the first three days, but we were finally able to fix our last Regimental Sports in Baghdad for the 5th.

The 5th opened with a dense chilly fog and at 10.30 hours the new 17th Divisional Commander made us a speech, which was the same for all units of the 17th Division who were returning to India on the termination of the operations down the River Hai.

We held our sports in the afternoon in glorious weather. Several General Officers were present, as well as many representatives of the Air Force and of General Headquarters, a very large gathering.

Amongst other events the handling of arms display by 100 men, the gymnastic display, and retreat by the Drums were all carried out with traditional thoroughness and created a good impression. Just before the sports the Royal Air Force gave a demonstration by twenty-four 'planes over the city.

On the 6th were held the Baghdad Troops Area Sports. We won the following events :—
1. Relay Race (1,000 Yards) 1st place.
2. Tug-of-War (final versus 50th Pack Battery) 1st place.
3. 100 Yards Race, 1st and 2nd places.
4. $\frac{1}{4}$ Mile Race, first four places.
5. 1 Mile Race, first four places.
6. Long Jump, 1st and 2nd places (equal).
7. Obstacle Race, 1st and 3rd places.

Thus in our last big Sports in Mesopotamia we won every event except the high jump.

On January 9th Captain C. A. Phillips, Lieut. C. S. Nash camped near Hinaidi railway station with 100 Indian Other Ranks and the Band and Drums (49 O.R.). They were to proceed straight down river with our dump of heavy kit to Basra under line-of-communication arrangements.

On January 10th " A " Company (Captain Fyldes) entrained in dull and threatening weather for Kut-el-Amara. The remainder of the Regiment were to have entrained in the evening, but at 09.00 hours orders were received for us to embark on the S.14 by 14.00 hours. This order was carried out, but owing to the non-arrival of the two barges till late, we remained tied up for the night off 17th Divisional Headquarters at Daura.

Proceeding early next morning we got as far as Bgailah and tied up. Our transport under 2/Lieut. Patterson passed us by train about noon. We arrived at Kut at 12 noon on the 12th, disembarked and joined " A " Company in camp.

The next three days were spent in camp whilst Kutcol concentrated. Officers and men were able to pay visits to the Pentagon, and to the Hai battlefields of 1916–17.

The composition of the Column to proceed down the River

Hai to meet another from Nasiriyeh, known as Kutcol, was as follows :—

Commanding, Brig.-General B. C. Dent, C.M.G., D.S.O.

Troops.

1 squadron 5th Cavalry.
131st Battery Royal Field Artillery (less one section howitzers).
50th Pack Battery.
61st Company Q.V.O. Sappers and Miners.
1 Company Machine Gun Battalion.
1st Battalion Royal Irish Fusiliers (approx. 500 rifles).
45th Rattray's Sikhs ,, 780 ,,
94th Infantry ,, 850 ,,
108th Infantry ,, 740 ,,
1/10th Gurkha Rifles ,, 550 ,,
with the usual ancillary services attached.

The transport was to be Mahelas (native boats) and the S.I (Army Commanders' ship) for Column Headquarters, two " Fly " gunboats and an ambulance steamer were to accompany the Column down the Shatt-Al-Gharraf or River Hai.

The object of this Column was as follows. During the insurrection the powerful Muntafiq Confederation of tribes had kept out of active participation. This Confederacy dwelt down the Shatt-Al-Gharraf between Kut and Nasiriyeh, and were both numerous and bellicosely inclined. Fortunately largely through fine work on the part of Political Officers concerned, these tribes did not join in, though at times it was a matter of touch-and-go. The Army Commander therefore decided to traverse their country with two Columns to show them that British Forces could and were able to do it.

Turkish Columns in the past had met with great disaster on more than one occasion over this same tract of country.

The Column commenced its southward march at 09.00 *January 16th.* hours. The Regiment did rear guard. The Column only did ten miles, and went into camp. The S.1 was left behind *See Map No. 15.* as it could not get over the bar at the confluence of the Shatt-Al-Gharraf with the River Tigris.

Very ominous black clouds appeared in the evening and rain appeared imminent.

January 17th.

The Column marched thirteen miles. We were left flank guard, and did a good eighteen miles over much plough and many canals. The rear guard actually arrived in camp before we did.

The S.1 stuck five miles back, and the gunboats and ambulance ship further back still. Brig.-General Dent, having no mess, dined with us.

January 18th.

The Column marched into Hai Town, we marched at the head of the main body. Just outside the town we halted for half an hour, to wait for a squadron of aeroplanes from Baghdad. When these arrived and circled over the town for half an hour, we marched through the town through dense gaping crowds of Arabs and camped one mile south of the town itself.

The river fell a further ten inches, and all the river craft got stuck, in fact some of our mahelas could not get up so we had no tents.

This caused a halt on the 19th, and again on the 20th. One company of the 94th were left as a garrison over all the derelict shipping about three miles north of Hai Town, and we proceeded on our march again on the 21st.

January 21st.

We marched as advanced guard to the Column to the new camp near Imam Saiyid Jawwad, about thirteen miles. The mahela convoy arrived in driblets and we got most of our kit and tentage. The weather was very close and stuffy with a following breeze.

January 22nd.

It was our turn for right flank guard to-day, but as the river ran so close to the road, we marched in the main body after the leading unit, the 1/10th Gurkha Rifles. We passed many populous villages on the river to-day mostly fortified by strong flanking towers. The men were a fine-looking lot and well armed, but the women and children were in the villages, and the flocks were out grazing. The crops were also well advanced.

After a march of about thirteen miles on a close day we encamped one mile north of Qalat Sikar, a standard river town with minaret and palm trees as is found everywhere on the Rivers Tigris and Euphrates. Just after our arrival in camp, two flights of aeroplanes (fifteen in all) arrived from Baghdad and circled over the town for half an hour before

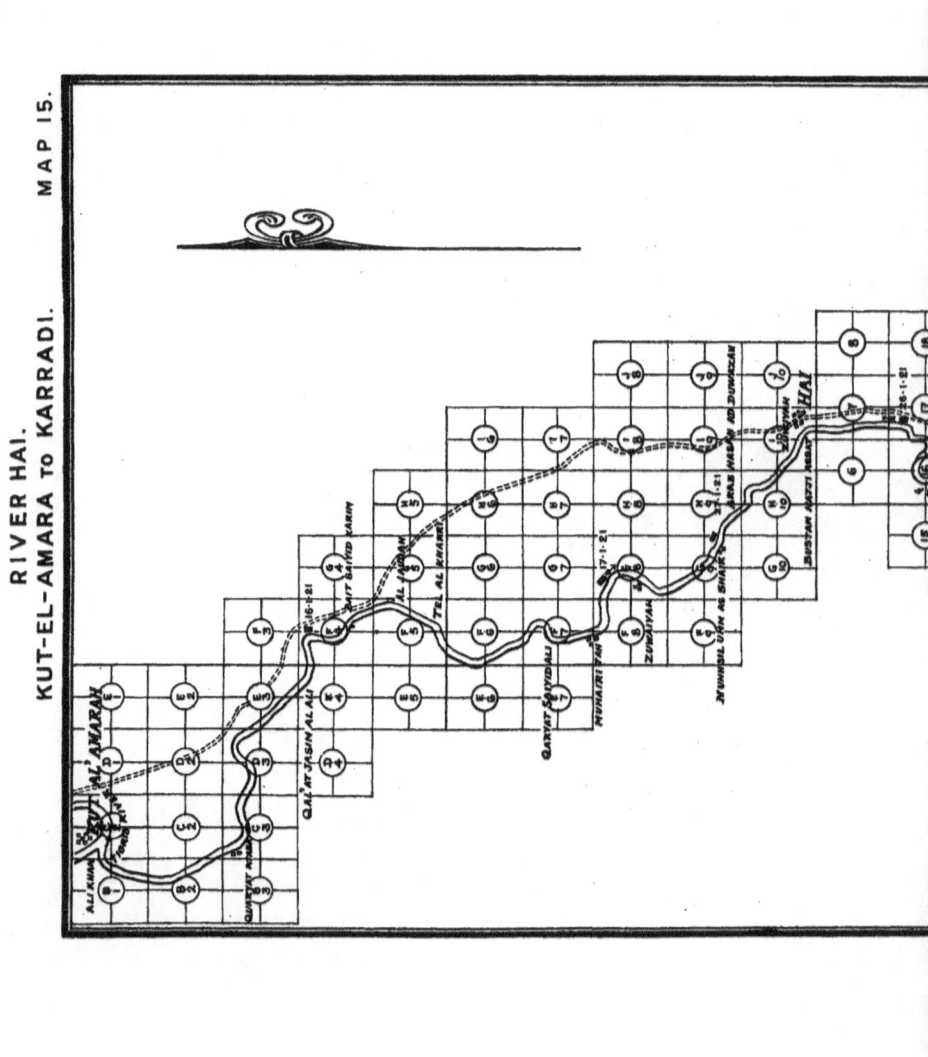

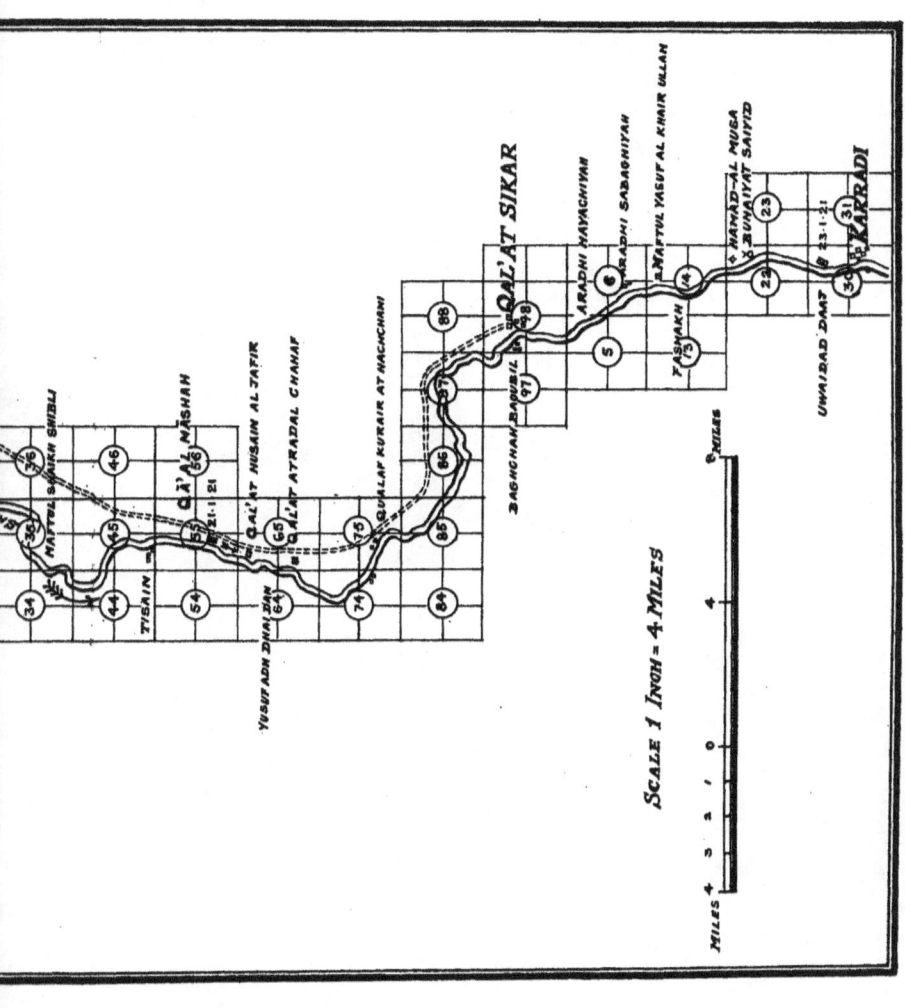

returning. Many sheikhs came in with their retinues to pay their respects to the Column Commander.

Lieut. Patterson was sent back in an ambulance to look after the bakery, which was stuck in shallow water five or six miles south of Hai Town. He had an escort of a few Royal Irish Fusiliers, and two Vickers guns.

The mahela convoy were well up to time for the first time since the Column left Kut.

January 23rd. The Column marched at 08.30 hours. We were rear guard and left camp at 09.45 hours. We made but little progress for two hours owing to the tortuous streets of Qalat Sikar, and the serpentine nature of the first part of the road. About half way we were nearly caught in a heavy thunderstorm, but the storm moved east across our front and then north, and we only got a few drops of rain.

We as rear guard got into camp, supposed to be ten-and-a-half miles, at 14.30 hours. All our mahelas were, for the first time, in before us, so we were quickly snugly settled in. We found the 34th Infantry Brigade Column encamped on the opposite bank, and in the evening Brig.-General Coningham came over to see us.

There was rain in the night, but fortunately not very hard.

January 24th. Both Columns marched at 08.30 hours, the 34th south to Nasiriyeh and our Column on the road back to Kut.

It was an unpromising-looking morning, but there was no rain. About noon the weather cleared, followed by a stiff northerly breeze and a curious haze which reduced visibility to under two miles.

We marched as a regiment immediately behind the transport and in front of the rear guard. We camped in the neighbourhood of Qalat Sikar.

Continuing our march on the 25th and 26th without incident we arrived in camp six miles south of Hai Town on the 26th. The same night we received orders to march at 07.00 hours seven miles to the scene of all the grounded vessels. A stiff breeze sprang up at night, which developed into a hurricane dust-storm with intense cold. We passed a truly beastly night.

January 27th. At 07.00 hours we marched (less one platoon per company) in bitter cold weather to a camp three miles north of Hai Town. All transport was sent back to the old camp, as the river was too low for mahelas, and our four platoons arrived in with our kit before dark.

Owing to the failure of the river transport and the shortage of land transport, it was decided to march the Column into Kut (twenty-five miles) in echelons, and to our joy we were detailed to march on the morrow.

January 28th. At 07.30 hours the following units of the Column marched to Kut.

131st Battery Royal Field Artillery (less one section).
50th Pack Battery.
" C " Company Machine Gun Battalion.
45th Sikhs.
108th Infantry.

The day was an ideal one for marching, and the whole echelon reached the old camp at Kut right bank at 16.30 hours.

Our dump was ready with hot tea, and we were all soon very snug in camp, having finished to the best of our knowledge our last march and operations in Mesopotamia.

February 1st. We stayed in camp for the next five days waiting for a ship to Basra. We spent February 1st, the anniversary of the attack in 1917, close to the scene of action. This happened to be our last day, for on the 2nd at 15.00 hours we got orders to embark on the P.S.55 immediately. As can be imagined the men got to work, and the whole Regiment, men and baggage, were on board by 17.30 hours. We had to leave our first line transport here. They had been through everything with the Regiment since September, 1917, and we parted with regret on both sides.

Brig.-General B. C. Dent came to say goodbye to us on board and we remained tied up for the night.

We got away at 07.00 hours on the 3rd on a glorious morning, one of Mesopotamia's very best, and passing all the familiar landmarks, the Pusht-I-Kuh range of mountains, Amara, etc., with a cheerful noise on the part of the men, which only ceased when they were asleep, reached Basra at 18.30 hours on the 4th.

Here we slept on board, and disembarking on the 5th,

marched by companies to the Demobilization Camp, Magil, where all the Regiment were billetted in huts.

Here we remained until the 19th waiting for a ship, when we received orders to embark on the H.M.T. *Hannover* on the 22nd. The time was spent with route marches, kit inspections and games and sports.

On the 8th the following wire from the Army Commander was received by Lieut.-Colonel McVean :—

"I regret that I am unable to come and thank you and your gallant regiment again for their good work before they leave Mesopotamia. Please convey to all ranks my regret at losing them, and give them my best wishes."

On the 20th the Board of Survey on our kit was held. The whole Regiment fell in with their kits laid out in lines, and the whole ordeal was successfully over in four hours.

On the 21st our heavy kits were loaded on the *Hannover*.

On the 22nd the great day arrived, the Regiment left camp at 07.30 hours headed by the magnificent band and drums of the 4th Battalion the Royal Fusiliers, kindly sent by Lieut.-Colonel Walker, C.M.G., D.S.O., and the Officers.

We were quickly aboard and ready to sail by 10.00 hours. We sailed at noon, but before sailing the whole of the 1/10th Gurkha Rifles came to see us off *en masse*.

We arrived at Karachi on the early morning of February 27th; it was almost five years to a day since the Regiment embarked there.

Disembarking and proceeding to the Rest Camp, we entrained for Multan on the evening of the 28th, arriving at Multan at noon on March 2nd, where we were played into our lines by the bands of five regiments.

Thus ended the fullest five years of the Regiment's existence, in which it may be truly said that they more than upheld their reputation as a fine fighting Regiment.

CHAPTER XI

THE EXPERIENCES OF CERTAIN OF OUR PRISONERS-OF-WAR
WHILST IN THE HANDS OF THE TURKS

No. 799 Sepoy Ujagar Singh, " A " Company, who escaped before his batch of prisoners reached Mosul.

" After the attack of the 36th and 45th Sikhs on the 1st February last, I was wounded and taken prisoner, after a small party of about twenty or twenty-five of us had been completely surrounded, and no help was forthcoming from the rear.

" Those of us who could walk were taken back along a communication trench to the Tigris, being first of all stripped of our uniform, boots, watches, and money, etc. The Turks murdered all our wounded who could not walk. I saw this with my own eyes; they bayonetted Subadar Ram Singh as he lay wounded, but the other names I cannot give as I did not personally know the men. We were then taken across the Tigris in ' bellums ' to some huts north of Kut-el-Amara, which appeared to be some big general's Headquarters. We slept in one of the huts that night, locked in and under escort.

" On February 2nd we were seen by a General and his staff, also lots of officers came to look at us, and we were much photographed. After this the badly wounded were put in carts whilst those of us who could, walked, and we were led round and shown to all the Regiments in the vicinity. We were then conducted in the same manner along a road to the River Tigris somewhere near Bgailah and put on a steamer about midnight on February 2nd or 3rd.

" The 3rd we spent on the ship, but were given no food whatever, and we arrived at Baghdad about 4 p.m., on February 4th.

"The wounded, myself included, were taken to a hospital and the remainder were sent to the jail.

"In hospital they cut off our kés and beards by force, although we did all we could to protest. They also took away our Punjabi kit, and in their stead gave us a suit of Turkish kit and a balaclava cap.

" We received three small loaves a day, and occasionally some rice-gruel, also very scant attention. Although my wound, a bomb wound on the right leg, had not healed, I was discharged from hospital to the jail about February 22nd. But in jail, an English Medical Officer, also a prisoner-of-war, and whose name I didn't know, looked after me very well, and I seldom went out on the fatigues with the others.

"About this time we knew that there was something in the wind, as the prisoners did heavy fatigue work on loading Turkish rations, household goods, etc., into railway trucks. The Jews who were made to guard us, also told us on the quiet, that the English were advancing, and that the Turks had lost so many men on one day, and so many on another.

"About March 2nd at 8 a.m., all the prisoners, English, Russians and Indians, were given the usual two small loaves each, and marched up the road towards Mosul between the Baghdad railway and the River Tigris. The first night we halted at a Police Post (? Qaleh Kermea) about eighteen miles from Baghdad. For four days we received no food whatever, and marched from 6 a.m. to 6 p.m., with two halts for the escort to eat their food. Our escort consisted of about twenty Turkish Cavalry.

"On the evening of the 6th (about) we arrived at Samarra, where, on the morning of the 7th, we received about six 'Chitaks' of wheat each. In Samarra we saw no formed bodies of troops, but only some officers and guards, and a good many Arabs were doing fatigue work. We stayed in Samarra for five days, and only received a ration of a little wheat daily, whilst we never had a blanket between us the whole time.

"On the morning of the 12th, we marched from Samarra, and each of us received ten small loaves, which was to be our ration as far as Mosul. About March 14th we arrived in Tekrit, where there were encamped about thirty German

Officers. One of them, who talked English and Hindustani very well, told us that the British Army had captured Baghdad.

"On the 15th we marched again, and two days later, I escaped with Havildar Kesar Singh, 24th Punjabis. Our guards had been most vigilant as far as Tekrit, but after Tekrit they got slack, and on the night we escaped the sentry was asleep.

"When we left Tekrit we had seven small loaves, which we had saved up, but we had absolutely no water arrangements whatever, not even a tin to drink out of. We chose the right bank to get back by, because we thought there would be fewer Turks there, and we kept well away from the river.

"We marched by night only, by day we used to lie up, and we guided ourselves by keeping the North Star behind us. The country was mostly undulating, and was much intersected by nullahs. We went for two days without finding water, and during this time a party of armed and mounted Arabs passed very close to us, but we lay very low and escaped their observation. At the end of the second day we came quite unexpectedly on a well in a nullah, which at the time was deserted by man, though some flocks were grazing about a mile off. Here we drank our fill, and washed ourselves and our clothes. We stayed there all day, and went on that night for about three days more without water. At the end of the third day we came upon an Arab encampment, and were so exhausted, that we decided to enter it, and ask for food and water, whatever the consequences might be.

"The Arabs threatened us with loaded rifles, and called us Kafirs and prisoners, and things looked dangerous, but we kept affirming that we were Faqirs on the way back to India from Mecca. They then made us repeat the 'Kalma,' which we did; Havildar Kesar Singh doing it particularly well, as he had learnt a lot of Arabic during his year's imprisonment. They then gave us food and water, and let us go, but made us give up our Turkish clothing, and gave us a complete outfit of Arab clothing including the 'Angad' instead.

"We walked on for some two or three days, and arrived at a large lake (? Lake Akarkuf). There we saw marks of artillery wheels, also empty bully beef tins, and empty cartridge cases of English make, so we followed this track. At night Havildar Kesar Singh felt seedy, and said he thought he had pneumonia, so we selected a dry spot to sleep on to find next morning that the water had risen on all sides and that we were cut off.

"There was however, a small Masjid close by, so we entered it and found a little salt there; we ate this, and drank a lot of water, as we were very hungry and thirsty, and our supply of bread was exhausted. We stayed there for the next night, and in the morning three unarmed and dismounted Arabs came into the Masjid. This apparently lay on a difficult and tricky track to Baghdad through the lake.

"We asked them to take us into Baghdad with the hopes of a reward, and though at first unwilling for fear of being shot by the English, they finally agreed, and that day took us to their village, which was about ten miles from Baghdad.

"They fed us and gave us water on our arrival. The inhabitants of this village treated us quite well, and kept asking us if the English Government would allow them to keep their rifles or not, to which we replied that we did not know. The next day they took us towards Baghdad, and they took us into the picquet line occupied by the 8th Gurkhas, which Regiment I found that a Major Keen was Commanding, who told me that he was a brother of Major Keen in my regiment. We reached Baghdad on March 27th, and there our troubles ended. The Arabs who took us in were given a reward of seventy rupees each."

No. 325 Naick Kaka Singh, and No. 461 Naick Narinjan Singh, who escaped after being recaptured.

"On February 1st we, both wounded and surrounded by the Turks after the attack by the 36th and 45th Sikhs, were taken prisoner by the Turks, and reached Baghdad about 4 p.m. on February 4th, 1917 [up to this date their story tallies with that of No. 779 Sepoy Ujagar Singh].

"On arrival we were taken to some cells in the Barracks for three days, where we were questioned daily by their Intelligence Officers. In this place were also many Arab prisoners. On February 8th, we were sent over to a big "Serai" on the right bank of the Tigris near the bridge of boats. Here we met about a dozen prisoners of our Regiment; there were also about twenty British soldiers, and some two hundred Russians in the place. On the top floor of this 'Serai' were about seventy Mussalman deserters from our army, but we held no intercourse with them, or they with us. They seemed to be under no kind of restraint, and were allowed into the city.

"For about three weeks all the prisoners were employed on making a protective 'Bund' outside the city on the right bank. We worked from early morning until dusk, on a small loaf of coarse bread, with a rest of half an hour at mid-day.

"About the 27th our work was altered, and we were put on to loading up German Officers' kit on the railway station, carrying it there from boats on the river. We saw the German Officers with the kit, and they left by train in batches. Their demeanour seemed to be downhearted. Many Turkish Officers came to see them off, and there seemed to be no enmity between them.

"Rumours reached us that the Turks were being forced back, and from the signs of increased activity we knew that the British Army was not far off.

"About midnight on March 2nd, we each received two loaves and were told that we were to march to Samarra. At about 8 a.m. on the 3rd we started, and were told that the rations we had been given were to last for five days, and that we should get no more.

"We arrived in Samarra on the 6th, and each received a handful of barley as a ration. On the right bank near the railway station was a big camp full of soldiers, we think all infantry. There were also many German Officers in camp there. We remained in Samarra about a week, and on the 12th Arabs told us that Baghdad had fallen to the British Army.

"On the 13th, we were each given ten small loaves as our ration, to last till Mosul was reached, and we marched on this date, arriving at Tekrit on March 15th.

"On the 16th we again marched for Mosul, and during the night a couple of days later, No. 799 Sepoy Ujagar Singh of our Regiment, and Havildar Kesar Singh 24th Punjabis escaped, and shortly after them, No. 788 Sepoy Kehar Singh, and No. 1355/15 Sepoy Wazir Singh, also of the 45th.

"These escapes became known to the Turkish guard at roll call before we marched, and in their anger they beat us a lot with their rifles. On the march this day No. 1187 Sepoy Udham Singh, 45th Sikhs, became very ill with fever, and fell down about noon. The Turkish guard lashed his hands together with a rope, and tied him to the crupper of a horse, and so dragged him along. He fainted after an hour or so of this treatment so they untied his hands, and having struck him over the head with the butt end of a rifle several times, and having stripped him of all his clothing, they left him on the ground. We do not know what his ultimate fate was, but he probably died then or shortly afterwards.

"Some of us made plans to escape, but I (Kaka Singh) had often carried Arjan Singh, who was sick, on my back for four marches, and it was not until a Havildar promised me he would look after him that I decided to go.

"On about March 21st we decided to escape that night, *Our first escape.* and No. 872 Sepoy Lal Singh, 45th Sikhs and Lance Naick Nikka Singh, 1st Sappers and Miners, agreed to accompany us. It turned out to be a very good night for the purpose, as it was raining hard and very dark.

"We decided to go out one by one some 200 yards and wait so as not to disturb the sentry. About midnight the sentry went to sleep, so Narinjan Singh went first, followed by Nikka Singh, and then Lal Singh and Kaka Singh. We had three small loaves each, and one small earthenware jar for water. We were all dressed in the rags the Turks had given us in Baghdad in exchange for our Punjabi clothing. We walked all night, and at dawn on the 22nd got into a hole in some broken ground, well away from the river and road, covering ourselves over with brushwood.

"In the evening after dark we went to the river (some three to four miles distant), drank our fill and filled our jar. On our way inland we saw a fire, so we made a wide detour into some hills (? the Jebel Makhul). We lost our way somewhat, and daylight of the 23rd caught us in these hills, where we hid in a nullah all day.

"We suffered greatly from the want of water all day on

the 24th, and not recognizing our position Naick Kaka Singh went up the biggest hill nearby before dusk to look round. He saw the river, so we made for it by way of a nullah. Here we drank our fill. We also hit the Mosul-Baghdad road, and kept a course about a mile west of it going south.

"In this manner we went along walking by night, and halting by day until about midnight on March 29th, when we saw what we took to be the lights of Samarra.

"We at once proceeded westwards to try and clear the flank of the Turkish lines, but first of all ran into a Turk. He called out 'Sher Ali' several times, and then ran back to a tent close by for his rifle. He shouted at us for some time, but we bent low and ran for our lives. We then came upon a fire, and again a second fire, so we made a very wide detour and hid in a hole in some broken ground until daylight.

"On the 30th after much walking we were almost mad with thirst, and seeing some Arab coolies we decided to ask them for water, thinking that if they detained us, we could get away again. So we crawled up to them, and asked for water. They gave us both food and water, but they would not let us go, as they said we were prisoners, though we loudly and often repeated the words 'Faqir' and 'Mecca.'

"On the 31st these same Arabs took us into the Turkish lines some thirty miles south of Samarra, and made us over to a Turkish Officer. He questioned us, and we again said that we were returning to India from Mecca. We were however, again made prisoners, and found in the same tent four British soldiers, and four Mussalman ship's Khalassis. We twelve prisoners were marched into Samarra, and put under escort in the lines of some regiment. Here we found No. 788 Sepoy Kehar Singh, and No. 1355/15 Sepoy Wazir Singh, who had escaped on March 16th (ante), and who had been recaptured in Samarra.

"About April 2nd, the fourteen of us were given the usual five small loaves as our ration as far as Mosul, and we marched up the same old road again with an escort of one Turkish N.C.O. and six men.

"We marched for five days, and thought that if we did not escape then, we never would as we were nearing Mosul.

These marches were extremely trying to us, as we were weak from the privations of our first escape, our bare feet were very bruised and cut about, besides which our Turkish escort were continually hitting us with their rifles.

"Lance Naick Nikka Singh, and No. 1355/15 Sepoy Wazir Singh agreed to accompany us again, but No. 872 Sepoy Lal Singh and No. 788 Sepoy Kehar Singh, who were also of our party before, were too exhausted to join us again. We four therefore decided that we would escape again on the night of April 6th/7th.

"On the 6th, we did a very long march. Having agreed to go out one at a time and meet, our chance came about midnight. Lance Naick Nikka Singh and Sepoy Wazir Singh, went out when the sentry went to sleep. Then, to our great consternation he woke up, and commenced pacing round us, so we two crouched down again. After what seemed to us an age, the sentry again went to sleep, so we (Naicks Kaka Singh and Narinjan Singh) also got out to find that the first couple had not waited for us, and we did not see them again until we met them in our own lines, for they got in all right a day or two before us. *Our second escape.*

"Profiting by our previous experience of lack of water we had, on the march up, taken a small leather 'Mushak' off an old Arab woman, and we had six small loaves between us. On this night we made about ten miles, reaching some low hills at dawn, where we lay up in a nullah.

"We think that on our escape being found out, that the alarm must have been given, for about 10 a.m. a patrol came out and searched the hills. One of them came and stood on a high hill just above where we were hiding, and looked round for quite a long time, but mercifully for us he did not see us crouching below him.

"We went on our way for six days very warily, going down to the river at dusk, and having the 'Mushak' we were very well off for water.

"After dusk on April 12th, we again came upon the lights of Samarra, and started to make a wide detour round the Turkish camp. We ran into two picquets and were challenged, and we had an uneasy time by running into two Turkish patrols, but we got through all right this time. Being frightened of being caught again, we made a very wide detour.

"We finished our loaves on the 12th, and from this date onwards suffered very acutely from hunger.

"From here we walked for five nights, hiding by day, with only our one 'Mushak' of water. Our only food was grass, except in one place where we found a long strip of leather on the site of an old Arab encampment, which we halved and ate.

"On the 17th, very weak indeed, and more dead than alive, we saw the railway track and made for it. Even then we were not sure if we had got behind the Turks or not, but soon we came upon some empty milk tins, and then felt sure that we had entered the British zone.

"Shortly afterwards we saw seven motor ambulances approaching us, and we stopped them. They took us for Arabs, and asked us what we wanted. We told them that we were escaped prisoners-of-war, and gave the name of our regiment, and the number of our brigade and division. Then a Medical Officer, a Captain, got out and congratulated us, and took us in an ambulance up towards the front to the camp of the 124th Baluchistan Infantry. We stayed there two days very weak, and very well cared for. We passed through several hospitals and eventually arrived in Baghdad, and thence to the Regiment at Amara.

APPENDIX I

BRITISH OFFICERS WHO SERVED WITH THE REGIMENT
1914-21

Lieut.-Colonel F. T. Stewart. Appointed Commandant L. of C. Defences, November 16th, 1916. Invalided to India.

Major H. B. Rattray, D.S.O. Commandant, November 17th, 1916. *Killed in action, February 1st, 1917.*

Major W. W. Van Someren, D.S.O. Wounded in France, December 21st, 1914; Light duty in U.K. Retired in 1920.

Captain F. C. Waterfield. Wounded in France, May 12th, 1915. *Died of wounds, May 21st, 1915.*

Captain H. C. Strong. With Burma M.P. *Drowned at sea, February 25th, 1915.*

Captain R. Rainsford Hannay. *Killed in action, February 1st, 1917.*

Captain J. E. Waller. Invalided to India, July 19th, 1916; Commanded Depot.

Captain K. G. Hyde Cates. With 15th Sikhs and afterwards Special Service Officer, E.E.F.

Lieut. R. A. Macausland. Staff Captain 37th Infantry Brigade, November 5th, 1916.

Lieut. G. H. Atkinson. Invalided to India, July 8th, 1916; Rejoined, October 25th, 1916. *Killed in action, February 1st, 1917.*

2/Lieut. A. C. Curtis, M.C. Wounded January 29th, 1917; Invalided to India, March 13th, 1917. Rejoined, October 2nd, 1918.

2/Lieut. R. H. L. Minchin. Invalided to India, May 4th, 1916.

2/Lieut. B. W. Key. Invalided to India, June, 1916; Rejoined, October 26th, 1917. Wounded, October 20th, 1918; Invalided to India, November 21st, 1918. Afterwards with 2/15th Sikhs.

2/Lieut. G. Mitchell. *Killed in action, February 1st,* 1917.

2/Lieut. A. H. Worster, I.A.R.O. Invalided to India, June, 1916.

2/Lieut. S. F. Criper, I.A.R.O. Invalided to India, July 22nd, 1916; Rejoined, March 12th, 1917. Adjutant Rest Camp, August 17th, 1917.

Captain J. G. Wilson. Joined Regiment in Field, May 14th, 1916. *Killed in action, February 1st,* 1917.

T/Lieut. V. M. Kaikini, I.M.S. Joined Regiment in Field, July 30th, 1916. Returned to India, July 2nd, 1917.

2/Lieut. J. W. Guise. Joined Regiment in Field, August 3rd, 1916; Wounded, February 1st, 1917. Invalided to India, February 20th, 1917.

2/Lieut. K. H. Preston, I.A.R.O. Joined Regiment in Field, September 13th, 1916. Transferred to 1/151st Sikh Infantry, May 15th, 1918.

2/Lieut. A. C. Stone, I.A.R.O. Joined Regiment in Field, September 21st, 1916. *Killed in action, February 1st,* 1917.

2/Lieut. B. W. Murdoch, I.A.R.O. Joined Regiment in Field, September 21st, 1916. *Killed in action, February 3rd,* 1917.

2/Lieut. C. W. W. Ford, 35th Sikhs. Joined Regiment in Field, October 29th, 1916. Proceeded to India, January 26th, 1918.

Captain R. H. Anderson. Joined Regiment in Field, December 25th, 1916.

2/Lieut. E. Hopkins, I.A.R.O. Joined Regiment in Field, January 24th, 1917. To Political Department Iraq, March 20th, 1917.

Captain W. R. Boswell, 28th Punjabis. Joined Regiment in Field, March 28th, 1917. To 28th Punjabis, December 16th, 1917.

Lieut. R. K. Henson, 25th Punjabis. Joined Regiment in Field, March 28th, 1917. Wounded, October 29th, 1918. Invalided, January 10th, 1919.

Lieut. J. G. Kilpin, 25th Punjabis. Joined Regiment in Field, March 28th, 1917. To 25th Punjabis, March 3rd, 1918.

Lieut. G. L. Watson, I.A.R.O. Joined Regiment in Field, March 28th, 1917. To Labour Corps, November 16th, 1918.

HISTORY OF THE 45TH RATTRAY'S SIKHS 247

Lieut. G. D. Pybus, 14th Sikhs. Joined Regiment in Field, May 14th, 1917. To 14th Sikhs, November 21st, 1918.

Lieut. J. E. Hughes, I.A.R.O. Joined Regiment in Field, May 19th, 1917. Invalided to India, August 19th, 1917.

Captain M. Saunders, 36th Sikhs. Joined Regiment in Field, May 29th, 1917. To Staff Employ, January 17th, 1918.

Lieut. R. B. Ramsbotham, I.A.R.O. Joined Regiment in Field, June 5th, 1917. Demobilized, March 26th, 1919.

Major D. A. D. McVean, D.S.O. Joined Regiment in Field, June 13th, 1917. Commandant, July 27th, 1917.

T./Captain Santokh Singh, I.M.S. Joined Regiment in Field, July 3rd, 1917; Wounded October 29th, 1918. Invalided, November 18th, 1918.

Major B. W. Shuttleworth. Joined Regiment in Field, October 21st, 1917. To British Siberian Mission, January 3rd, 1919.

2/Lieut. R. V. Fox. Joined Regiment in Field, February 23rd, 1918. Wounded July 7th, 1920.

Lieut. J. A. Finlay. Joined Regiment in Field, March 27th, 1918.

Lieut. C. Eastmead, 15th Sikhs. Joined Regiment in Field, March 29th, 1918. To 1/151st Sikh Infantry, May 15th, 1918.

Lieut. A. L. Butcher. Joined Regiment in Field, June 24th, 1918. Wounded, October 29th, 1918.

2/Lieut. G. W. Benton, I.A.R.O. Joined Regiment in Field, June 24th, 1918. Demobilized, March 26th, 1919.

2/Lieut. B. W. Kelly, I.A.R.O. Joined Regiment in Field, June 24th, 1918. Demobilized, March 21st, 1919.

2/Lieut. R. N. Moore, I.A.R.O. Joined Regiment in Field, November 21st, 1918. To 1/113th Infantry, July 31st, 1919.

Captain J. B. Mudge, R.A.M.C. Joined Regiment in Field, December 2nd, 1918. Demobilized, October, 1919.

Lieut. L. G. Mathews, I.A. (T.C.). Joined Regiment in Field, December 20th, 1918. To 1/5th Buffs, April 18th, 1919.

Lieut. C. A. Phillips, I.A. (T.C.). Joined Regiment in Field, December 23rd, 1918.

Lieut. G. M. Worden, I.A. (T.C.). Joined Regiment in Field, April 16th, 1919; Wounded, July 19th, 1920. Invalided, August 24th, 1920.

Lieut. H. St.-C. O. Will. Joined Regiment in Field, October 2nd, 1919.

Lieut. F. T. Birdwood, 36th Sikhs. Joined Regiment in Field, October 27th, 1919. To 36th Sikhs, February, 1920.

Captain J. B. D. Galbraith, R.A.M.C. Joined Regiment in Field, October, 1919. Demobilized, January, 1920.

2/Lieut. A. Patterson. Joined Regiment in Field, January 16th, 1920.

T./Captain M. V. Patakh, I.M.S. Joined Regiment in Field, January 20th, 1920.

Lieut. A. E. Blanchard, D.C.M. Joined Regiment in Field. September 2nd, 1920. To 77th Infantry Brigade Headquarters, November 13th, 1920.

Lieut. F. Adams, M.C. Joined Regiment in Field, September 2nd, 1920. Accidentally killed, November 29th, 1920.

Captain G. B. Fyldes, M.C. Joined Regiment in Field, September 9th, 1920.

Captain D. A. Christie, 14th Sikhs. Joined Regiment in Field, October 6th, 1920.

2/Lieut. C. S. Nash. Joined Regiment in Field, November, 1920.

APPENDIX II

INDIAN OFFICERS WHO SERVED WITH THE REGIMENT 1914-21

Rank	Name	No. or Unit	Date of Promotion Jemadar	Date of Promotion Subadar	
Subadar Major	Sundar Singh				*Wounded January 29th, 1917. To India on leave, June 30th, 1920. To Pension as Hon. Captain, January 6th, 1921.*
Subadar	Ishar Singh				*Invalided September 5th, 1916. To Pension, January 16th, 1917.*
Subadar	Nidhan Singh				*Invalided April 4th, 1916. Rejoined August 29th, 1917. To India on duty, July 8th, 1918. Rejoined May 1st, 1920. Wounded and died of wounds, July 7th, 1920.*
Subadar	Wariam Singh				*Wounded February 1st, 1917. Invalided February 17th, 1917. Rejoined August 29th, 1917. Transferred to 1/151st Sikh Infantry, May 15th, 1918.*
Subadar	Natha Singh, I.O.M.				*Invalided April 4th, 1916. To Pension, October 15th, 1916.*
Subadar	Narain Singh				*Wounded December 15th, 1916 and again February 1st, 1917. Invalided February 15th, 1917. Rejoined August 13th, 1918. Appointed Subadar Major in 1920. To Pension September 1st, 1922.*
Subadar	Lehna Singh				*Killed in action February 1st, 1917.*
Subadar	Bhag Singh				*Wounded February 1st, 1917. Invalided February 15th, 1917. Died of wounds at his home, April 25th, 1918.*
Jemadar	Thaman Singh			26.3.16	*Wounded and Prisoner-of-War, February 1st, 1917. Died in Turkey on June 6th, 1917, of his wounds.*
Jemadar	Ram Singh			19.6.16	*Killed in action February 1st, 1917.*
Jemadar	Karm Singh			25.8.16	*Killed in action February 1st, 1917.*
Jemadar	Lehna Singh				*Wounded Feb 1, 1917. Inv'lid'd Feb 18, 1918. To Pens'n, Jan. 1, 1919.*
Jemadar	Kehar Singh I				*Killed in action February 1st, 1917.*
Jemadar	Labh Singh				*Wounded December 16th, 1916. Invalided December 29th, 1916. Rejoined August 29th, 1917.*
Jemadar	Buta Singh				*To Base Depot, February 13th, 1917. To Pension.*
Jemadar	Sundar Singh	4058			*Invalided October 17th, 1916. Died at his home October 10th, 1917.*
Jemadar	Rur Singh				*Killed in action February 1st, 1917.*
Jemadar	Lal Singh				*Invalided October 17th, 1916. Rejoined April 8th, 1917. To India for duty, June 11th, 1918.*
Subadar	Lehna Singh	B.M.P.			*Invalided March 27th, 1916.*
Jemadar	Pritam Singh	B.M.P.			*Invalided May 4th, 1916.*
Jemadar	Mitt Singh	B.M.P.			*Invalided July 21st, 1916.*
Jemadar	Kehar Singh II	3799	17.5.16	2.4.16	*Killed in action February 1st, 1917.*

APPENDIX II.—*Continued.*

Rank	Name	No. or Unit	Date of Promotion Jemadar	Date of Promotion Subadar	
Jemadar	Wattan Singh	4092	28.5.16		Transferred to 1/151st Sikh Infantry May 15th, 1918.
Jemadar	Chanan Singh	B.M.P.			*Wounded February 1st*, 1917. Invalided February 18th, 1917.
Jemadar	Lal Singh	3826			*Killed in action February 1st*, 1917.
Jemadar	Jiwa Singh	B.M.P.			*Wounded February 1st*, 1917. Invalided February 18th, 1917.
Jemadar	Jaimal Singh	4063			Returned to India July 11th, 1917.
Subadar	Ishar Singh	3219	5.10.16		Transferred to 1/151st Sikh Infantry May 15th, 1918.
	Kehar Singh				Rejoined from 14th Sikhs February 20th, 1917. *Wounded October 29th*, 1918. Invalided December 17th, 1918. To Pension, June 23rd, 1919.
Jemadar	Kesar Singh	4214	2.2.17	8.7.18	*Injured in action July 8th*, 1920.
Jemadar	Bishan Singh	4115	2.2.17	26.4.18	To India for duty, January 2nd, 1918. Rejoined December 22nd, 1919.
Jemadar	Attar Singh [I.D.S.M.]	4399	2.2.17	30.10.18	Returned to India September 28th, 1920. To Pension, October 10th, 1920.
Subadar	Mehar Singh,				*Killed in action October 29th*, 1918.
Jemadar	Harnam Singh	4402	2.2.17	11.10.20	
Jemadar	Pertab Singh	3913	2.2.17	14.6.18	Invalided December 19th, 1919. Rejoined June 26th, 1920.
Jemadar	Harnam Singh	4114	2.2.17	30.10.18	
Jemadar	Sadhu Singh	4288	2.2.17		*Killed in action October 29th*, 1918.
Jemadar	Kundha Singh	4158	2.2.17		Transferred to 1/151st Sikh Infantry, May 15th, 1918.
Jemadar	Wadhawa Singh	4191	2.2.17		
Jemadar	Bishan Singh	3992	15.6.18		*Wounded July 19th*, 1920. Invalided August 3rd, 1920.
Jemadar	Sundar Singh	4301	15.6.18		*Wounded July 7th*, 1920.
Jemadar	Sant Singh	4306	8.7.18		*Killed in action July 7th*, 1920.
Jemadar	Surain Singh	4615	2.9.18		*Wounded February 1st*, 1917.
Jemadar	Gurmukh Singh	4422	2.9.18		
Jemadar	Bishan Singh	4773	30.10.18		
Jemadar	Buta Singh	4228	30.10.18		
Jemadar	Kesar Singh	4611	30.10.18		
Jemadar	Sadhu Singh	4565	23.6.19		
Jemadar	Tara Singh	4489	2.1.20		
Jemadar	Narain Singh	4612	8.7.20		*Wounded February 1st*, 1917 *and October 29th*, 1918.
Jemadar	Wazir Singh	4675	11.11.20		

N.B.—This list does not include the names of outside classes attached.

APPENDIX III

YEARLY CASUALTY RETURN

Year	Killed in Action			Otherwise Killed			Died of Wounds			Prisoners of War			Died of Disease			Wounded			Wounded and Invalided			Sick and Invalided		
	BOs	IOs	IORs	BOs	IOs	IORs	BOs	IOs	IORs	BOs	IOs	IORs	BOs	IOs	IORs	BOs	IOs	IORs	BOs	IOs	IORs	BOs	IOs	IORs
1914	—	—	1	—	—	—	—	—	—	—	—	—	—	—	1	1	—	7	—	—	—	—	—	—
1915	—	—	25	—	—	—	(A)1	—	6	—	—	—	—	—	4	(B)1	(C)1	106	—	—	—	—	—	—
1916	(G)6	—	5	—	—	4	—	—	2	—	—	—	—	—	5	—	(E)1	23	—	(F)1	2	(a)7	(b)9	556
1917	—	(H)7	121	—	—	1	—	(D)1	15	—	(I)1	39	—	—	14	—	—	144	(K)2	(L)6	205	(c)1	(d)2	105
1918	—	(M)2	39	—	—	—	—	—	7	—	—	—	—	—	6	(N)2	—	67	(O)1	—	75	—	—	46
1919	—	—	—	—	—	1	—	—	1	—	—	—	—	—	6	—	—	3	(Q)1	(P)1	9	—	(e)1	26
1920	—	1	27	(R)1	—	1	—	(S)1	32	—	—	—	—	—	4	(T)1	(U)2	93	(V)1	(W)1	103	—	—	19
1921	—	—	—	—	—	—	—	—	—	—	—	—	—	—	—	—	—	—	—	—	—	—	—	—
GRAND TOTAL	6	10	218	1	—	7	1	2	63	—	1	39	—	—	40	5	6	443	5	9	394	8	12	752

(A) Captain F. C. Waterfield. (B) 2/Lieut. S. F. Criper, I.A.R.O. (C) Jemadar Lal Singh. (D) Jemadar Mala Singh. (E) Subadar Narain Singh. (F) Jemadar Labh Singh. (G) Lieut.-Colonel H. B. Rattray, D.S.O.; Captain R. Rainsford Hannay; Captain J. G. Wilson; Captain G. H. Atkinson; Lieut. G. Mitchell; Lieut. A. C. Stone. (H) Subadar Lehna Singh; Subadar Ram Singh; Subadar Karm Singh; Jemadar Lal Singh; Jemadar Rur Singh; Jemadar Kehar Singh I; Jemadar Kehar Singh II. (I) Subadar Thaman Singh. (J) Subadar Major Sundar Singh and Subadar Lehna Singh. (K) Lieut A. C. Curtis; Lieut. J. W. Guise. (L) Subadar Wariam Singh; Subadar Bhag Singh; Subadar Narain Singh; Jemadar Lehna Singh; Jemadar Chanan Singh, B.M.P.; Jemadar Jiwa Singh, B.M.P. (M) Subadar Mehar Singh. I.D.S.M.; Jemadar Sadhu Singh. (N) Captain A. L. Butcher; T./Captain Santokh Singh, I.M.S. (O) Captain B. W. Key. (P) Subadar Kehar Singh. (Q) Captain R. K. Henson. (R) Lieut. F. Adams. (S) Subadar Nidhan Singh. (T) Lieut. R. V. Fox. (U) Subadar Kesar Singh; Jemadar Sundar Singh. (V) Lieut. G. M. Worden. (W) Jemadar Bishan Singh I.

(a) Lieut. R. H. L. Minchin; Captain W. D. Keyworth, I.M.S.; 2/Lieut. A. H. Worster, I.A.R.O.; 2/Lieut. B. W. Key; Captain J. E. Waller; Lieut. A. H. Atkinson; 2/Lieut. S. F. Criper, I.A.R.O. (b) Subadar Lehna Singh, B.M.P.; Subadar Nidhan Singh; Subadar Natha Singh, I.O.M.; Jemadar Pretam Singh, B.M.P.; Subadar Mitt Singh, B.M.P.; Subadar Ishar Singh; Jemadar Gopal Singh, B.M.P.; Jemadar Lal Singh; Jemadar Sundar Singh. (c) Lieut. J. E. Hughes, I.A.R.O. (d) Jemadar Pritam Singh, B.M.P.; Subadar Ramsurat Singh, 8th Rajputs attached. (e) Subadar Jangbahadur Singh, 8th Rajputs attached.

APPENDIX IV

REINFORCEMENTS, INDIAN RANKS

Year	Serial No. of Reinforcement	Date of Embarkation	Date of Arrival at Basra	Date of Joining Regt. in Field.	I.O.'s	I.O.R.'s	Folls.	Yearly Total I.O.'s	Yearly Total I.O.R.'s	Yearly Total Folls.	Indian Officers	Source of Supply
1916	1	22.2.16	11.3.16	28.3.16	3	136	4				Subadar Lehna Singh, Jemadar Pritam Singh, Jemadar Mitt Singh	B.M.P. from 15th Sikhs, E.E.F.
	2	25.4.16	3.5.16	?		30	1					Depot 45th Sikhs
	3	27.5.16	3.6.16	?		15	1					Depot 45th Sikhs
	4	27.6.16	3.7.16	3.8.16		50	3					Depot 45th Sikhs
	5	14.8.16	20.8.16	13.9.16		35	1					Depot 45th Sikhs
	6	31.8.16	6.9.16	21.9.16		49	2					Depot 45th Sikhs
	7	16.9.16	21.9.16	20.10.16		50	2					45th, attached 15th. Sikhs, Peshawur.
	8	2.10.16	8.10.16	29.10.16	1	50	1				Jemadar Lal Singh	Depot 45th Sikhs.
	9	12.10.16	17.10.16	29.10.16	2	72	2				Jem'd'r Jiwa Singh, B.M.P. Jem. Jaimal Singh, B.M.P.	Depot 45th Sikhs.
1917	10	29.10.16	3.11.16	?		15		6	554	18		Depot 45th Sikhs.
	11	2.12.16	7.12.16	25.12.16		52	2					Depot 45th Sikhs.
	12	16.12.16	21.12.16	16.1.17		70	1					45th, attached 15th Sikh. 15th Sikhs.
	13	3.1.17	9.1.17	12.3.17		30						Depot 45th Sikhs.
	14	4.2.17	13.2.17	12.3.17		12						Depot 45th Sikhs.
	15	25.2.17	4.3.17	29.3.17	2	50	1					8th Rajputs.
	16	3.3.17	13.3.17	29.3.17	2	112	2					2nd Rajputs.
	17	7.3.17	13.3.17	29.3.17	4	110	4					25th Punjabis.
	18	16.3.17	22.3.17	24.4.17	1	221	5				Sub. Mehar Singh, I.D.S.M.	Depot 45th Sikhs.
	19	23.3.17	30.3.17		2	72						11th Rajputs.
	20	2.4.17	8.4.17	24.4.17	1	98	3				Jemadar Lal Singh	Depot 45th Sikhs.
	21	23.8.17	29.8.17	21.10.17	3	175	3				Subadar Nidhan Singh, Subadar Wariam Singh, Jemadar Labh Singh	Depot 45th Sikhs.
						176	3					
	22	27.8.17	3.9.17	?		5						Depot 45th Sikhs.

HISTORY OF THE 45TH RATTRAY'S SIKHS

APPENDIX IV—Continued.

Year	Serial No. of Reinforcement	Date of Embarkation	Date of Arrival at Basra	Date of Joining Regt. in Field	I.O.'s	I.O.R.'s	Polls.	I.O.'s	I.O.R.'s	Polls.	Indian Officers	Source of Supply
1918	23	14.11.17	19.11.17	?	—	37	1				—	Depot 45th Sikhs.
	24	27.11.17	2.12.17	?	—	20	1				—	Depot 45th Sikhs.
	25	14.5.18	19.5.18		—	170	5				—	Depot 45th Sikhs.
	26	8.8.18	13.8.18		1	23	1				Sub. Narain Singh, I.O.M.	Depot 45th Sikhs.
	27	15.9.18	21.9.18		—	16	—				—	Depot 45th Sikhs.
	28	11.10.18	16.10.18		—	20	—				—	Depot 45th Sikhs.
	29			31.3.19	—	17	—	15	1188	23	—	45th att'd, 14th Sikhs, M.E.F.
1919	30	7.8.19	15.8.19		—	52	1				—	Depot 45th Sikhs.
	31	26.8.19	1.9.19		—	64	2				—	Depot 45th Sikhs.
	32	13.9.19	18.9.19		1	99	1				Subadar Bishan Singh	Depot 45th Sikhs.
	33	6.12.19	11.12.19	22.12.19	—	1	1				—	Depot 45th Sikhs.
								1	229	6		
1920	34	5.1.20	11.1.20		—	190	10				—	Depot 45th Sikhs.
	35	9.3.20	14.3.20		1	2	—				Subadar Nidhan Singh	Depot 45th Sikhs.
	36	27.4.20	1.5.20		—	101	6				—	Depot 45th Sikhs.
	37	23.8.20	28.8.20		—	50	4				—	Depot 45th Sikhs.
	38	12.10.20	19.10.20		1	35	7				Sub. Harnam Singh II	Depot 45th Sikhs.
	39	29.10.20	2.11.20		—	15	1				—	Depot 45th Sikhs.
	40	29.11.20	5.12.20		—	40	8				—	Depot 45th Sikhs.
								2	433	36		

TOTAL REINFORCEMENTS .. 25 2627 87

DETAIL.
From Depot 45th Sikhs 10 1848 67
From B.M. Police (Sikhs) 5 208 6
From 15th Sikhs — 30 —
From Outside Regiments 10 541 14

TOTAL 25 2627 87

APPENDIX V.

HONOURS AND AWARDS.

Nature of Reward	No.	Detail
Companion of the Star of India ..	1	Lieutenant-Colonel D. A. D. McVean, D.S.O.
Distinguished Service Order, Bar to	1	Lieutenant-Colonel D. A. D. McVean, D.S.O. (See Appendix VI.).
Distinguished Service Order ..	4	Major F. S. Keen, Staff Employ, East Africa, 1916.
		Captain (Acting Major) H. St. G. M. McRae, Staff Employ, France, 1917.
		Major J. G. Cadell, Staff Employ, East Africa, 1917.
		Major C. H. Watson, I.M.S., Cavalry Field Ambulance, Mesopotamia, 1917.
Military Cross, Bar to	1	Captain A. C. Curtis, M.C. (See Appendix VI.)
Military Cross	6	See Appendix VI.
Promoted Colonel	1	Lieutenant-Colonel D. A. D. McVean, D.S.O.
Promoted Brevet Lieut.-Colonel ..	2	Major B. W. Shuttleworth.
		Major R. H. Anderson, 1919.
Mentioned in Despatches	61	See Appendix VI.
Promoted Hon. Captain	1	Subadar Major Sundar Singh, I.O.M., Sardar Bahadur, 1920.
Promoted Hon. Lieutenant ..	1	Subadar Major Narain Singh, I.O.M., Bahadur, 1920.
Order of British India, 2nd Class	2	Subadar Major Sundar Singh, I.O.M.
		Subadar Nidhan Singh.
Indian Order of Merit, 2nd Class	18	See Appendix VI.
Indian Distinguished Service Medal	45	See Appendix VI.
Meritorious Service Medal ..	8	See Appendix VI.
Foreign Decorations	5	See Appendix VI.

APPENDIX VI

ACTIONS FOR WHICH REWARDS WERE GIVEN

Bar to the D.S.O.

Lieut.-Colonel D. A. D. McVean, D.S.O.

"For conspicuous gallantry and devotion to duty, and ability as a Battalion Commander during operations at Shergat, October 24th–30th, 1918. He led his Regiment into action after a series of most trying and arduous marches over difficult country, covering over sixty miles in seventy hours, and in the end through a heavy artillery and machine gun barrage. He displayed courage, and determination and leadership of a high order."

D.S.O. Gazetted September 2nd, 1902.

Bar to the M.C.

Captain A. C. Curtis, M.C.

"For conspicuous gallantry and devotion to duty on July 20th, 1920, during the relief of Rumaithah, and the subsequent withdrawal. During an attack by a numerically superior force of Arabs, though severely wounded early in the operations, commanded the whole force of cavalry and infantry engaged. The enemy were constantly driven off and checked within thirty or forty yards.

"Captain Curtis by his marked ability, determination and coolness under fire, was largely instrumental in organizing a successful attack, which ultimately drove the insurgents across a canal with much loss."

M.C. Gazetted July 3rd, 1915.

M.C.

Captain B. W. Key.

"For conspicuous gallantry and devotion to duty near Shuramiyah on October 20th, 1918. During a reconnaissance towards the Fat-Hah position he was ordered to advance and secure a ridge held by the enemy. Although exposed to heavy fire, the Company successfully reached its objective, where he moved about fearlessly in order to make his dispositions to the best advantage. He was eventually wounded, but refused to undergo treatment until his Company had been withdrawn to camp. His behaviour throughout was splendid."

Lieut. (Acting Captain) A. L. Butcher.

"For conspicuous gallantry and determined courage at Shergat on October 29th, 1918. He was in command of the leading line when its left flank was heavily counter-attacked by the enemy. He immediately collected a small party with three Lewis guns and firmly established himself, driving back the counter-attack, and killing three of the enemy himself. Although wounded, he refused to be evacuated until the Regiment was withdrawn into reserve."

Lieut. R. K. Henson.

"For marked gallantry and devotion to duty north of Shergat on October 29th, 1918. During an attack at dusk on the enemy's position, a heavy enemy counter-attack was delivered. He at once organized a party of scouts at Battalion Headquarters, and took up a position to stem the enemy's advance, maintaining his position with great determination until wounded. He had previously performed valuable services in carrying out reconnaissances."

Subadar Labh Singh. Village, Man. Tehsil, Kasur. District, Lahore.

"For conspicuous gallantry and devotion to duty north of Shergat on October 29th, 1918. When his Battalion was strongly counter-attacked on two sides, he took up a position on a flank, and eventually succeeded in driving back the enemy with considerable losses. He then went to the assistance of a garrison which was holding up the frontal attack, and again drove the enemy back. A critical situation was thus saved by his gallant action."

Subadar Kehar Singh. Village, Tudiala. Tehsil, Batala. District, Gurdaspur.

"For conspicuous gallantry and devotion to duty. During an attack on the enemy's position six miles north of Shergat on October 29th, 1918, he commanded his platoon with great skill and determination, although twice severely wounded. He held on to an important tactical position during a heavy hostile counter-attack, and by his coolness and his calm demeanour under fire averted what might have become a very critical situation."

Captain J. A. Finlay.

"For conspicuous gallantry and military ability on July 6th and 7th, 1920, near Rumaithah. When commanding an advanced guard he overcame by his initiative and bravery, a determined attack from the Arabs, and ensured the advance of the Column without any opposition. His courage, determination and leadership, were deserving of the highest praise, and the success of the operation was due to his disregard of danger, and coolness in action."

I.O.M. 2nd Class.

No. 525 Lance Naick Chanan Singh. Village, Khanpur. Tehsil, Ludhiana. District, Ludhiana.

"For conspicuous gallantry and resource in action on February 1st, 1917, on the River Hai. During an enemy counter-attack two men firing a Lewis gun in an exposed position were killed. This young Non-Commissioned Officer at once rushed forward for thirty yards, over the open under a hot fire, seized the Lewis gun, brought it into line with his own gun, and continued to fire it. But for his action the gun would certainly have been lost."

No. 77 Naick Bagga Singh. Village, Kalipur. Tehsil, Fatehabad. District, Hissar.

"For conspicuous gallantry and determination in action on January 29th and 30th, 1917. He behaved with great courage and coolness when in charge of a bombing party, holding off a much larger number of the enemy's bombers, although himself wounded early in the fight. He has displayed gallantry on previous occasions."

Subadar Major Sundar Singh. Village, Burj. Tehsil, Tarn Tarn. District, Amritsar.

"For conspicuous gallantry and dash in action on January 29th and 30th, 1917. He cleared the front line of one of our objectives with a platoon and a Lewis gun. He has always displayed the greatest coolness and courage in action, and has set a splendid example to all the ranks of the Regiment."

Subadar Narain Singh. Village, Assi. Tehsil, Ludhiana. District, Ludhiana.

"For conspicuous gallantry in action on February 1st, 1917. He led his platoon with courage, and though his British Officer was killed, he stemmed several counterattacks. He was eventually cut off, but succeeded in regaining our lines in the evening although severely wounded. He brought in five other severely wounded men with him."

No. 1197/15 Sepoy Baddan Singh. Village, Ram Garh Bela. Tehsil, Una. District, Hoshiarpur.

"For conspicuous gallantry in action on February 1st, 1917. A Lewis gun jammed at a critical moment and bombers were called for. None being available he immediately organized a bombing attack under heavy fire, and kept the enemy off until the Lewis gun was ready for action. He displayed marked courage throughout the day."

No. 615 Lance Naick Mall Singh. Village, Isapur. Tehsil, Malerkotla. District, Malerkotla.

"For conspicuous gallantry in action on February 1st, 1917. A Lewis gun jammed at a critical moment and bombers were called for. None being available he immediately organized a bombing attack under heavy fire, and kept the enemy off until the Lewis gun was ready for action. He displayed marked courage throughout the day."

No. 1002 Sepoy Darbara Singh. Village, Tagu Wala. Tehsil Chunian. District, Lahore.
Details not available.

No. 4402 Jemadar Harnam Singh. Village, Chaharke. Tehsil, Raya. District, Sialkot.

" For conspicuous gallantry and devotion to duty on October 29th, 1918. At a moment when an enemy counter-attack on our left flank was maturing, he led his platoon with great dash against it and broke it up. Afterwards he seized and held an advanced position, although most of his ammunition was expended. His conspicuously gallant conduct and skilful dispositions had the result of securing our right flank."

No. 4489 Havildar Tara Singh. Village, Jhoti Wal. Tehsil, Faridkot. District, Faridkot.

" For conspicuous gallantry and devotion to duty on the afternoon of October 29th, 1918. During an attack he was in charge of the Regimental Signallers, and displayed the greatest coolness under heavy fire. Later, during an enemy counter-attack, he rushed forward on his own initiative with his men, and took up a commanding position in a part of the line which was thinly held. By his prompt action he rendered valuable assistance in repelling the counter-attack. He had on previous occasions shown similar courage and resource."

No. 886 Lance Naick Ujagar Singh. Village, Bhangali. Tehsil, Kasur. District, Lahore.

" For conspicuous gallantry and devotion to duty on the afternoon of October 29th, 1918. He was sent forward with his Lewis gun section to cover the advance of his platoon. While advancing under heavy fire, he lost three men before reaching his position, and the remainder within fifteen minutes. He, however, held on to his position alone, and although exposed to heavy fire from front and flank, kept his gun in action until all his ammunition was expended. He then brought back his gun and reported to his Officer. By his brave and determined action he rendered valuable assistance to two platoons which were advancing to repel a counter-attack. His behaviour throughout the action was magnificent."

No. 1855 Sepoy Harnam Singh. Village, Sandaur. Tehsil, Malaud. District, Ludhiana.

"For conspicuous gallantry and devotion to duty on October 20th, 1918. Whilst his Company was acting as covering force to an artillery reconnaissance, both during the advance and withdrawal, he repeatedly carried important messages under heavy fire over long distances, displaying energy and marked determination. He behaved with consummate coolness throughout a critical period."

No. 304 Havildar Tara Singh. Village. Gharuan. Tehsil, Sirhind. District, Patiala.

"For conspicuous gallantry and devotion to duty on July 7th, 1920. During an attack on a column, he was often exposed to heavy enemy fire, but repeatedly established his signalling stations. On reaching the most forward position, he twice climbed up a telegraph pole under fire in order to 'Tap in.' He displayed great gallantry and initiative."

No. 2255 Sepoy Ram Singh. Village, Sahme Wala. Tehsil Sirsa. District, Hissar.

"For conspicuous gallantry and devotion to duty on July 7th, 1920. During an attack on a position, he was one of a Lewis gun team. By the accuracy of his fire, he materially assisted the advance of the line. He was severely wounded, but refused to leave his gun. His determination and courage were a splendid example to all."

No. 254 Havildar Ganga Singh. Village, Manan Wala. Tehsil, Ajnala. District, Amritsar.

"For conspicuous gallantry and devotion to duty on July 22nd, 1920. When the rear guard was heavily attacked

HISTORY OF THE 45TH RATTRAY'S SIKHS 263

and driven back, on his own initiative he took up a position, and brought such an effective fire to bear on the enemy that the latter were unable to advance. By his bravery and coolness, he so inspired the men under him, that the line was restored and the enemy driven back."

No. 4766 Havildar Harditt Singh.   Village, Thanan Wal.
Tehsil, Ludhiana.   District, Ludhiana.

"For conspicuous gallantry and devotion to duty on July 22nd, 1920. During an attack on a position his Platoon Commander was wounded. He at once took command, and by his skilful leading drove back the enemy. Later when the rear guard was driven in, on his own initiative he took up a position on the flank, and by his accurate fire materially assisted in stopping the rush. His leadership and courage were an example to all."

No. 733 Sepoy Chanan Singh.   Village, Buttar.   Tehsil,
Kharian.   District, Gujrat.

"For conspicuous gallantry and devotion to duty on July 7th, 1920. During an attack, when the firing line was unable to advance, he ran back fifty yards under heavy fire, and brought up a Lewis gun. Though wounded, he managed to get the gun into action, and his courage and coolness were beyond all praise."

This gallant Sepoy succumbed to his wounds.

No. 1777 Sepoy Mahna Singh.   Village, Charik.   Tehsil, Moga.
District, Ferozepur.

"For conspicuous gallantry on July 7th, 1920, in Mesopotamia, in rescuing wounded, who were lying within a hundred yards of the enemy's position. He displayed marked courage and initiative under fire in locating snipers, who were effectively enfilading the stretcher bearers. Two of them he killed and the remainder fled."

Mentioned in Despatches.

Lieut.-Colonel H. B. Rattray, D.S.O.   Killed in action.
Major R. H. Anderson.   Four times.
Captain R. Rainsford Hannay.   Killed in action.
Captain J. G. Wilson.   Killed in action.

264 HISTORY OF THE 45TH RATTRAY'S SIKHS

Captain C. H. Atkinson. Died of Wounds.
Lieut. A. C. Curtis, M.C. Three times.
Captain J. W. Guise.
Captain C. W. W. Ford, 35th Sikhs. Attached.
Lieut.-Colonel D. A. D. McVean, D.S.O. Three times.
Major B. W. Shuttleworth. Twice.
Lieut. R. V. Fox.
Lieut. H. St.-C. O. Will.
Lieut. G. M. Worden. Attached.
Major F. S. Keen, D.S.O. Staff Employ. Four times.
Major H. St.-G. M. McRae, D.S.O., Staff Employ. Three times.
Major J. G. Cadell, Staff Employ.
Captain K. G. Hyde Cates. E.E.F. Three times.
Captain R. A. Macausland, Staff Employ.
Jemadar Mehar Singh, I.D.S.M., killed in action. Twice.
1121 Sepoy Puran Singh.
948 Sepoy Sundar Singh, 14th Sikhs, M.E.F.
4538 Lance Naick Bhag Singh, 14th Sikhs.
Subadar Major Sundar Singh. Twice.
Subadar Narain Singh.
180 Havildar Sarup Singh
77 Naick Bagga Singh.
4369 Naick Hira Singh.
615 Lance Naick Mall Singh.
1197/15 Sepoy Baddan Singh.
4355 Sepoy Hakam Singh.
1002 Sepoy Darbara Singh.
1400 Bugler Kheta Singh.
525 Lance Naick Chanan Singh. Twice.
4594 Naick Jaga Nath.
Subadar Kehar Singh.
1500/B Naick Samund Singh.
Jemadar (4402) Harnam Singh.
1855 Sepoy Harnam Singh.
4489 Havildar Tara Singh.
886 Lance Naick Ujagar Singh.
4228 Jemadar Buta Singh.
4611 Jemadar Kesar Singh.
15 Bhisti Duni.

HISTORY OF THE 45TH RATTRAY'S SIKHS

Awarded the I.D.S.M.

1001 Sepoy Ujagar Singh. France, 1915.
1036 Sepoy Fateh Singh. Killed in action. France, 1915.
Jemadar Mehar Singh. Killed in action. N.W.F., 1915.
1121 Sepoy Puran Singh, N.W.F., 1915.
948 Sepoy Sundar Singh, Gallipoli, 1915.
4538 Lance Naick Bhag Singh, Gallipoli, 1915.
180 Havildar Sarup Singh, February 1st, 1917.
325 Havildar Kaka Singh, February 1st, 1917.
77 Havildar Bagga Singh, Shergat, October, 1918.
52 Havildar Prem Singh, Shergat, October, 1918.
614 Naick Indar Singh, Shergat, October, 1918.
268 Sepoy Bassant Singh, Shergat, October, 1918.
1109 Sepoy Nahar Singh, Shergat, October, 1918.
4828 Havildar Rur Singh, Shergat, October, 1918.
4675 Havildar Wazir Singh, Shergat, October, 1918.
1144 Sepoy Banta Singh, Shergat, October, 1918.
1821 Sepoy Gurditt Singh, Shergat, October, 1918.
1538 Sepoy Kala Singh, Shergat, October, 1918.
813 Sepoy Narain Singh, Shergat, October, 1918.
1501 Sepoy Rattan Singh, Shergat, October, 1918.
797 Sepoy Surain Singh, Shergat, October, 1918.
Jemadar Kesar Singh, Shergat, October, 1918.
828/B Sepoy Harnam Singh, February 1st, 1917.
360/B Sepoy Kirpal Singh, February 1st, 1917.
161 Havildar Ishar Singh, Rumaitha, July, 1920.
4441 Havildar Jiwan Singh, Rumaitha, July, 1920.
520 Naick Lal Singh, Rumaitha, July, 1920.
770 Naick Jaswant Singh, Rumaitha, July, 1920.
696 Naick Maghar Singh, Rumaitha, July, 1920.
785 Naick Bakhtawar Singh, Rumaitha, July, 1920.
817 Naick Tahel Singh, Rumaitha, July, 1920.
1075 Naick Hazura Singh, Rumaitha, July, 1920.
1124 Lance Naick Chattar Singh, Rumaitha, July, 1920.
1680 Sepoy Ganga Singh, Rumaitha, July, 1920.
2335 Sepoy Bhag Singh, Rumaitha, July, 1920.
1037 Sepoy Sewa Singh, Rumaitha, July, 1920.
1343 Sepoy Seta Singh, Rumaitha, July, 1920.
1405 Sepoy Indar Singh, Rumaitha, July, 1920.
1154 Sepoy Kishan Singh, Rumaitha, July, 1920.

1668 Sepoy Kehar Singh, Rumaitha, July, 1920.
2284 Sepoy Makhan Singh, Rumaitha, July, 1920.
3281 Sepoy Jit Singh, Killed in action, Rumaitha, July, 1920.
1212 Sepoy Mehar Singh, Rumaitha, July, 1920.
20 Bhisti Wiru, Rumaitha, July, 1920.
4611 Jemadar Kesar Singh, Rumaitha, July, 1920.

Awarded the M.S.M.

355 Drummer Phuman Singh, 1917.
413 Sepoy Anokh Singh, 1917.
4489 Havildar Tara Singh, 1917.
525 Naick Chanan Singh, 1918.
1084 Sepoy Bhan Singh, 1918.
1012 Lance Naick Teja Singh, 1918.
4523 Havildar Major Dharta Singh, 1919.
401 Naick Massa Singh, 1919.

Awarded Foreign Decorations.

Lieut.-Colonel F. T. Stewart : The Order of St. Stanislas, 3rd Class (with sword), Russia, 1917.
Captain R. A. Macausland : Staff, Croix de Guerre, France, 1917.
928 Sepoy Sham Singh : Medaille Militaire, France, 1917.
1036 Lance Naick Fateh Singh : Bronze Medal for Military Valour, Italy, 1917.
Major R. H. Anderson : Croix de Guerre, France, 1919.

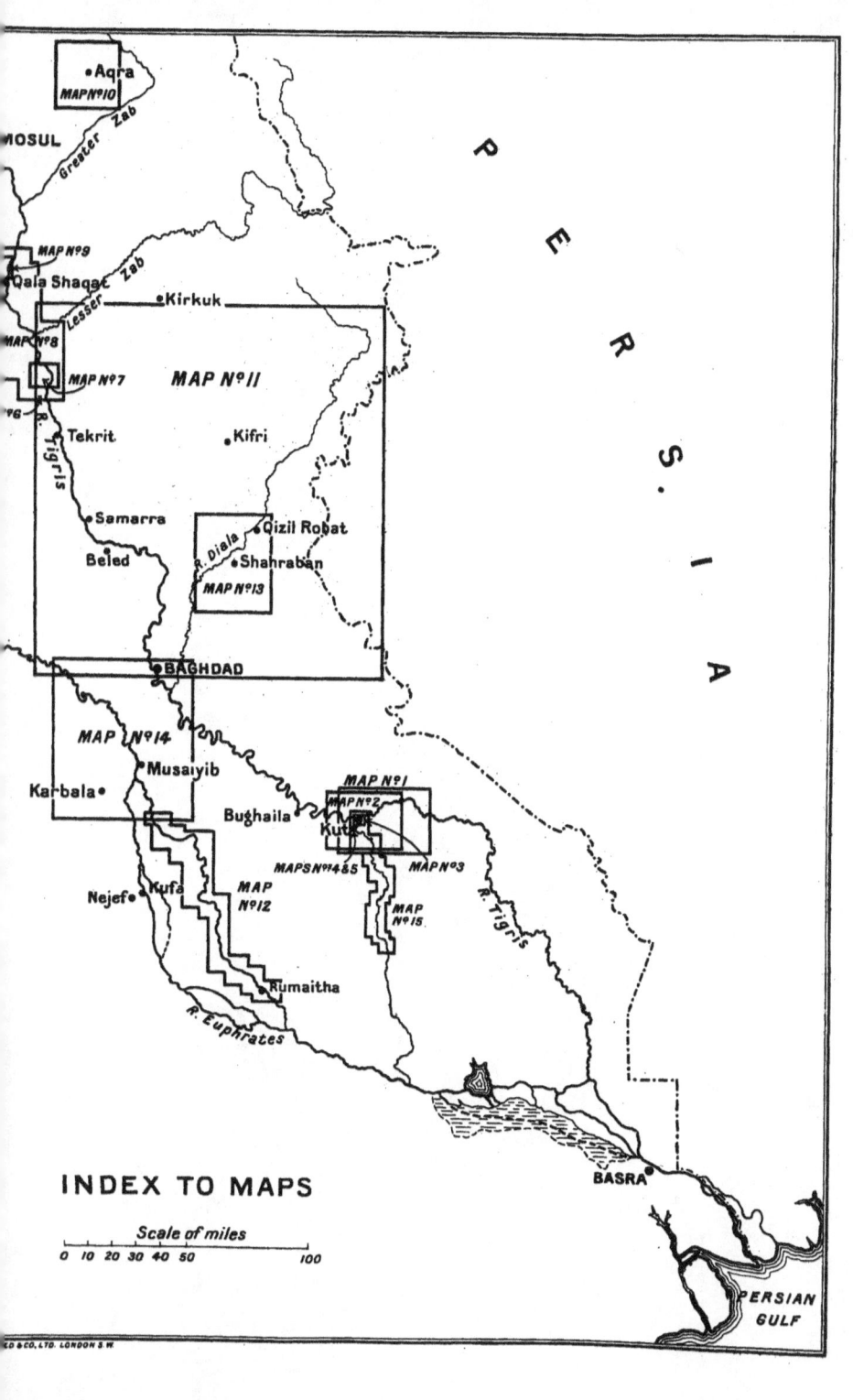

www.ingramcontent.com/pod-product-compliance
Lightning Source LLC
Chambersburg PA
CBHW021955220426
43663CB00007B/819